A Guest
at Cambridge

A Guest
at Cambridge

Dr. George H. Guest

PARACLETE PRESS
Orleans, Massachusetts

1st Printing, April, 1994

Copyright © 1994 by George H. Guest
Cover photo credit: Nigel Luckhurst, Cambridge, England
Library of Congress Card Number: 94-66305
All rights reserved.
Published by Paraclete Press
Orleans, Massachusetts

ISBN: 1-55725-038-3
Printed in the United States of America

Acknowledgements

My grateful thanks are due to Mrs Jane Rogers, who skilfully prepared my manuscript for publication; and also to Mr Stephen Cleobury who (although in no way responsible for any of the opinions expressed in it) carefully checked the text. Mr Michael Page was kind enough to contribute some photography, and Mrs Glyn Daniel to read the proofs.

I was urged to write this book by my wife, Nan; my children, David and Elizabeth; and my sister, Gwendolen Jorss. Without their encouragement it would not have been written.

Table of Contents

Part III

Foreword

A mong the many events which paid tribute to George
Guest on his retirement as Organist of St. John's College
was a dinner in Hall attended by a large number of former
Choral Students and Organ Students. I was honoured on
that occasion to speak, as I am now to write. I observed
then that George has become a legend in his lifetime. This
status flows not only from his personal and musical
characteristics but also from the fact that, rarely for these
days, he has given the whole of his professional life to
one institution: St. John's. As the reader will discover, it
was not only his musical direction of the Choir, but also
the essential work of establishing the new Choir School
and of ensuring proper recognition of the Chapel music
within the College as a whole which were the main strands
of a career which has made his work and the Choir of
St. John's so justly renowned. Largely through the Choir's
recordings and tours, and his own freelance work, his
influence on succeeding generations of choir trainers has
been immense.

This volume gives us a tantalising glimpse of some of
his techniques: it will quickly become apparent that
phrasing, tempo and vocal quality are of crucial importance
to him. I have met few who have such an *instinctive* approach

to music, though there is always a strong musicological foundation to his interpretations as well.

There are many of his pupils who, like me, are greatly in George's debt. I hope I may associate them with this tribute to him.

Stephen Cleobury
Director of Music
King's College, Cambridge

The King to Oxford sent a troop of horse
For Tories own no argument but force:
With equal skill to Cambridge books he sent
For Whigs admit no force but argument.

William Browne (1692-1774)

Part I

1

Bangor, Chester and the Royal Air Force

Un funud fach cyn elo'r haul i'w orwel,
Un funud fwyn cyn delo'r hwyr i'w hynt,
I gofio am y pethau angofiedig,
Ar goll yn awr yn llwch yr amser gynt.[1]
Waldo Williams

I suppose it all began when I was a small boy in Bangor, North Wales, in the early 1930's. My father had been, for many years, an enthusiastic and gifted amateur organist and was always happy to deputize in local churches. At that time, however, few small instruments in the district boasted an electric blower, and it was usually necessary to pump the organ by hand. Clearly I was the obvious person to undertake this very important task, and it became my introduction to the music of Matins and Evensong (there

---

[1] A short moment before the sun sinks below the horizon,
A gentle moment before the evening takes its course,
To remember those forgotten things, now lost in the dust
of former times.

3

were very few sung Communion Services at that time) and was doubtless responsible for initiating and nurturing a passionate interest in what subsequently has become my life's work. My parents (my mother also had an abiding love of music, and was a keen singer in her earlier days) encouraged me to have piano lessons from an elderly lady who called once a week at the house. These soon gave way to a much stricter regime, and I became a pupil of Mr John Williams FRCO—he was never referred to without the letters of his diploma. John Williams FRCO was one of the old school of teachers, and was an extremely strict disciplinarian. He was not averse to administering sharp taps with a ruler on errant fingers in both scales and arpeggios, but he was basically a kind person and was highly regarded in the district both as a teacher and as the skilled organist of Capel y Tabernacl, Bangor (long since, alas, given over to secular use).

Bangor itself was something of a backwater in those days. Traffic was minimal, and it was always possible to play football in the streets. There were few, if any, *tai haf* (second homes) in the district, and the Welsh language was taken for granted—though there was a growing feeling amongst parents that English was the language in which to become fluent if one wanted to "get on in the world." Welsh lessons in Hirael Infants School and Ysgol Santes Fair were virtually non-existent, and those offered in Friars School (the ancient grammar school of the city) were formal, dull and always non-conversational. It was, nevertheless, a wonderful place in which to grow up; there was Bangor mountain above the city, the Menai Straits with its splendid Victorian pier, Port Penrhyn and its busy slate trade and colourful variety of ships and, on a Saturday afternoon, Bangor City F.C., on whose sloping ground were re-fought the old English/Welsh wars (for some reason the City were, at that time, members of the Birmingham League). There was little connection between the University College, standing so impressively on its hill in Upper Bangor, and the rest of the city—indeed Bangor at that time still tended to be a city of finely demarcated and fiercely independent enclaves—Garth, Hirael, Glanadda, Penchwintan, to name but a few. There were a large number of Nonconformist chapels, most boasting a considerable membership, but with little in the way of music except for their congregational hymns. These, in which the matchless poetry of William Williams Pantycelyn, Ann Griffiths and others was sung to noble and dignified tunes whose gravity and basic simplicity perfectly fitted the words, were the chapels' staple musical fare.

The Church in Wales tended to look eastward across the border, and the choral services in the ancient cathedral of Saint Deiniol were held entirely in English. Nevertheless, the Cathedral Choir in the 1930's was a flourishing body and congregations tended to be large. There was, generally, no lack of applicants either for Choristerships or for Lay Clerkships. Dean Griffith Roberts, a kindly old gentleman who had been appointed as long ago as 1903, was the guiding spirit of the life of the cathedral in those days, and Bishop Green, later to be enthroned as the second Archbishop of Wales, ruled the Diocese with dignity, equanimity and attention to detail. The music was in the hands of the young Mr Leslie Paul; he was a native of Bangor and had been a pupil at Friars School, subsequently becoming a Music Scholar at Clifton College. He studied at the Royal Academy of Music, London, later taking his degrees from Keble College, Oxford. In 1927 Dr Roland Rogers, who had been Organist of Bangor Cathedral from 1871 to 1892, and from 1906 to 1927, died, and Leslie Paul was appointed in his place. It was my good fortune to become a treble in his choir.

We sang what was a very representative repertoire of church music at that time, with Tudor music taking very much second place to 18th and 19th century pieces. Perhaps the most abiding memory I have of my period in Bangor Cathedral Choir is that, quite without realising it, I began to commit the Psalter to memory. Other, less appealing, aspects of my time there were the frightening "initiation ceremonies" which senior choristers imposed on newly-joined Probationers. These included being locked in a dark and smelly surplice cupboard, with a lighted taper being introduced through the keyhole; having Dean Roberts's chamber pot filled with water and poured over one's head seemed, by comparison, to be quite innocuous!

In 1935 my father, who had for many years worked as a commercial traveller for a Liverpool wholesale grocery firm on the North Wales coast, decided to move just over the English border to Chester. There were a number of reasons for this, one of the chief being that, given my continued progress in music, it was considered advantageous for me to become a chorister in Chester Cathedral Choir, an altogether larger and more prestigious establishment than that at Bangor, and presided over by a wonderfully gifted musician in Malcolm Boyle, a pupil of Sir Walter Parratt, and formerly Assistant to Sir Walford Davies at Saint George's Chapel, Windsor. I well recall singing the Verse in the Magnificat of *Harwood in A flat* at my Voice Trial and, to my great joy, was accepted. The Choir School was small and cramped, but the teaching, presided over by the awesome Headmaster, the Revd A. Jessop Price, was adequate, and I spent five happy years there. Malcolm Boyle's influence was immense and the essence of his personality and perhaps his character was seen in his rehearsals. Boyle's way was always the way of reason, and this, coupled with an approach as compassionate as it was courteous, enabled him to achieve extraordinary results. His talent, his sunny personality and his supreme optimism (even in the face of dire personal anxiety) were magnets which drew young and old alike. His improvisations were products of genius, models of such construction, and many a time did a visitor, thinking he had been listening to a printed piece, wait at the bottom of the organ-loft stairs to ask the name of the work he had just heard. At the end of his last service as cathedral organist, he improvised a masterly voluntary of heart-rending poignancy based, characteristically, on the intonation to the Creed. He won friends in all walks of life, and never tired of regaling them with anecdotes which brought to life his days as a chorister in Eton College Choir, his association with Parratt, E. H. Fellowes, Sir Walford Davies, and his early days at Chester Cathedral. It was a supreme irony that Dean Tubbs, for whose Installation he wrote the splendid anthem *Thou, O God, art praised in Zion*, should be in charge of the Chapter which subsequently dismissed him for announcing his second marriage, his first wife having deserted him, and from whom he was eventually divorced.

Dr Roland Middleton was Sub-Organist of the cathedral, and also Organist of Mold Parish Church, Flintshire. He was not a good choir-trainer, being totally unable to keep discipline; indeed, Monday afternoon boys' rehearsals must have been as much dreaded by him, as looked forward to by us! Although he was a good improviser, his organ-playing tended to be scrappy. On the other hand, he was a first-rate teacher. He had much more patience than Malcolm Boyle, and his lessons in harmony and counterpoint were models of clarity as, paradoxically, were his organ lessons. I learnt a great deal from him, and it was largely due to his skill and encouragement that I was able to pass my ARCO in January 1940 whilst still at school (I had, by this time, moved to the King's School, then on its traditional site in the Abbey Square).

With great regret, I have to say that I tended to waste my time at school, and left at 16 without having taken any Higher School Certificate (A-level) examinations. It was natural, therefore, that my parents should expect me to get a job, and I became a Temporary Clerk in the local Army Audit Office (Chester was and is the headquarters of Western Command). This was routine work, consisting largely of checking vouchers for pieces of equipment issued to soldiers. Some of these vouchers related to events which had taken place in the 1920s, so my work probably was not of vital national importance. Nevertheless, I enjoyed my time there, particularly the mid-morning period when I would be sent out to buy the office cakes for the "elevenses" of the more senior staff.

I was, at this time, working for my FRCO, and wickedly writing harmony and counterpoint papers under cover of a large ledger during office hours, but eventually my parents gave me leave to resign from this employment in order to devote more time to my FRCO preparation. This I took in July 1941, and was, happily, successful.

By this time, I had become Organist and Choirmaster at Connah's Quay Parish Church, Flintshire, and used to bus there from Chester twice a week. The choir was good, and we were usually able to sing an anthem on Sundays, together with the appropriate Psalms and a large repertoire of hymns; but the pay was meagre, and I could never understand why there were, apparently, never any funerals or weddings at the church, for the fee of 2 guineas a service was well worth having. I found out, just before I left, that these were, by tradition, 'perks' of the Vicar's wife, who not only played, but took all the fees as well!

Meanwhile, the Second World War was increasing in scope; much of Europe had been over-run and it was clear that there was to be no early end to hostilities. I had become 18 years of age in February 1942, so I decided to join the Royal Air Force as soon as possible and was called up on 1 August 1942, and music, for some 4 years, naturally took second place. A slightly defective left eye rendered me unfit for air-crew duties, and I was put on to Radar work, though, not being in any way scientifically minded,

I found much of what I was called upon to do was in many ways incomprehensible. By 1944 it became clear that all our training was directed towards a Second Front somewhere in Europe, and by late May of that year the Fighter Direction Tender (a kind of flat-bottomed type of landing craft fitted with the latest radar and designed to direct fighters on to enemy targets) to which I had been assigned had reached Weymouth, and had joined the enormous number of craft of all descriptions then assembling for D-day. The weather was atrocious, and the landings had to be postponed for 24 hours because of it, but finally, on 6 June, and encouraged by a printed message of support from General Eisenhower, we set sail, and served for a fortnight just off the coast of Normandy. A brief return to England was the prelude to another tour of duty. This was abruptly terminated on the night of 7 July by an aerial torpedo which sank us within a quarter of an hour. I happened to be on deck at the time, assisting a sailor who was firing an Oerlikon gun. He saw the track of the approaching torpedo, and in colourful but highly effective language advised me to duck immediately. The torpedo struck almost simultaneously and entered the craft through the paint store, the contents of which were catapulted through the air and landed on those on deck. I must have presented a strange sight to my parents when I arrived back in Chester on Survivors' Leave. I was, however, luckier than some; there were fatalities, and some swam away in the wrong direction and it was said that they were taken prisoner by the Germans.

A quiet period in Cornwall followed, with two events remaining very clearly in my mind. Firstly, the murder of a WAAF by the Commanding Officer of the station; and secondly the very great pleasure I had from getting to know that extraordinary eccentric, Guillaume Ormond, Organist of Truro Cathedral. He was a splendid musician but extremely forgetful, and it was said that the clergy had by them a button which showed a red light in the organ-loft (then by far the highest in any English cathedral). An intermittent flashing meant "You're playing the wrong chant/hymn-tune"; and an unwavering red light meant "Stop playing immediately!" I remember, too, a rude and officious verger interrupting an excellent performance of Mendelssohn's *Organ Sonata No.3 in A* by a loud clapping, and, when Guillaume stopped playing (this was at the end of a Saturday Evensong), shouting "We're locking up now, Mr Ormond." To my very great surprise, Guillaume's only answer was "Right-o Mr G. . . ."

Then, in January 1945, I was posted to India. The journey to Bombay in the Empress of Scotland took the best part of a month and conditions in the grossly overcrowded troopship were primitive in the extreme. I celebrated my twenty-first birthday in Port Said, and there followed an extremely hot and uncomfortable week in the Suez Canal and Red Sea before arriving in the sticky humidity which was normal in Bombay. The war in Europe had ended, and that in the Far East was in its last stages, so there was little of a military nature to do and I found myself in charge of what were called "soft furnishings"—that is to say, making sure that the curtains, cushions and carpets in the little RAF station of Juhu, in north Bombay, were kept clean and in good order. I was also the Commanding Officer's chauffeur, as well as acting pianist for the somewhat infrequent Church Parades. During this period I was also sent to a film studio in Poona to learn how to act as a cinematograph operator, and in the evenings I would frequently be hired to play quiet dance music in a local night club which existed largely for the amusement of wealthy Bombay cotton magnates. Bombay itself was a fascinating, noisy, dirty metropolis, the poor were very poor, and the rich very rich (no member of the Forces under the rank of Sergeant was allowed in the Taj Mahal Hotel, and I well remember a prominent notice at all entrances

"Dogs and South Africans not admitted"). But the general poverty and squalor was appalling.

I spent just under two years in India. In retrospect it was a wonderful period of my life, though at the time the uncertainty about repatriation was a worry. But at last, in November 1946, my time came, and we crowded with eager anticipation on to the troopship which was to carry us home. There was an air of euphoria everywhere, and I recall that, as we passed Gibraltar and entered the dreaded Bay of Biscay once more, we threw, with ill-concealed pleasure, all our tropical kit into the sea. Once home, we were kitted out with ill-fitting civilian clothes, and I remember that this was the first time that I had owned a trilby hat (not, of course, that I ever wore it!). And at last I was home, and thankful at my good fortune in having survived unscathed.

2

Chester and Early Years at Cambridge

When in the slipp'ry paths of Youth
With heedless steps I ran,
Thine arm unseen convey'd me safe,
And led me up to Man.

Joseph Addison

During my time in India I found I had been appointed Organist and Choirmaster at Christleton Parish Church at a salary of £52 p.a. Christleton is a small village some two miles out of Chester, then a distinct entity, now a suburb of the city, and at that time it had a vigorous church life, with a large, enthusiastic choir; the Rector, the Revd A. A. Guest-Williams, had been an undergraduate at Saint John's College, Cambridge (of which I had not previously heard!). In addition, Malcolm Boyle had offered me the position of Sub-Organist at the cathedral at a salary of £120 p.a. which, needless to say, I accepted with great alacrity, and I looked forward to a quiet period when I could perhaps put down roots, begin to assemble a teaching practice and, above all, build up a repertoire of organ pieces.

The Choir at Christleton consisted of boys, girls, men and women, and it very quickly reached the standard of being able to sing an anthem at each service. The pieces were mostly simple, but I can recall an excitingly successful performance of S. S. Wesley's *Blessed be the God and Father.* Music for Communion Services was less attractive, and it was an extremely difficult job to persuade the Rector that the Merbecke setting was not a "Roman Catholic piece," but that it was, in fact, a product of a composer who had become violently anti-Catholic, and who had even published an anti-Catholic pamphlet entitled "Conference between the Pope and his Secretarie," in the introduction of which he writes "In this lyttle Volume I have collected . . . and somewhat have touched also the Luciferous pride of that monstrous Dragon of Rome . . . to awake him out of his deadly errours, wherein he hath snorted so long."

A number of the children became quite good musicians, and one in particular, Kenneth Woollam, the distinguished operatic tenor, was perhaps the most noteworthy. He left us after a while to join the Cathedral Choir but his initial musical impetus came from his time in Christleton Parish Church Choir.

Chester Cathedral Choir in the late 1940s consisted of six Lay-clerks, sixteen Choristers and some eight Probationers. The duties were heavy, and on most Sundays there were as many as six services—8 am. Communion in Saint Anselm's Chapel (Merbecke), 9.30 am. Military Parade Service, 10.30 am. Choral Matins (Sunday School during the Sermon), 11.30 am. Sung Eucharist, 3.30 pm. Choral Evensong (without Sermon), 6.30 pm. Nave Evensong (with Sermon). In addition there were five Choral Evensongs during the week, and a number of morning services as well. The repertoire was larger than that of Bangor; it contained many more Tudor pieces, though few continental works of the same period. Virtually no contemporary music was sung—none by Herbert Howells, nor Benjamin Britten, nor even any of the superb William Harris anthems. Nevertheless, the standard repertoire of the time became ingrained in one, and because the Service List (always known as "The Scheme") invariably included the years of the particular composer's birth and death, I quickly learned that Maurice Greene lived from 1695-1755, John Goss from 1800-1880, and S. S. Wesley from 1810-1876—though remained sadly ignorant of similar details concerning Haydn, Mozart, Beethoven and the other 18th- and 19th-century giants.

Malcolm Boyle was then at the height of his powers. His organ playing was always superbly exciting, and he was able to maintain this standard in spite of rarely, if ever, practising. The organ at Chester Cathedral was almost a semitone sharp, and so most pieces had to be transposed down. *Stanford in G* became *Stanford in G flat, I was glad* (Parry) had always to be played in A. I remember Malcolm on one occasion absent-mindedly beginning *How lovely are Thy dwellings fair* (Brahms) in C major, and returning to D major via Eb major in the course of the performance; few detected anything odd in the harmonic structure of the performance. His registration always tended towards the Romantic, the Mixtures were always kept a little out of tune, and therefore unusable, and there was a complete veto on the use of the Tremulant.

The Lay-clerks were of the old school. They had one rehearsal a week, from 3.15 pm. to 4 pm. on a Saturday, and saw no reason why this in any way should be thought somewhat inadequate. There were indeed some outstanding soloists amongst them, but their lack of numbers precluded any real choral subtleties in the Choir's singing. The clergy were a mixed bag; perhaps the most memorable character was Minor Canon Aubrey Baxter. He was extremely old, and had sung in the Choir of King's College Cambridge at the same time as lay-clerks who had sung under T. A. Walmisley (1814-1856). His voice was true (which was more than could be said of some of the other Minor Canons), but he was a real eccentric. Amongst his many interests was Etymology, and I recall him accosting a harassed mother, who with her children was looking round the Cathedral one Bank Holiday, with the startling observation "Good morning, madam, do you know how we came by the word 'journeyman'?" And, without waiting for an answer, went on to answer his own question "It comes from the French word, jour = day, and signifies a person who is paid by the day, rather than by the week, month or year. Good morning." And off he went, leaving behind one very perplexed lady.

I had been back at Chester for less than three months when Malcolm Boyle told me that a competition for the Organ Scholarship (or Studentship as the college liked to call it) was to be held at Saint John's College, Cambridge. Apart from the occasional comment by the Rector of Christleton, I had never heard of Saint John's and was surprised to find that there was a Choir, even a Choir School, but, in any case, I had no desire to leave Chester. I had, as I thought, attained my goal in life, and was perfectly happy. But Boyle in his wisdom persisted and, not entirely with enthusiasm, I entered the competition.

To my surprise there were only three candidates, and I played the only piece I was confident in at the time, the *Prelude and Fugue in A minor*, by J. S. Bach. There were the usual keyboard tests, and, given my unique experience in downward transposition, I was fortunate to be asked to play a given hymn-tune a semitone lower. Academically I was equally fortunate, for my FRCO plus War Service was sufficient to exempt me from the necessity of obtaining Higher School Certificate passes. A few days later I received the following telegram "Congratulations on being selected by Examiners for appointment to Organ Studentship (signed) Thistlethwaite, Saint John's College." A new life was opening up before me, though I had little idea that it heralded the start of a lifetime's work at Saint John's. To stay in one job for 44 years shows either lack of ambition or job satisfaction, and it is the latter, rather than the former, which has always applied in my case.

Cambridge in the late 1940s was full of young men who, by then in their early or mid-twenties, had survived the War, and had arrived, noisily, to resume or make a belated start on their studies. Food rationing, as well as clothes and coal rationing, was still in force and college menus tended to be unimaginative and somewhat sparse. As far as Chapel music was concerned, everyone looked up to the choral pinnacle that was King's, with the fearsome but immensely gifted Boris Ord producing a standard of performance which most of us found awesome in its apparent nearness to perfection. He had a superb, inborn sense of rhythm which he communicated to the members of his choir by his hands, by the subtlety of his bodily movements, but especially by the magnetism of his eyes which drew sounds from his singers which not only provoked immense admiration for their splendid vocal technique, but which, at the same time, moved listeners by his ability to inject into a performance those elements of interpretation which bring a performance to life, but which can hardly be notated, let alone be described in words. Boris also conducted the Cambridge University Musical Society, its orchestra and its chorus, to great effect, and every undergraduate could hear, during his three years at Cambridge, Bach's *Mass in B minor*, and his *Saint Matthew Passion*. He also found time to conduct the University Madrigal Society, though it cannot have been easy for one who was surely a misogynist to endure sopranos and contraltos, rather than trebles and male altos. Many were the anguished tears and veiled threats which emanated from those ladies who had borne his sarcasm almost to breaking point. His end was tragic and a wasting disease brought about his premature death in December 1961.

But Boris was only one of a brilliant group of musicians working in the Faculty of Music at that time. There was Philip Radcliffe, the classical scholar turned musician, of King's also; the historian whose erudite lectures, always delivered without notes, were illustrated on the piano in his inimitable way. It was odd that one with such a razor-sharp mind should possess such a slapdash piano technique. He was able, however, to illustrate any point in his lectures, whether of opera, symphony, concerto, string quartet, organ or piano music, or song—all played, it goes without saying, without a note of music. Philip met a tragic death in 1986; he had been going on holiday to France in a car driven by his elderly sister. On emerging from the ferry on the French side his sister absent-mindedly continued driving on the left hand side of the road. Their car was hit by a heavy lorry, and both were killed instantly.

Then there was Hubert Middleton, of Trinity, who taught Harmony and Counterpoint. His position as Organist of that college had previously been held by such great men as C. V. Stanford (1852-1924) who, although Professor of Music, was never elected a Fellow, and because of this, it is said, he refused to teach in Trinity and insisted on holding his composition classes in the waiting room of Cambridge station. Alan Gray (1855-1935) followed Stanford, and carried on the choral tradition which, at that time, made the Trinity Choir the most famous in Cambridge. It was a tragedy when their choristers were done away with, and their choral library given to Great Saint Mary's Church, where it gathered dust but was never used, until I was able (by permission of a later Vicar) to rescue it and incorporate it into the Saint John's Choir Library. The Choir of Trinity College now exists as a body of young ladies and young men, and, under the direction of Richard Marlow, has acquired a deserved reputation for excellence.

Thurston Dart, the mathematician turned musician, was

perhaps the most brilliant lecturer of the time. He was a wonderfully original scholar whose book *The Interpretation of Music* is indispensable to any who aspire to historically correct performances. Dart was also a superb harpsichordist, and I recall two incredibly exciting concerts in which Bach's *Six Brandenburg Concerti* were played in the newly-opened Royal Festival Hall, London by the Boyd Neel Orchestra (then at the height of its fame) with Dart playing as soloist, and myself as continuo at a second harpsichord. Some of his improvisations tended to be outrageous (he never hesitated to put down a chord in a rest if he felt that it increased the musical tension and excitement), but they were products of a sharply brilliant mind, and I shall always treasure the lessons in continuo playing which I received at his hands.

The Professor was Patrick Hadley, friend of Delius, friend of Vaughan Williams. "Paddy," as he was known to all, has become a legend, and many are the anecdotes told of this wildly eccentric, but very gifted, composer and lovable man. His music, pathetically small in amount though it is, is distinctive in its sweep of the harmonic essence of late Romanticism. "No questions now," he would admonish an eager enquirer at one of his lectures, "kindly reserve them until the end of the lecture." Usually by then the questioner had forgotten his question, but if he hadn't, and repeated it, Paddy would always reply "No questions, I fear, I hear my taxi outside and I have to catch a train to Norwich. Good morning!"

His behaviour at Choral Scholar Trials was equally bizarre. Not many candidates in those days put down Gonville and Caius College (of which Paddy was the Precentor) as the college of their first preference, but just occasionally one did, and the Chairman would say "Professor Hadley, I think this is your candidate." Paddy, with a somewhat confused air, would lurch to his feet, and, approaching the understandably nervous young man would say, in what he took to be an encouraging tone of voice "Come this way, my dear fellow, let us see where the voice lies." Now Paddy had an artificial leg and, on one never-to-be-forgotten occasion, welcomed the candidate, then turning to the rest of us who were his co-examiners said, to our considerable surprise, "I say, have any of you boys got a drawing pin?"[1] None of us had, of course, but one was eventually discovered on the mantelpiece whereupon, to our astonishment, and to the candidate's particular horror, he lifted his artificial leg on to the piano stool, pulled up his trouser leg and his sock, and stuck the drawing pin with great force into his leg, in order to prevent his sock from slipping. Paddy's bathroom always had in it a selection of legs, some with brown shoes on and appropriate socks, one, I remember, had on it a pair of black shoes with black silk socks, and there were others of many colours and textures which did duty for most occasions.

Paddy's predecessor as Professor had been the redoubtable E. J. Dent. Dent was an unbeliever and Paddy frequently, and with mischievous glee, told the story of Dent's coffin on its last journey, slowly disappearing from view in Golders Green Crematorium to the strains of the last few pages of the Angel's Farewell from Elgar's *Dream of Gerontius,* played on an electronic organ.

For many years Hadley taught at the Royal College of Music one day a week, and he was usually to be seen in the bar of that famous train "The Fenman" on his return journey in the evening. His reply when asked if he would take a drink was always the same "A double-double Scotch, if you please, my dear fellow, I've had a very hard day!"

It is high time for a revival of Patrick Hadley's music. Much of it is of stunning beauty, particularly the large scale works for orchestra and choir. His eccentricity of manner should not be his only memorial.

---

[1] that is, a 'thumb-tack.'

As a young man I learned a great deal from all these musicians, but I learned most from Robin Orr, whose Organ Student I was from 1947-1951. A skilled composer who had been a pupil of both Alfredo Casella and Nadia Boulanger, a fine choir trainer, and an organist who had been a pupil of Sir Walter Alcock, Robin Orr was also a patient and understanding teacher. On his return from service in the RAF in 1946 he had inherited a somewhat run-down choir, kept going during the war-years by the Headmaster of the Choir School, the Revd Sam Senior, and the week-end visits of Herbert Howells, later to become an Honorary Fellow of the College. The College Choir consisted of three ancient Lay-clerks (one of whom, a tenor with a glass eye, had known Vaughan Williams when the latter was an undergraduate at Trinity), six rather dispirited Choral Students, and fourteen local boys who were educated at our tiny day choir school. Services were only sung on Sundays (though there had been week-day Evensongs before the War), and the Choir, I recall, would sometimes even sing a unison anthem. But, undeterred by this mediocrity, Robin Orr set about improving things, and, gradually things *did*, slowly, begin to improve. Congregations tended to be small, with rather more undergraduates than is the case today, but many fewer visitors. The music of Saint John's Chapel just was not known, and I remember that a number of people in the town were under the firm impression that the services were for members of the college only. Matins was the Sunday morning service, rather than a Sung Eucharist, and everything that went on in the Chapel was "low church." C. B. Rootham, Robin's predecessor, had begun the tradition of always having the Psalms unaccompanied, and this, to my private regret, was continued. But, that apart, I derived nothing but benefit from my four years as Robin's Organ Student, and the lessons learned were by no means musical ones only. It was indeed a blessed period in my life.

3

Saint John's College Choir

The Choirmaster stood at the pearly gates
His face was worn and old,
He stood before the man of fate
For admission to the fold.
"What have you done," Saint Peter said
"To gain admission here?"
"I've been a Choirmaster, sir," he said,
"For many and many a year."
The pearly gates flew open wide
Saint Peter touched the bell.
"Come in," he said, "and choose your harp
You've had *your* share of hell."

Anon. (20th century)

During my last year as Organ Student, in 1951, I was summoned to the Master's Lodge, to be told, to my considerable surprise, that Robin Orr had decided to retire in order to devote more time to composition, and that the College Council had it in mind to offer me the vacant position. Not wishing, presumably, to risk a refusal, the Master then said "If you were to be offered the position would you feel inclined to accept it?" I replied, perhaps too eagerly, that I should be honoured to accept, and so began what became for me a life's work as Organist (and Choirmaster) of Saint John's College.

My first Dean was Edward Raven, a somewhat shy man whose voice was certainly not of the highest quality. He sometimes surprised us in Chapel, and I can recall a Sunday Evensong when, after the usual announcements, he said in his clipped and rather formal voice "The preacher next Sunday will be," and, shuffling furiously through a pile of papers, finally, and with a distinct air of triumph, said "myself!" And while we were all digesting that, he went on to say "The Choir will now sing the anthem *Agnus Dei, qui tollis peccata mundi,* words by William Byrd!"

Dean Raven's family invariably attended Sunday morning Matins, and it was always something of a trial for the choristers to keep straight faces whilst singing the Psalm which includes the words "He feedeth the young ravens that call upon Him," with the Dean's charming daughters sitting only a few feet away from them.

The President at that time, Martin Charlesworth, had recently taken Holy Orders and occasionally he would take the service. His voice was pleasant but he had the un-nerving habit of scooping up to every accented note. His sense of pitch also tended to be unreliable, and I recall an Evensong in which he began to intone a Collect on a high D. In the middle of it he became tired and dropped a fifth to G, but as the end of the prayer approached, he felt that somehow he should get back to the original pitch in order that the Choir could sing the Amen. So, to everyone's astonishment, we heard

Through Je - sus Christ   our Lord

I still remember the look of disgust on the senior Lay-clerk's face as he refused to bring in the choir, and in a voice somewhat louder than was necessary *said,* with sarcastic deliberation, "A-men." But Martin Charlesworth, a classical scholar of considerable renown, was the kindest of men and he would go to endless lengths to put nervous undergraduates at their ease; one of his more bizarre efforts in this direction was to mimic any regional accent that he heard, being fully convinced that this made the young man "feel at home." It was Martin, too, who one Sunday morning, leaving Chapel after an 8 am. said Holy Communion service, met me, still dressed in pyjamas and dressing-gown, creeping through the courts in order to buy my Sunday newspaper. "Good morning" he said "you have just got up, no doubt you will have had breakfast, in which case there will be some dirty dishes in your gyp-room (kitchen). Do give me the honour of washing them up for you!" And this from the President of the College!

The little day choir school, just across the road from the college, was ruled over by the Revd Sam (*never* Samuel) Senior, a tiny Yorkshireman who also acted as Precentor. Sam's school had in it between 35 and 40 pupils who were taught the 3 r's, together with good manners, in the two classrooms which comprised the school; by far the greater part of the building consisted of the Headmaster's house. Sam was permitted by the College to augment his salary by admitting as many non-singing boys as he liked, with the inevitable result that conditions were incredibly cramped, there was no aisle in either classroom and desks were jammed together to such a degree that, in the main classroom, the master was obliged to enter through one door, whilst the boys contrived (some by climbing over desks) to enter by another.

Sam was a good musician of the old school, and his singing in Chapel was excellent, always true in pitch and phrased musically. Although his was a small voice he had the gift of being able to project it, and his diction (which always had a hint of a Yorkshire accent in it) was never less than clear. The excellence of the present College School is very different from the situation which Miss Maria Hackett, known as "the Choristers' Friend," found during her series of visits in the early nineteenth century to the choral establishments of England and Wales. She visited Saint John's in 1821 and reported as follows: "There is no mention of a Choir in the original Foundation and Statutes of this College, but in the reign of Charles II, a Music Master and six Choristers were added to the former establishment by Dr Gunning (22nd Master of the College) and Doctors Turner and Barwick, who gave a rent charge to the Society for the purpose.

The Choristers are to be chosen by the Master and senior Fellows within a month after any vacancy, the trebles to be about nine years of age, and to continue no longer until about sixteen; and the counter-tenors to be chosen of such whose voices are strong, and like to hold, and not to continue longer than their voices hold good. From Saint John's College I have not been honoured with an answer to my enquiries, and the accounts which have been transmitted to me respecting the present state of the School, under the superintendence of this Society, are such as I forbear to publish."

Some years later Miss Hackett, under the heading of "Trinity College and Saint John's College" wrote, "Two sets of boys, ten and eight, are now attached to the two colleges, but all attend the same schoolmaster, and are taught Latin, mathematics and drawing. They have a good school library, and are kindly permitted to use the Fellows' cricket-ground."

The subsequent history of the school is vague until 1873 when the tiny day choir school mentioned earlier was established in Bridge Street, in the middle of a block of property owned by the College, and situated conveniently a short walk from the Chapel; but, good though it had undoubtedly been, it was in the 1950s clearly becoming inadequate, chiefly due to a chronic lack of space and an absence of modern facilities. Changes of a radical nature were unavoidably imminent!

There had been changes in the Choir, too. One of Robin Orr's last acts before resigning was to induce the three Lay-clerks to retire, and the College had sensibly decided to increase the number of Choral Students to 12, four of each voice. There were 20 boys available, and, rather than have 14 Choristers and 6 Probationers, we changed to 16 Choristers and 4 Probationers. And this, apart from introducing 2 volunteer basses in addition to the four bass Choral Students, has constituted the College Choir ever since.

Dean Raven had died in the Michaelmas Term 1951, as had Martin Charlesworth, and Edward Knapp-Fisher (later to be Bishop of Pretoria, and subsequently Canon of Westminster) combined the offices of Chaplain and Acting-Dean until the arrival of Canon James Stanley Bezzant from Liverpool Cathedral as Dean. Bezzant was a remarkable man; he had a distinguished war record, but his home life had been saddened by an unsuccessful marriage. He was a very considerable scholar, and a marvellous preacher, one who always preached without notes—but he was not easy to work with. There were numerous occasions, even in Chapel, when he did not appear to be quite himself or, as the contemporary jargon has it, "excited" and at those times he would usually join in with the Choir, somewhat raucously and not always with the right notes. After a while I found it necessary never to put down on the Chapel List *Harwood in A flat, Noble in B minor, Stanford in B flat* and *Whitlock in D*, all of which were favourites of Bezzant's, and in which he could never resist taking part. He was, in many ways, a frightening man, and I well remember returning to Cambridge from an outside engagement to find the Organ Student in a state of nervous collapse. Bezzant had during the Service, stormed up to the organ loft and in a voice audible in the Chapel below had accused the young man of accompanying the plainsong Psalms "in a Roman Catholic manner."

On another occasion I had left the then Organ Student, the late Brian Runnett, in charge for Ash Wednesday Evensong, at which Allegri's *Miserere mei* was sung. As the quiet last chord died away the Dean was heard to say, quite audibly, "Bloody rubbish!" This, as Brian told me, quite destroyed the mood of the service. The Choir filed out after the Grace, and Bezzant, after a prayer, began "Gentlemen and boys, you may have noticed an observation escape from my lips after the Allegri. It was in no way a comment on what was a very beautiful performance, but I have long been of the opinion that the last verse of Psalm 51 is a later interpolation by someone who was not a scholar. For you will recall that in verse 16 we read 'For thou desirest no sacrifice, else would I give it thee: but thou delightest not in burnt-offerings,' and yet only three verses later, in verse 19, there are the words 'Then shalt thou be pleased with the sacrifice of righteousness, with the burnt-offerings and oblations, then shall they offer young bullocks upon thine altar.' Surely, its either the one or the other! Good evening."

But Bezzant had many endearing qualities. At the end of each term he gave, at his own expense, a most lavish dinner to all the senior members of the Choir and to the Chapel staff. These were wonderful occasions, and James Bezzant added to them by presenting books to all those Choral and Organ Students attending one of these dinners for the last time.

He was also Dean of Discipline and he would, from time to time, take a Porter and lurk in the shadows near a well-known climbing-in place in the Forecourt (this was in the days when the gates of the college were locked at

10 pm., and late arrivals were required to pay a fine). On one evening the two men duly waited, and presently they were rewarded by seeing a young man climb, at considerable risk to life and limb, over the spikes. He dropped down inside the college with a sigh of relief. At that moment Bezzant and the Porter stepped forward. "Good God!" said the young man, on seeing them. "No, my dear fellow" said Bezzant "simply his representative here on earth. Your name, please?"

It was during Bezzant's time at Saint John's that the whole future of the College Choir came into question. Sam Senior was due to retire as Headmaster in 1955, and it was clear that the College could no longer maintain the old Choir School. It so happened that a large house, appropriately named Saint John's House and situated in a convenient position on Grange Road, became vacant at about this time. It belonged to the College and was ideally suited to be a Choir School, particularly as the College's extensive playing fields lay just across the road from it. A committee was therefore formed to decide whether to move the school to Grange Road, or to close it completely; this would, of course, have meant the end of the choral tradition at Saint John's. Things looked distinctly unpromising at first, and Robin Orr and I were initially the only two people urging a move to Saint John's House. Finally, we had a stroke of good fortune; a distinguished Professor who was a member of the committee said "I'm a plain botanist, I know little of these matters, I hear Orr and Guest telling us about the Saint John's choral tradition, and how necessary it is to have a Choir School in order to maintain it. I'd like to see some written evidence to that effect." This was our golden opportunity and letters soon began to arrive at the Master's Lodge from distinguished musicians, all urging, in their different ways, the college to keep the Choir School. Finally, the Master telephoned me to say he had just received a telegram from Italy reading "Save Saint John's Choir

School at all costs," and signed by a Ralph Vaughan Williams. "Would this be a relation of the composer, do you think?", he asked innocently. As we had asked the old man to write, it was not a relation of the composer, but the composer himself, and this telegram, together with the letters of the other musicians, turned the tide of opinion in favour of moving the school to the new site. It was re-opened in 1955 in Saint John's House, Grange Road.

Saint John's College School has been a conspicuous success since beginning its new life. Three splendid Headmasters—the Revd C. F. Walters, Mr Alan Mould and now Mr Kevin Jones have built it into one of the best preparatory schools in the country. Byron House, a small pre-prep. school situated between King's College School and Saint John's College School, was acquired in the course of time and there are now over 400 pupils, boys and girls. The College during this period of growth has been immensely supportive, and it has indeed been heartening to observe that those Fellows who initially opposed the move were, and are now, amongst its greatest supporters. The scholarships given to Probationers and Choristers are substantial, amounting to two-thirds of the annual fee, and there is a constant stream of boys, mostly of very high calibre, seeking entry.

A sign of the times was the first Sung Eucharist on 6 March 1955. For some time subsequently there was just one a term, then two, then four, then from the Michaelmas Term 1969 Matins gave way to a Sung Eucharist on each Sunday of Term. The first Advent Carol Service was held on 2 December 1956. From the outset it had been decided to make this an 'admission by ticket only' event, and close on 1100 people attended what has now become an annual service. Since 1981 it has been broadcast, and is now relayed to most radio stations in the United States and Canada, as well as to other countries throughout the world.

One of the consequences of University Terms is that

the colleges are never in residence during Holy Week, and it was with this in mind that the present Dean, the Revd Andrew Macintosh, and I conceived the idea of holding a Lenten Carol Service, built around the story of the Crucifixion and interspersed with carols and other suitable music. This service was held for the first time in 1985 and attracts a large congregation; it was broadcast for the first time in 1993.

There are three other traditional services which deserve mention. First, there is the Ascension Day Carol. At midday the Choir, a brass group, some handbell ringers (there are no bells in the Chapel Tower) and the Chaplain climb to the top of the tower to sing an Ascension Carol by Praetorius. This is thought by many to be an ancient custom, but it dates back only to the beginning of this century, as will be seen from the following letter from the then Organist, C. B. Rootham to the then Master:

May 30 1927

Dear Master,

I am sorry that I have no exact record of the first time when our Saint John's Choir sang on the top of the Chapel Tower on Ascension Day: but it must have been early in the 1900s. I came back to Saint John's in October 1901. It was then the custom for the choristers to ascend the tower as a little treat on Ascension Day morning, after the morning service which ended about 11.45. William Bateson and (Sir Joseph) Larmor at High Table one night were talking about whether voices could be heard from a height. I suggested that they would be heard all right from the Chapel Tower: they thought not. I said no more: but when Ascension Day came round I trained the Choir in the motet of Palestrina *O Rex gloriae* (which is, of course, proper to Ascension Day) and asked the Choral Students and Lay-clerks to accompany the boys up the tower, with their copies of the motet. As far as I remember, I told no one but the members of the choir of my plan; and immediately after the clocks had finished striking 12 (midday), I started the choir in the motet. While conducting it I kept an eye on the courts below, and was interested to see everyone stop and look about, then upwards, to see where the singing was. I particularly kept an eye on Larmor's windows in his rooms in the Second Court, and presently was rewarded by seeing his head come out, and look about also to see whence the sound of voices came! This is the origin of the singing on our Chapel Tower! It is now, as you know, an established custom, dating, as I have written, from *about* 1902.

Yours sincerely, C. B. Rootham

The Sunday morning service for the Commemoration of Benefactors, held on the Sunday nearest to 6 May (Saint John ante Portam Latinam), is traditionally followed by Madeira and seed cake in the Master's Lodge. It is a service more highly regarded by the Fellows than by the undergraduates, perhaps because of the lengthy list of Benefactors which is traditionally the central part of the service. All choirs have a keen eye for the bizarre, and careful watch is always kept to see if the reader declaims "Hamlet Horace Mayor, of Wigan" or "Hamlet Horace, Mayor of Wigan." I was privileged to preach at this service in May 1985, taking as my text the first verse of Psalm 41 "Blessed is he that considereth the poor and needy: the Lord shall deliver him in the time of trouble."

Saint John's College has always had a strong connection with Wales, and many are the Welshmen who have studied within its walls. There was the martyr Saint Richard Gwyn, who on 15 October 1584 was dragged through the streets of Wrecsam to the Beastmarket to suffer with conspicuous bravery a horrible death.

And we celebrated, in 1988, the 400th anniversary of the first complete translation of the Bible into Welsh by William Morgan in 1588. An undergraduate of Saint John's, his name is rightly venerated in Wales, as is that of his friend and contemporary Edmwnd Prys (also of Saint John's) who took his BA in 1567 and is renowned for his Metrical version of the Psalms. There is a copy of Morgan's Bible in the College Library and it was used at the bilingual service which was held annually until 1991 on Saint David's Day, March 1. This service, in which the Choir sang two anthems and a hymn in Welsh, was justly popular and always attracted a large congregation. The disappointment at its recent abandonment has been widespread amongst the Welsh community, especially when one recalls that, with Italian and Spanish, the regularity of Welsh makes it one of the easiest of all languages to pronounce—quite apart from its being one of the official languages of Great Britain.

One of the questions which seem to delight interviewers is an enquiry about the relationship between the two choirs of Saint John's and King's. It is said that when Rootham and Ord were in charge of their respective college choirs the relationship was sometimes less than friendly, and Mrs Rootham, C. B. Rootham's widow, used to say that the only time she ever entered King's Chapel was when Rootham's *Evening Service in E minor* was being sung, and that she always, without exception, after the service complained to the King's authorities that the chapel was "beastly cold." But relations could not have been more friendly since the war, and especially in recent years. David Willcocks and Philip Ledger were both good friends to Saint John's, and the fact that we have been able to supply King's with their present distinguished Organist, Stephen Cleobury, former

Organ Student of Saint John's, has always been a matter of considerable pride to us.

When Sir David was in charge "down the road" (the phrase by which King's is affectionately known to all members of Saint John's Choir) he was invited to a Banquet in Saint John's College Hall which was the culminating event in a Conference of the Old Cathedral Choristers' Association. This took place in the early 1960s, at the time when we were just beginning to build up our reputation, and clawing our way to some kind of national, and even international, reputation. There had been a Festival Evensong in Chapel beforehand, and no stone had been left unturned in the choir rehearsals which preceded it. The Chapel was full and, to my relief and delight, the Choir sang beautifully; and at the Banquet, speaker after speaker spoke in glowing terms about the singing. The speaker before Sir David (who was, of course, Guest of Honour) even went so far as to say that "the singing was out of this world." My head grew larger and larger until David stood up to speak. "As Organist of King's" he began, "I was interested to learn that the singing of Saint John's Choir at Evensong was like nothing on earth!"

I shall always remember Philip Ledger for a most generous gesture, made to us at a time of considerable tribulation. It was a Lent Term and our Choristers had been stricken with a flu bug. Very important services were imminent, and, with there only being four or five of our boys available, it was clear that we were in deep trouble. This got to the ears of Philip, who telephoned me to say that he had heard of our dilemma, and would we like to audition half-a-dozen King's boys and, if found satisfactory, borrow them for a few days. Needless to say, I told him that I would not dream of *auditioning* King's boys, but that I would borrow them with great pleasure. The King's boys came, and with consummate musicianship adapted to our ways and enabled us to keep our services going. They subsequently returned to King's and became King's boys again. We now lend each other Choral Students and music and, although rivals, are the best of friends. I believe strongly that the presence of Saint John's Choir in the same city is a factor in keeping King's Choir up to the very high international standard that it has attained—just as the knowledge that there is a choir of such excellence "down the road" has been an inspiration to us at Saint John's. The joint Evensong which we sing alternately in Saint John's Chapel and King's Chapel is an event to which we always look forward, as is the music provided by the two choirs at the Honorary Degree Congregation held each June in the Senate House.

It is the responsibility of the University Organist to arrange this, and during my tenure of the post I was obliged to write each year to the Master of Saint John's for permission for our Choir to take part, mentioning that, as far as I knew, the Organist of Saint John's had no objection! The two choirs sing two five-minute spots and the National Anthem, accompanied by a brass group which also plays before and after the ceremony. Not a wildly taxing programme, but it does add greatly to what is already a colourful event.

4

Organ and Choral Students, Choristers and Other Matters

If one's aim in life is to become a cathedral organist there is no training better than by way of an Organ Scholarship. It is by being involved daily with choir rehearsals, by coming to grips with a wide repertoire of pieces, by observing and listening to other choirs and organists, that one, almost unconsciously, learns the job. It is impossible to 'teach' choir-training; the *sine qua non* is the particular type of personality that one either happens to be born with, or not. We have been very fortunate in our Organ Students at Saint John's and many have gone on to reach positions of high eminence.

Sir David Lumsden, Assistant at Saint John's in the early 50s, went on to become, successively, Organist of Saint Mary's Church, Nottingham, of Southwell Minster, of New College, Oxford and subsequently Principal of the Royal Scottish Academy of Music and Drama, before moving to become Principal of the Royal Academy of Music, London.

Also from the 1950s came **Peter White,** Assistant Organist at Chester Cathedral, Director of Music at Merchant Taylor's School, and now Organist of Leicester Cathedral, and the late **Brian Runnett,** so tragically killed in a car accident near Lichfield in 1970. He had also been Assistant Organist at Chester Cathedral, before first becoming a Lecturer at Manchester University and then Organist of Norwich Cathedral. **Jonathan Bielby,** Assistant Organist at Manchester Cathedral and now Organist of Wakefield Cathedral, followed Runnett at Saint John's.

Stephen Cleobury was steeped in the cathedral tradition, having been a Chorister at Worcester Cathedral. After leaving Saint John's he became Organist of Saint Matthew's Church, Northampton, then Sub-Organist at Westminster Abbey, Organist of Westminster Cathedral, and is now our colleague "down the road" at King's College, Cambridge.

Jonathan Rennert, now Organist of Saint Michael's Cornhill, London followed; then came **John Scott,** a Chorister at Wakefield Cathedral, Assistant Organist at Saint Paul's Cathedral, London and also at Southwark Cathedral, subsequently Sub-Organist of Saint Paul's, and later succeeding Christopher Dearnley as Organist of Saint Paul's Cathedral.

Although **David Hill** was never a cathedral chorister he brought many gifts to his work at Saint John's. He is a skilled violinist, and quickly showed his prowess as an orchestral conductor. He later became Sub-Organist of Durham Cathedral, Organist of Westminster Cathedral, and Organist of Winchester Cathedral. **Ian Shaw** followed David Hill as Sub-Organist at Durham Cathedral, but has since left the cathedral world for another branch of the profession. The 1980s produced two more Cathedral Organists in **Adrian Lucas,** Assistant Organist of Norwich Cathedral, and now Organist of Portsmouth Cathedral, and **Andrew Lumsden** (son of Sir David Lumsden), Assistant Organist of Southwark Cathedral, Sub-Organist of

Westminster Abbey, and now Organist of Lichfield Cathedral. The tradition is being maintained by **Andrew Nethsingha,** Assistant Organist of Wells Cathedral.

A number of the Choristers have become professional musicians, and I mention particularly the operatic producer, **David Pountney,** and the conductor **Robert King.** Others who promise to follow in their distinguished footsteps include **Paul Plummer,** now Organ Scholar at New College Oxford, **Richard Mayo,** formerly Organ Scholar of Corpus Christi College, Cambridge, and **Allan Walker,** recently appointed Organ Student at Saint John's.

Amongst the Choral Students who have become professional singers are (in chronological order) Kenneth Bowen, John Noble, Mark Deller, Michael Rippon, Rupert Forbes, Michael Pearce, Peter Knapp, Richard Suart, William Kendall, Michael Earle, Mark Tucker, Charles Naylor, Andrew Greenan, Simon Keenlyside, Jonathan Best, Charles Pott, John Davies, David Guest, Andrew Gant (now also a successful composer), Lynton, Atkinson, Stephen Gadd, Nicholas Gedge and Jeremy Huw Williams. Dale Adelmann has become Organist of Saint Paul's Cathedral, Buffalo, New York, U.S.A. But perhaps the most famous of Chapel singers was John Gostling, born in East Malling, Kent in about 1650. He was admitted to Saint John's College in October 1669, aged 18. He was sworn in as a Gentleman Extraordinary of the Chapel Royal on 25 February 1679 and, having taken Holy Orders, became a Minor Canon at Canterbury Cathedral, Chaplain to King Charles II, Sub-Dean of Saint Paul's Cathedral and Prebendary of Lincoln.

The compass and volume of Gostling's voice was remarkable, and a number of anthems were written by Henry Purcell for him; *They that go down to the sea in ships* is perhaps the most famous. He became a favourite of the King and twice accompanied him to Windsor. By way of thanks the King is said to have presented Gostling with a silver egg, filled with guineas, together with the dry comment that he had heard that "eggs were good for the voice."

Choristers' and Probationers' rehearsals were, until 1991, held in the Song School, a splendidly appointed building in the Forecourt which contained the very extensive Choir Library. The boys marched in twos from the Choir School in time for an hour's rehearsal from 8.30 am. to 9.30 am. on five mornings a week. This was an extremely beneficial arrangement, for it gave everyone much needed exercise, and in summer provided a very distinctive opportunity for camera shots to the many visitors enjoying the beauties of the Backs. Choral Students were required to "learn their notes" in their own time, so that the full rehearsals in Chapel could be devoted entirely to interpretation. There was one 'men only' rehearsal for three quarters of an hour before Wednesday Evensong; otherwise there was, as a general rule, a full rehearsal before each service at which the whole choir was present. This we found sufficient for the term's music, and for the various recordings and recitals undertaken by the Choir.

The Senior Chorister was always a very important person. He had the difficult job of controlling, by the force of his personality and by his personal example, the others. Not only had he to be a good musician with, if possible, a decent voice, but also able to ensure that all were punctual, all were clean and tidy, and that all behaved themselves. There are countries where such a system would be forbidden by law, but I am firmly of the opinion that it works well; it teaches self-discipline, and certainly teaches the Senior Chorister to take responsibility. Discipline in Saint John's Choir was very different from that in the Choir School of Saint Thomas' Church, Leipzig, when J. S. Bach was Cantor there. The Cantor's duties were to teach singing (seven hours weekly); to be present with the boys at church on Thursday mornings at 7 am; to give some of the Latin lessons . . . the boys rose at 5 am. in summer, at 6 am.

in winter.

A list of faults and their fines is worth reprinting:

1. For losing the key or leaving it in the door: 4 groschen
2. For failing to shut the door when the last to leave the room: 2 groschen
3. For being sick (qui vomitat): 2 groschen
4. For swearing, loud or improper speech: 6 pfennigs
5. For impertinent language, in Latin or German: 6 pfennigs
6. For not getting up in the morning and missing prayers: 3 pfennigs
7. For not tidying the cubicle before 10 in summer and 12 in winter: 6 pfennigs

Over the years we have had a succession of splendid Chaplains, a number of whom have gone on to become bishops. Henry Hill, who later became Bishop of Ontario, Canada, was Dean Bezzant's first Chaplain. He tended sometimes to be nervous, and I well recall his singing, on the day on which King George VI died, "O Lord save the King, I mean the Queen." Others who have reached the Bench of Bishops include Philip Goodrich (Bishop of Worcester), and Keith Sutton (Bishop of Lichfield). Stephen Sykes, our former Dean, is now Bishop of Ely. One of the most interesting and most popular temporary Chaplains was Donald Coggan, Honorary Fellow and former Archbishop of Canterbury, who came for a term on sabbatical leave. His reading of the Lessons was always memorable, and he delighted us by his request to sing at Evensong from time to time. He would rehearse assiduously, and his voice was always true. Donald Coggan became so popular with the Choral Students that he was rewarded with the supreme accolade; he was invited to the Baron of Beef public house towards the end of his stay in Saint John's for a parting drink. The manner of his refusing was a model of tact!

Cardinal Hume's visits to preach have always been special

occasions, and his sermon at the service of Thanksgiving for the life and work of Saint John Fisher to mark the 450th anniversary of his death will long be remembered. This service, on 8 June 1985, commemorated one who, with the Lady Margaret Beaufort, was responsible for the foundation of Saint John's College. As the Fellows of the time wrote to Fisher, in prison shortly before his execution "We acknowledge ourselves obliged to you for so many benefits that we cannot even count them or express them in words. You are father to us, teacher, counsellor, lawgiver, indeed the pattern of every virtue and all holiness. To you we owe our livelihood, our learning and every good thing that we have or know."

There have, of course, been many Memorial Services over the years, but there is one in particular which demands mention here, that of Herbert Howells. He had been Acting Organist at Saint John's during the absence of Robin Orr in the Royal Air Force at the time of the Second World War, and had subsequently been elected an Honorary Fellow of the College. Howells' Memorial Service took place on 7 May 1983, and the music, all of it by H.H., centred around his *Take him, earth, for cherishing.*

Marriages in Chapel, though much less frequent than Memorial Services, have increased of late. Formerly only children of Fellows or Fellows themselves were permitted the use of the Chapel, but permission has latterly been extended to junior members. My own wedding on 31 October 1959, to Nancy Mary Talbot, of Cambridge, was solemnised by Dean Bezzant, and it was an odd experience to kneel in the sanctuary, hear the Choir sing and yet have no control over it. We have had two children, David, now a professional singer in London, who was both a Chorister and a Choral Student—and Elizabeth, a professional violinist, formerly living in Bloemfontein, South Africa, but now teaching in England.

My own work, apart from that with the College Choir,

has included a good deal of adjudicating, both in Welsh Eisteddfodau and in English Festivals. For the former one needs three qualifications: to be a professional musician, to hold a position outside Wales and to be able to speak the Welsh language. The increased use of Welsh has brought sharply into focus the third requisite of late, and especially is this true in the Eisteddfod Genedlaethol (the National Eisteddfod). The so-called International Eisteddfod, held at Llangollen, has virtually nothing at all to do with Welsh culture, and might just as well be held in Scunthorpe or Wick. The only Welsh I heard on the one occasion at which I adjudicated there was the Welsh National Anthem sung as an "own choice" piece by a Russian choir!

In the late 60s I was invited to direct a newly-formed choir in Massachusetts, USA. This was called the Berkshire Boy Choir and consisted of some forty boys and a group of professional men. We rehearsed daily for a month, and gave concerts in the following month. The boys came in twos and threes from various locations, some from choirs such as that of Washington Cathedral, others from under-privileged homes. There was, rightly, an attempt to mix black and white, regardless sometimes of their musical prowess, and I recall one little black boy, Willie, who came from a notorious district of Chicago. He, poor fellow, was found to be tone-deaf and was a 'growler'; there was no question of his singing with the Choir so he was given the job of distributing programmes in the foyer of the various locations in which we sang. I shall always remember Willie, standing nonchalantly, chewing gum and accosting the incoming audience with a welcoming grin and (out of the side of his mouth) "Yuh wanna *proh*-grem?"

The Philippines was a country I had always wished to visit, and so when an invitation came to take part in the Bamboo Organ Festival in Manila I accepted with alacrity. This particular and somewhat unique organ is housed in the Catholic Church of Las Piñas, Metro Manila. It has one manual and eleven pedal notes only and, out of a total of 1032 pipes, 902 are made of bamboo wood, chosen particularly because of its climate-resistant properties. The instrument was restored by the firm of Johannes Klais, of Bonn, Germany in 1975. There are a number of divided stops, and the voicing itself shows a strong Spanish influence. The specification is as follows:

MANUAL (Bass FF-C′)

Flautado Violin	8′	Docena 2	$1^1/_3$′
Flautado Major	4′	Quincena 1	1′
Octava 1	2′	Quincena 2	1′
Octava 2	2′	Bajon cillo	4′ (horizontal)
Docena 1	$1^1/_3$′	Clarin Campana	2′ (horizontal)

MANUAL (Treble C′-F³)

Flautado Violin	16′	Docena	$2^2/_3$′
Flautado Major	8′	Quincena	2′
Travizera	8′ (beating)	Corneta	8′ (mounted)
Octava 1	4′	Clarin Claro	8′ (horizontal)
Octava 2	4′	Clarin Campana	8′ (horizontal)
Octavina	4′		

PEDAL

Contras	4′ (11 pipes) + Pajaritos (Bird song-7 pipes)
	Tambor (3 pipes)

The concerts in Las Piñas Church were well attended, with the *ad hoc* choir singing well, especially in Haydn's *Nelson Mass,* though the orchestra, the Metro Manila Symphony Orchestra, could not be included amongst the world's finest, and I remember that in a subsequent concert I was surprised to find that the horns were totally unable to play the well-known Hornpipe in Handel's *Water Music,* and that the First Oboe complained that the little Aria was beyond him because he had only seen the music for the first time that very morning!

One of the most frightening cities on earth is Los Angeles, and my one visit there was to conduct a concert performance of Purcell's *Faery Queen*. I remember excellent orchestral playing and a splendid chorus, but the whole occasion was spoiled by perhaps the most incompetent solo singing I had ever heard. The streets of Los Angeles were dangerous but I was able to visit the Spanish quarter and, best of all, to take a trip to San Francisco. The famous redwood trees were a delight, and I also journeyed the very short distance to visit Alcatraz Island and its bleak, abandoned prison. The cells themselves seemed to be rather more comfortable than those in similar establishments in Britain, though the punishment cell was appalling—steel floors, steel walls, completely dark, completely empty. The guide asked if any of us wished to experience a few minutes in this place; I started to sidle away, but felt a tug on my arm and saw that my wife had no intention of missing this treat. We went in—the massive door clanged shut—and we were alone, completely cut off. Would the guide lose the key, I thought? Would it perhaps break in the lock? Would the guide forget about us? But no, we were let out after a few minutes to our great relief, though I am convinced that my tendency to claustrophobia in confined spaces dates from this event.

I have long had a close connection with the very good Choir of Liverpool Metropolitan Cathedral, and from time to time I have had the pleasure of spending a long week-end with them, taking their rehearsals, and directing them at High Mass on the following Sunday. I quickly learned that one of the important things was to be able to talk sensibly to the boys about the players and achievements of Liverpool F.C. and Everton F.C.

Two other events in Wales gave me great pleasure at their inception. First, in 1984 there was formed a new youth choir, Côr Cenedlaethol Ieuenctid Cymru (the National Youth Choir of Wales). Auditions were held and it seemed as if the Choir would go from strength to strength. A few concerts were given, but after a while the authorities decided that no conductor would be in charge for more than three years! This ridiculous rule, which destroyed any kind of artistic continuity, has been responsible, in my view, for the fact that the Choir, so promising in its early days, has never really fulfilled its true potential—though on the credit side it has produced two superb baritones in Bryn Terfel and Jeremy Huw Williams.

The other event was the Llandaf Festival, which I was asked to direct in 1984. Much of my work for it was, of necessity, done from Cambridge, and the day-to-day organisation was left to others in Cardiff. I will not comment on the latter, suffice it to say that audiences were abysmally small, and I was glad to retire after one year from what had become a thankless task. The Festival itself committed assisted suicide—and another local Welsh Festival died, a great pity, for I cannot believe that Festivals of this kind are any less necessary to Welsh culture than are the massive international events which now take place so regularly in Cardiff and elsewhere in Wales.

Since retirement from Saint John's I have worked increasingly abroad, directing youth choirs in Holland, Belgium, Switzerland and the USA. There is a growing call for master-classes, especially in conducting and in choir-training, and I have had the pleasure on more than one occasion of being invited to conduct the splendid Choir of Saint Thomas, Fifth Avenue, New York City, for weekends and to lecture to visiting choir-masters; Gerre Hancock, its superbly talented Director, is perhaps the most prestigious church musician in the country. A development of extraordinary interest and musical importance has taken place on Cape Cod, Massachusetts, on the east coast of the USA, at Rock Harbour, near Orleans (where Liverpool,

England, is nearer than is San Francisco). The Community
of Jesus, an ecumenical foundation founded in 1970,
decided a few years ago to develop its choir and I was
invited to give what help I could. The singers were all
amateurs, some living under a Rule, others living in
associated families. Never have I known a group to work
harder, and they soon began the custom of travelling to
Cambridge for a month each year, in order to be rehearsed
by Stephen Cleobury and myself on alternate days.
Gradually their competence improved, so that they reached
the necessary standard to give concerts. Things were hard
at first, for although they by now were singing extremely
well, their name was not known, and it was necessary in
these early concerts to "paper the house." I had the pleasure
of touring Austria, Hungary and Yugoslavia with them in
1989, and subsequently what was then the Soviet Union
in 1990. The highlight of our visit to Yugoslavia was our
stay in Medjugorje, where Our Lady is said to have appeared,
and still to appear, before a group of young people in
the village. It was at the time of our visit rapidly becoming
another Lourdes, with thousands of pilgrims arriving from
all parts of the Catholic world. Its subsequent fate is clearly
in the balance, and one can only hope for a return to
a just peace in that ravaged land.

Moscow and Leningrad were equally noteworthy, and
we were indeed fortunate to be in these lovely cities
(especially the latter) at a time when there were the first
beginnings of a move from Communism. I was thrilled
to have the opportunity of conducting in the Conservatory
Hall and the Tchaikovsky Hall in Moscow, and the Kapella
Hall in Leningrad. This choir, known as the *Gloriæ Dei
Cantores*, continues to give concerts of an extremely high
standard throughout the world under its conductor
Elizabeth Patterson.

My connections with Wales continue to be strong, and
on my election as President of the Royal College of

Organists in 1978 I was honoured to have an *englyn* written
by two of Wales' most distinguished bards to mark the event.
The internal rhyming of consonants, as well as the more
familiar (to English ears) rhyming of vowels at the ends
of lines, is a characteristic of this ancient Welsh literary
form. It was composed by Dic Jones and T. Llew Jones
in a quarter of an hour in a noisy pub bar at the time
of the 1978 Eisteddfod Genedlaethol in Caerdydd in 1978:

> Enaid mawr y nodau mân—hwn â'i ddawn
> A ddwg fawl o'r organ;
> Sior Guest yw saer y gân
> Sy'n tywys yn Sant Ioan.[1]

A similar englyn was written at about the same time
by the late W. J. Jones, Y Bala:

> Sior Guest, un o sêr y gân—ddaw yma'n
> Ddiomedd o'i drigfan,
> A'i lafar nawr ar lwyfan
> Mae; erglyw, fel Cymro glân.[2]

It is not generally known that most villages and towns
in Wales have their own local eisteddfodau. Audiences are
usually large and competition keen, and prizes, usually of
money, tend to be larger than those offered in similar

---

[1]   Friend of the little notes (ie. the keyboard)-this person with his gift
Brings forth praise from the organ;
George Guest is the architect of song
And he leads (the choir) in Saint John's.

[2]   George Guest, one of the stars of song—comes here
Generously from his home,
And now his work on stage (ie. the Eisteddfod stage)
Is; listen!, as that of a sincere Welshman.

Festivals in England. A characteristic is that eisteddfodau frequently continue until the early hours of the following morning; at a local eisteddfod a few years ago I heard the comment that that particular eisteddfod was something of a failure; it had ended by 2 am., whereas that of the previous year had gone on until 3 am.—and the astonishing thing is that there is normally a sizable audience present until the singing of "Mae hen wlad fy nhadau" at the end of proceedings, however late. One of the most popular events is the 'Hymn-tune for the over-60s'. A dedicated band of elderly singers go from place to place, usually singing the same hymn on each occasion, and competing against the same people. The appeal of this particular competition is largely sentimental, though there are, of course, other hotly-competitive events for soloists and for choirs. Many have been the professional singers who took their first steps in public performance at local eisteddfodau, before venturing to appear in the National Eisteddfod, not least being Geraint Evans, Kenneth Bowen and Bryn Terfel.

There are various competitions for *Cerdd Dant,* that unique and wholly characteristic art form which is peculiar to Wales, and is of great antiquity. The competitions devoted to Welsh folk-song are always popular, and are usually of an extremely high standard. Their very simplicity makes a polished performance vital, and the fact that the texts almost always deal with the fundamentals of human life is perhaps the main reason for the appealing and often moving quality of these beautiful songs. Changing economic conditions have been largely responsible for a certain weakening of the old tradition of Corau Meibion (male-voice choirs), but many of the old names still appear in 'the National,' though what many believe to be a fear of being placed other than first is almost certainly a reason for the absence of others.

I was appointed an Assistant Lecturer in the Faculty of Music at Cambridge in 1953, and subsequently a Lecturer.

The custom in those days was that the Organists of Saint John's and King's Colleges were so appointed though, perhaps temperamentally, I never found the work easy. I was required to be a kind of 'musical G.P.', and found myself lecturing on a variety of historical topics, Form and Analysis, Ear Training, Harmony and Counterpoint, as well as holding classes in such keyboard skills as Transposing (how useful my Chester days proved in this particular discipline!), improvising upon a Figured Bass, Harmonising melodies and basses, and reading an orchestral score at sight on the piano. I served under four Professors—Patrick Hadley, Thurston Dart, Robin Orr (who, more than anyone drew together the Faculty—both junior and senior members—into one cohesive and friendly unit) and Alexander Goehr, the present holder of the Chair. The move from the rather cramped but cosy premises in Downing Place to the much more sumptuous Music School in West Road has not, in my view, been an unmixed blessing, chiefly because of its much more remote situation and a certain coldness of atmosphere. There has been, too, a subtle change in the teaching and in the examinations. In the 40s and 50s the Mus.B. degree was the goal of most undergraduates; nowadays it tends to be something of a backwater, and no longer do potential cathedral organists regard the degrees of BA(MA), Mus.B., as absolute necessities.

It was possible to take early retirement from my Lectureship in 1982, and I quickly took advantage of this; there was no longer any sense in continuing to pretend that being Organist of Saint John's College was anything but a full-time occupation.

5

Concerts and Foreign Tours (1951-1973)

> Though we travel the whole world over
> to find the beautiful we must carry it
> with us or we find it not.
> *Ralph Waldo Emerson*

Concerts are nowadays an integral part of every choir's year, though in the early 50s they were by no means common, and foreign tours even less so. One of the major events of 1951 was the Festival of Britain, and our Choir gave an extremely successful concert in Chapel, under the direction of Robin Orr; it was his last concert as Organist, and my last as Organ Student. Little subsequently happened until 1954, when the Court Circular in the Times of 28 July 1954 included the following: "Sandringham, Norfolk July 27, Queen Elizabeth the Queen Mother, accompanied by the Princess Margaret, this evening attended a choral concert given by the Choir of Saint John's College, Cambridge in Saint Margaret's Church, King's Lynn." Alan Hemmings was organist, and Robin Orr returned to play his *Te Deum* and *Jubilate*. This work, newly-composed, proved something of a trial to Basil Maine, the eminent music critic, who wrote "just as I seemed to be coming to grips with its wilful dissonance . . . it suddenly ended upon an unashamed concord, and in the circumstances it was this final harmony I found disturbing." A similar programme was given in Chapel for that year's Cambridge Festival.

In 1955 the Choir visited the famous church of Saint Peter Mancroft, Norwich, and this recital was especially noteworthy for the first performance of that splendid unaccompanied motet by Robin Orr, *I was glad*. 1957 included a visit to Saffron Walden Parish Church, and in 1958 we journeyed to the Isle of Wight to sing in Freshwater Parish Church (one of the College's numerous livings). Apart from a concert in Great Dunmow Parish Church little of note happened until we paid a second visit to Freshwater in 1960, though part of an anonymous letter to The Listener on 7 May 1959, is perhaps of historical interest. "As choristers at Saint John's," he writes, "we had our initiation ceremony, carried out in solemn pomp. One became a full-fledged choirboy on a dark evening after service, when the verger had gone home. The chapel lights were switched out, a candle or two produced, and the choir formed a double line in forbidding silence before a statue in the ante-chapel. In the echoing gloom the fledgling was ordered to advance with stiff upper lip, to bow to his colleagues and kiss the statue's toe which had grown smooth and shiny from the custom. The victim was then tapped smartly on the back of the head by heavy books which had been concealed behind the backs of the more senior choristers. He was then, in every sense, a Chorister of Saint John's College Choir."

Saint Mary's Church, Shrewsbury, now sadly closed to public worship, was visited in 1961, with Brian Runnett at the organ, as he was at All Saints' Church, Newmarket.

1962 was a very special year, for Saint John's was celebrating the 450th anniversary of its foundation in 1511, and to mark that event the College had in the previous year commissioned Robin Orr, Herbert Howells and Michael Tippett to compose works for the Choir; these were all performed for the first time at a concert in March 1962. Orr's *Come and let yourselves be built as living stones,* written for choir and organ, is built on the scale D, E, F, G, A flat, B flat, C flat and is in that composer's inimitable astringent style. The text of Howells' *Sequence for Saint Michael* is taken from Alcuin's *Sequentia de Sancto Michaele, quam Alcuinus composuit Karolo imperatori.* The name Michael was never very far from Howells' mind, and it is impossible to believe that the impassioned cry 'Michael'— the choir's first utterance—does not refer to the composer's dead son as much as it does to the saint.

Splendid though these two works are, it is perhaps the *Magnificat and Nunc dimittis (Collegium Sancti Johannis Cantabrigiense)* by Tippett which has achieved the most widespread popularity. The composer himself wrote: "Occasions and problems. The 450th anniversary of the founding of Saint John's College is clearly an occasion for jubilation. The problem would be to compose a reasonably fitting means to express jubilation through a Magnificat and Nunc dimittis without disturbing their character. If we feel jubilation needs a great volume of sound, then that can most easily come from the organ, especially the fine organ of Saint John's. Jubilant sound from the choir is effectively smaller but, all the same, in its own right entirely sufficient. So part of the solution of the self-imposed problem was not to match the choir with the organ, but rather to let each speak proportionately. Then, again, the Evening Canticles are songs. Although these are traditionally so well known that we can indeed forget the personal occasion of their origin, I have wanted to retain their song-like character by reserving any complex polyphony to the quite impersonal Gloria. The *Magnificat* is a song of rejoicing and praise. But Simeon's song is rather of renunciation. I have given the song to an optional solo boy, or small number of boys, accompanied by solo men's voices, as in old Verse anthems, while the organ, in contrast to the display of the *Magnificat*, is reduced to primitive onomatopoësis of the 'thunderings' of God." This magnificent setting, which owes nothing to any of its predecessors, is now deservedly sung throughout the world and is a landmark in sacred choral music. Brian Runnett accompanied, and played solo pieces by Orr, Howells and Tippett.

Later that year the Choir sang at Guildford Cathedral. Howells' *A Sequence for Saint Michael* was repeated, and subsequently the following letter appeared in the local press "Sir—No doubt your musical correspondent will report elsewhere on the excellent choral recital in Guildford Cathedral . . . but how many who were present, we wonder, noticed how delightfully topical was their last item *A Sequence for Saint Michael*, particularly in view of the fact that on the following day the new branch of Messrs Marks and Spencer was due to open in the High Street, Yours etc., Surrey Churchman."

1963 brought another concert at Saint Peter Mancroft Church, Norwich, one at Saint Matthew's Church, Northampton, and one at Saint David's Cathedral, Wales, all with Brian Runnett at the organ. For the Saint David's visit we all stayed at nearby RAF Brawdy. I was put into the Officers' Mess, Mr Rossiter (our excellent Chapel Clerk) was put into the Sergeants' Mess, and everyone else (including the Regius Professor of Divinity, Craddock Ratcliff) was put into the Seamens' Mess.

Saint Albans Abbey, Saint Matthew's Church Northampton and the Whitworth Hall, Manchester University were visited in 1964, and the usual Cambridge

Festival concert was given in the Long Vacation, followed by a second visit to Saint David's Cathedral. Jonathan Bielby was the excellent accompanist at all these concerts.

Coventry Cathedral was full for our first 1965 concert. This was followed by our first collaboration with the Academy of Saint Martin-in-the-Fields orchestra, led by Neville Marriner, in a programme which featured Haydn's *Theresa Mass* (with Erna Spoorenberg, Bernadette Greevy, John Mitchinson and Tom Krause as soloists). The final concert of the year was at Blackburn Cathedral; this will always remain in my mind as the occasion on which the first item was to be the Verse Anthem *O God, which by the leading of a star* (John Bull). As the boy soloist opened his mouth to enunciate the first word, not tone came out but vomit! He had indeed been too lavishly entertained, and it became necessary there and then to alter the programme, something I have always hated doing.

1966 saw us in Monmouth School, where the Senior Chorister's father was Headmaster, and his sister (now the distinguished conductor, Jane Glover) was just developing an interest in music. The Cambridge Festival concert saw us again working with the Academy, this time in Haydn's *Harmoniemesse,* with Erna Spoorenberg, Helen Watts, Alexander Young and the Canadian Joseph Rouleau as soloists. It has always been a pleasure to sing with the Choir of King's College, and together we gave a concert in Westminster Abbey later that year, with David Willcocks and me sharing the conducting. Waltham Abbey was visited in November 1966, and the final concert of the year was in Leeds Parish Church. Our visit to Leeds was particularly appropriate, for the Parish Church organist, Donald Hunt, had a son in our Choir, and he was soon to have his younger son, too, joining us as a Probationer.

For some quite unknown reason we have not, over the years, given many concerts in London, but we visited Saint Clement Danes Church in early 1967. The Times critic wrote about this concert "How much does it really matter what kind of sound a choir makes, as long as it is polished, musical and euphonius? What . . . is the point of comparing say, the Choir of King's College Cambridge with that of, say, Saint John's College . . . so long as both are as excellent as they undeniably are? Silly questions, perhaps, but relevant to last night's programme, because its content was very much geared to the type of sound this fine choir makes." There was the usual Cambridge Festival concert in the summer and, because I was working in the USA with the newly-formed Berkshire Boy Choir at the time, the final concert of the year at the magnificent church of Walpole Saint Peter, Norfolk was conducted by Robin Orr.

1968 was an extremely busy year, with concerts at Carlisle Cathedral (with our new Organ Student, Stephen Cleobury accompanying), Aldeburgh Parish Church (as part of the Aldeburgh Festival, and with Peter Pears reading). This particular concert was based on music and words by the Wesley family, and it was after this concert that Benjamin Britten delighted the Choristers by enthusiastically giving his autograph on scraps of paper; there were multiple signings on each bit of paper "they'll do for swops!" said the composer. Barnack Parish Church was also visited, as was Huddersfield Town Hall. And then came our first overseas tour; we had been working for this and finally our opportunity came when we were invited to take part in an ecumenical week of services just before Christmas in Holland. We sang Evensong in the Church of the Dove at Amsterdam, and I recall a particularly effective *Stanford in G*. After a strenuous rehearsal the senior members of the Choir were strolling along one of the canal banks in search of a decent place in which to have a drink, when eventually we came across a place with the familiar name of the George the Fifth Bar. The noise inside was deafening and we were initially astonished to find that the very crowded bar consisted entirely of men. We did not intend

to stay long, but our departure was even more precipitate
when Mr Rossiter, our Chapel Clerk, said in a somewhat
puzzled tone of voice "You see that barman over there,
he's winked at me three times already!"

We visited Saint Matthew's Church, Northampton again
in 1969, and I was particularly pleased to be giving concerts
in Bangor Cathedral and Saint Asaph Cathedral on
successive days in March. Another visit to Wales, this time
to the south, took place in August. We were invited to give
a concert in Llandaf Cathedral as part of the Investiture
Celebrations, the concert being presented by the Royal
College of Organists and the Cardiff City Council. And,
to end a busy year of recitals, we visited Norwich Cathedral
in December. Stephen Cleobury accompanied throughout,
and contributed some superb organ solos, none more
memorable than the *Fantasia and Fugue in G minor* (J. S.
Bach) which he played at the Norwich concert.

Our first recital of 1970 was in the large church of Saint
Mary, Nottingham, and in April we visited France for the
first time, to sing in Houdan (Rambouillet) Parish Church
in aid of the restoration of the ancient but decrepit Cliquot
organ in that church. I well remember that a number of
notes were dumb and that the pedals had only some seven
or eight notes which worked. Nevertheless Stephen
Cleobury, by adapting some pieces and transposing others,
worked wonders and the programme was given as
advertised. The following day we had the great pleasure
of providing the choir for High Mass at Chartres Cathedral,
and it was sad to learn that the long and distinguished
musical tradition at that wonderful cathedral had been
largely abandoned as a result of the reforms in the Roman
Catholic Church. Whilst at Houdan we were honoured by
a Civic Reception, and with considerable trepidation, I made
a short speech in French in reply to the Mayor's welcome.
This entire visit had been arranged by the late Professor
J-B.M. Barrère, Professor of French Literature and Fellow

of Saint John's. The Barrères were always supporters of the Chapel and its music, and were particularly keen that the College Choir should sing abroad as much as possible. And it was with that wish in mind that they, most generously, gave in 1971 £10,000 to enable the Choir "to undertake singing engagements in Europe, and elsewhere in the world."

In June 1970 we crossed the Atlantic, some by air, and others (including myself) by sea on the Empress of Canada. We began with a CBC recording, followed by a concert in the enormous cathedral of Mary Queen of the World, Montreal, a concert which will always be memorable for me because of a superb performance of Mendelssohn's *Hear my prayer* by our leading treble, Andrew Brunt; the British High Commissioner gave us a most lavish Reception later that evening. There were subsequent concerts at Montreal Anglican Cathedral and Kingston Cathedral, before we crossed into the United States and arrived in Buffalo for the 1970 Convention of the American Guild of Organists. We sang services for much of the week, and I lectured on Choir-training to the 2000 or so delegates.

There followed a concert in Saint Joseph's Old Cathedral, reported under the odd title of "Young Voices Sanctify a Choral Chronology" in the Buffalo Evening News of 1 July 1970. Other recitals took place at the State University College, Fredonia (N.Y.), Chautaugua Amphitheatre, the Saratoga Springs Performing Arts Centre, Hartford Cathedral (Conn.), and we then paid our first visit to the Church of Saint Thomas, 5th Avenue, New York City. This concert was described by the New York Times critic, Raymond Ericson, as "one of the finest concerts given in New York this year." Our tour ended with recitals at Salisbury (Conn.) and the Shed at Tanglewood, the enormous summer home of the Boston Symphony Orchestra; it had been quite a financial success, and the invested profit has enabled the Choral Students, Organists and Clergy to enjoy a yearly Choir Dinner from that time onwards.

Further recitals in 1970 were given in Saint Edmundsbury Cathedral and the Victoria Hall, Halifax; and Saint Paul's Church, Bedford was visited in February 1971. There followed another journey to Leeds Parish Church and the wonderful hospitality of Donald Hunt, before we travelled to Worcester for Stephen Cleobury's wedding in the Cathedral. Stephen had been Senior Chorister in the Worcester choir, so it was entirely appropriate that the two choirs should join on this occasion and, by coincidence, the Organist and Choirmaster at Worcester Cathedral at that time was none other than Christopher Robinson, who was to succeed me at Saint John's in 1991. Later in 1971 we sang in Clare Parish Church, Suffolk, gave the usual Cambridge Festival concert, and finished the year with recitals and a Sung Eucharist at Brecon Cathedral, Wales, a second visit to the newly-extended Blackburn Cathedral, and a concert in Wakefield Cathedral, after which I met for the first time a young man named John Scott, who was inquiring about the possibility of an Organ Scholarship in Cambridge. Jonathan Rennert was our accompanist by then.

The first outside event in 1972 was a broadcast of Choral Evensong from Framlingham Parish Church, as part of the Aldeburgh Festival. This was followed by a Cambridge Festival concert, and an invitation by Yehudi Menuhin to sing at his Gstaad Festival in Switzerland. This latter was a splendid occasion—the singing was first-class, and we were enabled to see something of the country and to enjoy the numerous ski-lifts and cable-cars. Further concerts in 1972 were given in Saint Asaph Cathedral, Wales, at the Gŵyl Gerdd Gogledd Cymru (North Wales Festival of Music) newly inaugurated by William Mathias (this concert included the first performance of the *Three Latin Motets*, written for our Choir by Lennox Berkeley), and at

Chesterfield Parish Church, where we were given the opportunity of examining the inner construction of that grotesquely mis-shaped spire.

1973 began with two events in the Midlands. First a concert at Saint Leonard's Church, Bridgnorth and a Sung Eucharist at the Collegiate Church of Saint Peter, Wolverhampton. We next gave a recital in Ely Cathedral in connection with their Thirteenth Centenary Celebrations, to be followed by one in Canterbury Cathedral, and a second visit to Brecon Cathedral, where we gave a concert and sang a Sung Eucharist on the following morning, including for the first time a hymn in Welsh *Cofia'n gwlad, Benllywydd tirion*. The Cambridge Festival concert this year included music by Britten, Tippett, Berkeley and featured a performance of Robin Orr's *Festival Te Deum* (1951). This exciting work, with its demanding organ part (played on this occasion by Jonathan Rennert) certainly deserves to be better known. I was honoured to be its dedicatee, and the first performance was given by the Lady Margaret Singers, a very talented choir of mixed voices, based on Saint John's, which flourished in the late forties and early fifties.

In August we paid a visit to the Netherlands and Belgium, giving concerts in Saint Salvator's Cathedral, Bruges; the Sacramentskerk, Breda; Saint Joseph's Church, Helmond (where we first met Mr & Mrs Jan Smit, later to be so helpful to our Choir); and Saint Bavo's Cathedral, Haarlem. This, the Catholic cathedral (and not to be confused with Saint Bavo's Church in the same city), is the only place in the Netherlands which retains its Choir School, and which still preserves an enviable choral tradition.

6

Concerts and Foreign Tours (1974-1985)

Bradford Cathedral was visited in January 1974. "When it comes to the Top of the Church Pops" wrote the music critic of the Bradford Telegraph and Argus "they don't come any better than Cambridge's famous Saint John's and King's College Choirs." This was closely followed by another recital in Northampton, this time in Saint Giles' Church.

A little while later I received a request from the Holland Festival for a boy treble to sing some of the solos in a number of performances of Handel's *Messiah*. It so happened that we had at the time a splendid solo boy, by name Lynton Atkinson (now a distinguished international tenor), so he and I, accompanied by my wife as Matron, crossed over and Lynton sang with great aplomb and considerable artistry in De Doelen, Rotterdam; the Concertgebouw, Amsterdam; and the Kurzaal, Scheveningen. Later in the year two performances were given in Belgium—in Ghent and in Dendermonde. There were financial difficulties in Dendermonde, and I remember that the orchestra refused to play for Part III until they were paid. They were, eventually, in small coins and notes, and a catastrophe was averted.

Norwich Cathedral was visited in July, and the Cambridge Festival concert consisted of works by Tye, Liszt and Duruflé (the *Requiem Mass*). At the end of the Long Vacation Term we travelled to the Netherlands and to France, beginning our tour in the massive, impressive but incredibly cold cathedral of 's-Hertogenbosch. There followed a recording in Hilversum, a concert in the Sacramentskerk, Breda, and another recording, this time for Radio OMROEP. One of the works being recorded was the long and difficult *Western Wind Mass,* by Christopher Tye. We had just got to the end of a very successful "take" of the *Agnus Dei,* and the last chord was being sustained with great skill when suddenly I noticed the gentle sobbing of one of the Choristers. That particular "take" was spoiled, of course, and I soon discovered the reason for the boy's distress— the event had been too much for him, and a gentle stream was descending down his leg and on to the studio floor. The ever-resourceful Mr Rossiter soon appeared with a mop and bucket, and the boy was taken away to be dried out and comforted.

We then travelled south to Maastricht to sing in the extremely dark church of Our Lady. For some reason I was obliged not only to conduct, but also to take the priest's part at this Evensong. A concert at Our Lady's Church, Helmond concluded the Dutch part of our tour, and we then travelled to Paris and gave a concert in the secularized La Sainte Chapelle. We took the opportunity, too, of visiting Versailles and, quite without permission, sang Farmer's version of the *Lord's Prayer* in the Royal Chapel—then dispersed quickly before we could be admonished! A 'Songs of Praise' televised by the BBC was followed by a concert in the Chapel of Rossall School, Fleetwood, and so another year ended.

1975 began with a visit to Capel Penmount, Pwllheli, Wales, to give a concert to aid the Eisteddfod Genedlaethol Cymru which was to be held in the district later that year. The chapel was packed, and the congregation was delighted by the programme, which included *Iesu, drud ddifyrwch dynion* by J. S. Bach—the composer would be as little likely to recognise these words as he would *Jesu, joy of man's desiring,* of which it is a translation! And the congregational singing of the final hymn was a revelation to our Choir!

Saint Peter's Collegiate Church, Wolverhampton was again visited in March, and there followed concerts in Ealing Priory and Hitchin Parish Church. We travelled to Holland and Germany in June, beginning our tour with a High Mass at the Altenberger Dom, Germany. There followed concerts at the Concertgebouw, Amsterdam; De Doelen, Rotterdam; the Kurzaal at Scheveningen, and Our Lady's Church Helmond (where we once again experienced the kindness of Mr and Mrs Jan Smit). The tour continued with concerts at 's-Hertogenbosch Cathedral; the Kreuzeskirche, Essen (the only time we have been late for a concert—this being entirely due to the fact that we were given a driver who was not only semi-literate, but who had difficulty in distinguishing his right hand from his left). Our final concert was in Aachen Cathedral, "a demonstration of consummate *a capella* art," as the critic of the Aachener Volkezeitung described it.

The Cambridge Festival Concert for July featured Fauré's *Requiem,* whilst there were further summer recitals at Chichester Cathedral for the Chichester Festival, and at Chester Cathedral for the Incorporated Association of Organists. But perhaps the most important event of the year was the BBC Promenade concert given in September at Saint Augustine's Church, Kilburn, sung to a huge audience and broadcast live. The programme consisted of Tye's *Western Wind Mass*, Purcell's *Funeral Sentences*, Britten's

Missa brevis, and Tippett's *Saint John's Magnificat* and *Nunc dimittis*—together with notable contributions from the Alan Civil Brass Ensemble. The year ended with a visit to Saint Mary's Church, Swansea, Wales; John Scott again accompanied with great skill, as he had done throughout the year.

1976 began with a concert in All Saints' Church, Northampton, and in June we paid another visit to Worcester Cathedral, and followed this in July with concerts in Westminster Cathedral (for the 16th International Congress of Pueri Cantores, and with an estimated audience of 5000 people); and in Saint George's Chapel, Windsor, where I recall an inspired performance of J. S. Bach's *Trio Sonata No. 1 in E flat* by John Scott. The Cambridge Festival concert was a mixed bag this year, but featured the music of Robin Orr—three of his anthems, and his brilliantly effective *Te Deum in C.*

There followed concerts in Bromyard Parish Church and in Wrecsam Parish Church (which included an excellent performance of Mendelssohn's *Hear my prayer* by Jonathon Bond). This was again a concert given in aid of funds for the Eisteddfod Genedlaethol Cymru. December saw us in the Netherlands once more, where we found 's-Hertogenbosch Cathedral if anything colder than ever. We gave further recitals in the Church of the Holy Heart, Boxtel; the Janskerk, Utrecht; the Katholieke Hogeschool, Tilburg; the Wallonian Church, Amsterdam; and sang an Evensong in the Embassy church of Saint John and Saint Philip, The Hague.

1977 opened quietly and our first tour took us to France, to the lovely countryside of Normandy, first to Coutances Cathedral, then to Caen to sing Evensong in the Abbaye aux Hommes, followed in the evening by a concert. July saw us in the south of France, at the Abbaye aux Dames in Saintes (having stopped to hear a little of the music at Solesmes en route). Later that month we joined with the choirs of Magdalen College, Oxford (conducted by Bernard Rose) and Saint Alban's Abbey (conducted by Peter Hurford) in a concert in the Abbey. The Cambridge Festival recital was built around Tallis' *Missa Salve Intemerata Virgo* and Vaughan Williams, *Five Mystical Songs,* in which the soloist was a former Choral Student, Peter Knapp. Our final engagement was a TV Anglia programme of music and words, assisted by Donald Houston. This was pre-recorded in the village of Heydon, Norfolk, and I well remember the panic caused by the fact that it snowed on the first day of the recording, but not on the second. The placing of the Choir seemed somewhat fussy, and we were obliged to sing from the church, a stable, the pub and the village green. Mr Rossiter was pleased to be allocated a walk-on part.

It had long been my ambition to get Saint John's to Australia, and I finally succeeded in March 1978. The Choir was in good form, and included the identical twins, Mark and Hugo Tucker. Mark has since become an international tenor, whilst Hugo, a distinguished scholar, is a Fellow of Downing College. Each voice was identical, and I was later told that they used to change sides with impunity, just as the whim took them. Audiences throughout the tour were immense, largely, I suppose, because this was the first visit of an English choir of this kind to Australia. We began with a recital at the Concert Hall, Perth, then sang in Adelaide Cathedral and Adelaide Town Hall. We then gave a concert in the Canberra Theatre, before moving on to the Sydney Opera House; we were told that the attendance there was 2700, and that some 2500 people were turned away. Following this concert a correspondent wrote to the Sydney Morning Herald "Sir, As a regular subscriber to the Australian opera, I am wondering if the opera authorities could perhaps employ someone like Dr Guest . . . to train our opera singers. It is most frustrating to attend opera after opera and to hear only an occasional word, even when the opera is sung in English. And, in this regard, the supposedly greatest soprano in the world is one of the worst offenders. However, last week what joy it was to hear every phrase, every word, and even every syllable, even though all the singing was in Latin. If little boys of nine or ten can be taught perfect diction, just what is wrong with our opera stars?" I have to say, with regret, that no offer of employment ever reached me from the Opera House authorities. Easter Sunday was a day of extreme heat, and vivid musical contrasts, as well as marked differences of churchmanship. We sang a Sung Eucharist at Christ Church Saint Lawrence, Sydney in the morning. This is an extremely 'high' church and the clouds of incense were inhaled stoically by the Choir, who were fascinated to see the thurifer vigorously swinging through 360 degrees. Evensong at Saint Andrew's Cathedral was completely different, so 'low' was it in churchmanship that in the large congregation of some 1400 people we were the only persons to turn east for the Creed. We sang a further Evensong on the following day at Saint James', North Sydney.

It was at Sydney that one of our Choristers came by a funnel-webbed spider, one of the most dangerous of all insects, and proposed to bring it home and care for it. His hosts reacted with some horror to this, and insisted that it be taken to the Zoo and killed. Great distress was caused by this news, but the spider's remains were immersed in an appropriate liquid, bottled and brought back to this country, where presumably they still are.

Melbourne was our final port of call, and we sang in the Robert Blackwood Hall and gave two concerts in Saint Paul's Cathedral. We enjoyed Melbourne and some of us were lucky enough to visit the Melbourne cricket ground, given over at that time of the year to Australian rules football. The cricket museum was fascinating, but for some reason ladies were barred from entry.

1978 was a quieter year. The Cambridge Festival concert

in June had as its main works Liszt's *Missa Choralis* and Lennox Berkeley's *Five-part Mass.* We gave another concert in aid of funds for the Eisteddfod Genedlaethol, this time in Capel Jeriwsalem, Blaenau Ffestiniog, Wales. A number of Welsh pieces were sung, and the concert ended with William Mathias' *Ave Rex* (1970). It was disappointing to learn subsequently that, although we had made no charge for our services, the chapel authorities had insisted on making a charge for the use of the Chapel, based on a sliding scale according to the size of the audience.

By now David Hill had become Organ Student, and he accompanied the Choir in its recital in Snape Maltings in December. This was followed immediately by another tour of the Netherlands and Belgium. We began with a concert in the Grote Kerk, Sittard (near the German border), followed with six concerts in Belgium, at Saint Martinus Church, Lede; Hasselt Cathedral; Saint Bavo's Church, Noorderwijk; the Cultural Centre at Brussels; Saint Pieter's Church, Woluwe; and the Cultural Centre at Turnhout. This was the one and only tour arranged by Azymuth; audiences tended to be small, largely because of a lack of advertising and the choir arrangements could, in every respect, have been improved. The organisers were however left in no doubt as to their shortcomings by our Matron on this tour, Mrs Vera Marsh. We did nevertheless manage to visit the battlefield of Waterloo, a most interesting excursion, though it was doubly hard to prevent the boys from buying assorted junk in the form of small pieces of metal all, according to the local shopkeepers, being authentic souvenirs of the battle.

Our first tour in 1979 took us to Eindhoven where we gave a concert in Saint Joris' Church. There followed two recordings, one in Sankt Peter's Church, Cologne and the other in Brussels. In this latter recording I shall long remember a magnificent treble solo by Richard Perry (later to be a Choral Scholar in Trinity College Choir, Cambridge) in S. S. Wesley's *Blessed be the God and Father.* July saw us once again in Chichester Cathedral at the Chichester Festival, and it was the occasion of the first performance of John McCabe's lengthy, unaccompanied motet *Solomon, where is thy throne?* This excellent work was written for our choir, and clearly the composer approved of the performance, for he wrote to me: "This is just a short note to thank you all very much indeed for the magnificent performance of my Motet in Chichester the other day— it really was the best possible send-off the work could have had and I was absolutely delighted." The Cambridge Festival concert, with David Hill at the organ, was largely built around the music of French and Belgian composers—the *Messe Basse* by Fauré, three Poulenc motets, organ music by Vierne, and the *Missa Festiva* by Flor Peeters.

In June we were away to the United States and Canada once again, and began our tour with a concert in Washington Cathedral. There followed recitals in the Church of the Holy Comforter, Richmond, Va.; Christ and Saint Luke's Church, Norfolk, Va., and Saint Michael and All Angels, Baltimore, Md. It was at this stage of the tour that we were shown over the nuclear aircraft carrier, the Nimitz, and also visited the Langley Space Research Centre. Concerts followed at Trinity Church, Princeton, NJ and Indianapolis Cathedral, before we crossed over to Canada, and gave another recital in the Cathedral of Mary Queen of the World, Montreal, in front of an audience of over 2000 people. The reception given by the British Consul General was indeed memorable, and was attended by the High Commissioner, Sir John Ford, and Lady Ford. On our return to the USA we gave further concerts at Albany Cathedral; Saint Paul's Church, Troy, N.Y.; the First Baptist Church, Brattleboro, Vt., before ending the tour with our second appearance at Saint Thomas Church Fifth Avenue, New York City.

Our final overseas journey of the year was melancholy.

The death of Admiral of the Fleet the Earl Mountbatten of Burma, at the hands of the I.R.A. was mourned throughout a large part of Europe, and particularly was this so in France, where an official memorial service was held in L'Eglise Saint Louis des Invalides. It was an especial honour for Saint John's College Choir to be invited to sing at this service, and although I was on sabbatical leave and the Choir under the direction of Peter Hurford, it so happened that I was conducting in Paris at the time and so was enabled to attend the service, and also the dinner afterwards. The meal was, as one might expect, splendid, but the occasion was especially noteworthy for the fact that suddenly the elderly but immensely dignified widow of General Leclerc without warning stood up and, in a voice quivering with passion, sang some half-dozen verses of a French patriotic song. This was received with rapturous applause by the Choir, and the Dean responded in his usual kindly and fluent way. The meal then continued.

1980 brought our first tour of Japan. We flew out via Anchorage and arrived at Narita Airport, Tokyo in the company of a pop group. On arrival we were accosted by some thirty young Japanese girls who made a bee-line, not towards the pop-group, not towards even the Choral Students, but towards the Choristers. They showered them with little gifts, and then followed our coach to the hotel in Tokyo, from which they were eventually ejected by the management. Notwithstanding this rebuff they then, having discovered the windows of the boys' bedrooms, began throwing small gifts up to them, all which of course delighted the Choristers, unused as they were to such personal attention. Three concerts were given at the Ishibashi Memorial Hall, Tokyo; the Cultural Centre at Fukushima; the Miyagi Gakuin College, Sendai; the Ishikawa Kosei Nenkin Hall, Kanazawa; the Culture and Art Hall, Kyoto; the Civic Hall, Takamatsu and the Civic Hall at Matsuyama. The tour itself was wonderful, and we experienced many delights, including a journey on the famous 'bullet train' which took us past the snow-capped Mount Fujiyama, but we were bedevilled by illness and I recall that at one of the Tokyo concerts we were obliged to change a number of items, and I was backstage, just before the concert started, desperately looking for one of the Japanese 'cellists (the continuo player). She was nowhere to be seen, and it was vital to find her. Presently there came round the corner an elderly Japanese cleaner, dressed in traditional fashion, I put my question, but clearly she had no English so I was obliged to mimic 'cello playing with my arms. Her face lightened at once, and a few minutes later she returned—bearing, in triumph, a Hoover! My last memory of Japan is of a small boy sitting in the waiting area of Narita airport, holding hands with a Japanese girl clearly some years older than himself, and with tears running down the cheeks of both of them. We were fortunate not to experience an earthquake, but there were minor tremors all the time, and I recall the Senior Chorister of the time, Nicky Gedge, coming to tell me "Please, sir, the pictures keep falling down in our room, and we haven't touched them, really." The flight home, over the vast spaces of Siberia, was thrilling; we flew non-stop to Moscow (the reception there was chilly in more ways than one, with armed soldiers at all the exits, and what appeared to be retired lady weight-lifters in evidence at most of the airport shops).

We visited Germany in June 1980, giving concerts in Saint Lorenz Church, Nürnberg and Eichstätt Cathedral, and we provided the choir for Mass at the other great Nürnberg church, that of Saint Sebald. The excellent sermon was preached in German by our Dean, Andrew Macintosh. This was followed by our first visit to the Republic of Ireland. We sang at High Mass in the Catholic pro-Cathedral, Dublin. The Archbishop of Dublin, the Most Revd Dermot Ryan (who sadly died just before being elected a Cardinal) was a gracious host, both in the cathedral (where a congregation of more than 1500 stood and clapped in welcome to the first Anglican choir ever to sing in the pro-Cathedral), and subsequently at a sherry party given in the Choir's honour. Later that day we gave a concert in Saint Patrick's Cathedral. The Irish Times critic, in his notice the following day, wrote "The Saint John's College Choir has claims to be the premier Anglican cathedral-style choir of the world today."

We welcomed an old friend in the harpist, Marisa Robles, at our Cambridge Festival concert to play Britten's *Ceremony of Carols*. Other works were by Howells, Mathias and Tallis. At all these 1980 concerts David Hill accompanied the Choir splendidly, and played organ solos with musicianship and skill. The final tour of the year, just before Christmas and following a concert in Saint Nicholas Chapel, King's Lynn, was to Germany and the Netherlands. We began at the church of Saint Marien, Kempen, then moved into Holland and sang at Meppel Dutch Reformed Church; the Scottish Church at the Begijnhof, Amsterdam; Saint Jacob's Church, Utrecht; Saint Martin's Church, Doesburg; and Saint Antonius' Church, Dordrecht.

Our first concert in 1981 was a return visit to Capel Penmount, Pwllheli, Wales to sing in aid of the Eisteddfod Genedlaethol yr Urdd (a youth Eisteddfod which was to be held later in that year in Pwllheli). By this time, the Choir's pronunciation of Welsh was excellent, and the pieces sung in "the language of heaven" were especially appreciated. In June we made a short visit to northern France, singing at the wonderful Abbey Church of Saint Ouen, Rouen; at Montivilliers Abbey, le Havre, and at L'église Saint Jean, Caen. The Choir was able to inspect the Bayeux Tapestry, and to see what remained of Mulberry Harbour and the D-day landings (all planned in their final stages in the Senior Combination Room of Saint John's College, from which, of course, the Fellows of the time were barred). The usual Cambridge Festival concert was held, the Chapel once more being full to capacity. Our next trip was a return visit to Saint Asaph Cathedral, North Wales, where we sang a programme of music by Poulenc, Tallis, McCabe, Duruflé and Howells. Ian Shaw had succeeded David Hill as Organ Student, and accompanied the Choir with great skill.

We gave a further concert in Saint Nicholas Chapel, King's Lynn in the pre-Christmas period before breaking new ground with a visit to Greece. The flight was uneventful, but an incident at Athens airport will long remain in the memory. A fussy lady official insisted on reading our names, and requiring us to acknowledge them. Her pronunciation of English tended to the bizarre, and many of us had become hysterical by the time she reached the name of one of our best-ever altos, Owen Pugh; to hear the poor fellow referred to as "Mr Poof" was almost more than any of us could bear! We gave two concerts in the Louzitania Theatre, Athens, and also sang in Saint Mark's Basilica, Heraklion, Crete. It was a wonderful experience to be in Greece at this time of year and the absence of visitors on the Acropolis made it possible for us to view the glories of ancient Athens in peace and tranquillity, and we were fortunate to be able to visit Knossos in Crete in a similarly relaxed way.

In July 1982 we gave a concert in aid of an Appeal for the Home Farm Trust for mentally handicapped people at All Saints Church, Hertford. A few days later our Cambridge Festival concert featured two Masses, the *Missa Pange lingua* by Josquin des Prés, and the *Western Wynde Mass* by John Sheppard. The main tour of 1982 was our second visit to Australia. We gave concerts in the Concert Hall, Perth; two in the Festival Theatre, Adelaide; two in the Melbourne Arts Centre; the City Hall, Hobart (where the Mayor clearly relished his role as leading citizen in admonishing one of our basses to "take your hands out of your pockets when you're speaking to the Mayor of

Hobart!"); Sydney Town Hall, and Sydney Opera House, Saint Monica's Cathedral, Cairns (north Queensland); Saint James Cathedral, Townsville; the Pilbeam Theatre, Rockhampton; the Mayne Hall at Brisbane, the Civic Theatre at Newcastle and the School of Music at Canberra. This was one of our longest overseas tours and included no less than fourteen concerts; but there were compensations and the boys were again fascinated by the variety of kangaroos and koala bears that inhabited the many game parks. It was a great pity that rough seas at Cairns made it unsafe, as we judged, to take the boys over to the Great Barrier Reef; the adults made the crossing and were rewarded by the glittering splendour which goes to make up this enormous reef. It was at Cairns too that the local Catholic priest gave us the benefit of the party-piece with which he habitually regaled visitors to the town. He placed one of the Anglican clergy some distance away with a cigarette in his mouth. He then produced a thickish rope, and without further ado, aimed it at him and neatly cut the cigarette in two! As I was about to step forward to thank him, he asked, to my horror, for a volunteer from the Choristers to act as his assistant in a repeat performance. A boy stepped forward—I feared the worst, and began to rehearse in my mind how I could explain the loss of a nose or an eye to his parents on our return to Cambridge. But my fears were groundless, again the cigarette was cut cleanly in two, and the boy was rightly regarded as a hero by all.

Our pre-Christmas tour was again to the Netherlands, and concerts were given in the Dutch Reformed Church at Meppel; the Martini Kerk at Groningen; the Nieuwe Church at Amsterdam; the Janskerk at Utrecht; the R. K. Kerk at Aardenburg; and Saint Martinus Kerk at Weert. We also provided the choir for High Mass at Saint Bavo's Cathedral, Haarlem. So ended a busy but extremely interesting year, and we led a quiet existence (apart from the full round of Chapel services) until June 1983, when we paid our first visit to Sweden. With Adrian Lucas now Organ Student we sang six concerts: at Stora Kopparbergs Kyrka, Falun; at Göteborg Cathedral; at Sancta Maria Kyrka, Ystad; at Saint Jacob's Kyrka, Stockholm; at Brunnby Church, and at Falkenberg Church. One of the memorable experiences we enjoyed on this tour was a visit to the famous copper mine in Falun. We were, of course, obliged to dress for the occasion, and we looked a strange sight in our yellow capes and hard hats. The commentary was delivered in a slightly bizarre fashion, which made it difficult for us to concentrate on what was being said!

One of the most famous of Saint John's undergraduates was William Wilberforce, and it was entirely appropriate that we should give a concert in his church, Holy Trinity, Clapham Common, London in aid of the Anti-Slavery Society for the Protection of Human Rights, the musical items being interspersed with readings given by our Dean. The summer brought the yearly Cambridge Festival concert at which the main work was a set of motets by Jean Langlais under the title of *Corpus Christi.*

This was followed by our first visit to Oxford where we gave a concert in the unhelpful acoustic of Christ Church Cathedral. Gibbons, Taverner, Langlais and William Harris were the featured composers in a recital described by the critic of the Oxford Times as "a stunning, virtuosic concert." Bedford School was visited just before Christmas, together with Capel Bethlehem, Rhosllanerchrugog, Wales; then came our usual pre-Christmas foreign tour, this time to Spain (or, more properly, to Catalonia).

We expected favourable acoustics here and we were in no way disappointed. Our three concerts took place in the immense Church of Santa Maria in Barcelona, in the Basilica of Sant Esperit, Terrassa, and in Tarragona Cathedral. It was indeed fortunate that the Choral Student with the responsibility of making a short speech of thanks to the very large audiences at the end of each concert did so in Catalan, rather than in Spanish. In many ways the most interesting part of our tour was our visit to the Abbey of Montserrat. The Abbot invited us to sing at Conventual High Mass, with their own very distinguished choir. Our contribution consisted of works by Byrd, Parsons and Bruckner, and the Montserrat choir sang Segarra's *Salve Regina*. Subsequently our Choristers met their Choristers socially, and were escorted by the Catalan boys up to the pinnacle of the extraordinary mountain on which the Abbey stands; it did not seem to matter in the least that none of our boys knew a word of Catalan, nor their boys a word of English.

In March 1984 we gave a recital in Uppingham School Chapel, following this by a concert and a recording for NWDR in Kempen Church, Germany. Concerts were subsequently given in Saint Martins Church, Weert; the Dominicankerk, Zwolle; and at the Abdij van Berne, Heeswijk. The Cambridge Festival concert took place in late July, with works by Tallis, Orr, Vaughan Williams and Stravinsky. Andrew Lumsden was the accompanist, both in the German and Dutch tours, and in the Cambridge concert. Christ Church Cathedral, Oxford was visited again during the Long Vacation, and just before Christmas we paid our second visit to the very distinctive Chesterfield Parish Church. Our Senior Organ Student, James Cryer, had been taken ill and into his place, at a moment's notice, stepped Philip Kenyon, who had only been a member of the college for some two months.

Andrew Lumsden came back to help us in our Christmas tour of Canada. The tour began with concerts at Saint Peter's Church, Kitchener, Ont.; Saint Paul's Cathedral (could there be any other dedication?) London; Saint Paul's Cathedral, Buffalo (the usual visit to see the Niagara Falls was paid); Saint Peter's Church, Brockville; Christ Church Cathedral, Montreal; and finally the Roy Thomson Hall in Toronto (the Toronto Globe and Mail described this concert as being "something between extraordinary and miraculous").

1985 opened with a concert consisting entirely of the music of J. S. Bach. This was held in our College Chapel, and was one of a series in celebration of the 300th anniversary of the composer's birth. It was a heavy programme, and included *Motets 3 to 6* inclusive, as well as the *4 Duetti for organ,* played by James Cryer. The first overseas tour of the year was to Germany and Italy. We gave our initial concert in Saint Lorenz Church, Nürnberg; there followed a drive down to Milan and a recital in the Basilica of S. Simpliciano. We then travelled to Modena and sang in the Cathedral, before returning to Germany— but, through the kindness of our excellent coach driver Mr Rex Fishpoole, we made a detour to visit Venice for a couple of hours. Just as we had done in the Royal Palace at Versailles many years before, we grouped together and sang John Farmer's *Lord's Prayer,* before dispersing hurriedly in all directions, and so back to Germany and the Liebfrauen Dom in Munich. This was a difficult building in which to sing; its size is enormous, and the acoustic not particularly helpful. We then crossed into East Germany and drove along the extremely ill-kept roads to West Berlin (where we were staying), before making the tedious journey over the border at Checkpoint Charlie to give a concert in the French cathedral in East Berlin. There was no organ, and the building had only recently been restored after its almost total destruction in World War II. In the Crypt afterwards the Choral Students sang a selection of currently popular songs to an enthusiastic audience, though it was quite clear from their glum faces that there were plain-clothes police also in the audience. A splendid lunch was provided by Mr Tony Ford, Counsellor of the British Embassy, though because his house was bugged throughout we were only able to talk freely in his garden, which was overlooked by a large house in which could be seen two men with telescopes who were clearly 'watching points'. Mr Ford also told me that his house staff had been appointed by the Communist Government, and that he was watched night and day. Our German driver (from East Berlin) refused our invitation to lunch, clearly because he was afraid of being seen in the building!

We then returned (it took one hour to re-cross the border) to West Berlin to sing in the Kaiser Friedrich Memorial Church. In writing about this concert the Lippische Rundschau music critic wrote "there are many famous boys' choirs; from Saint Thomas, Windsbach, Vienna and Kruzian, but the crown definitely belongs to Cambridge." Other concerts were given at the Martin Luther Church, Detmold and Heilsbron Minster.

The Cambridge Festival concert was made up of works by D. Scarlatti, Britten and Fauré (the *Requiem Mass*). Philip Kenyon was the skilled accompanist, as he was at yet another concert at Christ Church Cathedral, Oxford. December 1985 saw us singing in Saint Woolos Cathedral, Newport, Wales, and also taking part in a Christmas programme at the Royal Festival Hall, London. A further tour of the Netherlands took place just before Christmas, and we gave concerts at Saint Laurenskerk, Rotterdam, a Carol Service at the Kloosterkerk, The Hague (where the 8th Lesson was read by the British Ambassador, Sir John Margetson (former bass Choral Student in the College Choir). There was a magnificent reception in the Residence a few days later, and we were all delighted that the Ambassador joined the ranks of our basses for the carols which were later sung. Other concerts were given at the Westerkerk, Amsterdam; the Janskerk, Utrecht; Onze Lieve Vrouwe Kerk, Aardenburg, the Pieterkerk. Leiden; the Martinikerk, Groningen, and the Grote Kerk, Doesburg.

7

Concerts and Foreign Tours (1986-1991)

For some reason we had never worked for any length of time in Switzerland, so it was a special pleasure to be invited to sing in Zurich in June 1986. Evensong was sung in the very beautiful Fraümunster, and a concert given in the Tonhalle. This visit was in connection with an exhibition arranged in Zurich by the Fitzwilliam Museum, Cambridge, entitled "Fitzwilliam—a Cambridge Collection of Music" and was brought about by the good offices of my predecessor Professor Robin Orr and Mrs Doris Orr. Again there was a Reception by the British Consul General, attended by the British Ambassador, Sir John Rich, who had been so kind to us in Montreal in 1979.

The summer of 1986 saw further concerts in the Sheldonian Theatre, Oxford (Howells, Bach and Liszt) and in our Chapel for the Cambridge Festival. Meanwhile we had been preparing for another tour of the United States and gave our first concert in Yantic, Conn., before moving south to Saint Paul's Church, Lynchburg, Virginia, where the warmth of our welcome will long remain in our minds. We then travelled north to sing in the Church of the Covenant, Cleveland, Ohio, and to enjoy a Reception later given by the Consul-General. Our concert in the First United Methodist Church, Evanston, Chicago, gave us the opportunity the following day of ascending what was then the world's tallest building, the Sears Tower (1353 feet above ground level). The Basilica of Saint Mary, Minneapolis, Minn., was one of the most memorable buildings of this particular tour; its helpful acoustic was a joy, and it was an equal pleasure to meet the distinguished American composer, Paul Manz, after our concert. We then flew over the Rockies to San Francisco and to Grace Cathedral. There were many delights here for the Choristers, and they particularly enjoyed the street cars and the waterfront with the former prison of Alcatraz in the distance. We continued with concerts in the Wornall Road Baptist Church, Kansas City, Mo. and in Saint Paul's Cathedral, Buffalo, NY, making the almost obligatory visit to Niagara Falls at the same time. Next it was the turn of the Mechanics' Hall at Worcester, Mass., where we had the pleasure of welcoming a large number of friends from the Community of Jesus who had made the journey from Cape Cod in order to attend the concert. The tour ended with a recital at Saint Thomas Church, Fifth Avenue, New York City. Throughout the tour Philip Kenyon had been the excellent accompanist, and we enjoyed the most lavish hospitality from his father, resident in the city, and from the Rector and the Organist of Saint Thomas (The Revd Dr John Andrew and Dr Gerre Hancock).

1987 began with a concert in the newly-opened Corn Exchange in Cambridge. This was shared between the Choir of King's College (directed by Stephen Cleobury) and ourselves. King's were responsible for the first half, and they gave an extremely good performance of Haydn's *Nelson Mass*; our share in the second half consisted of a moving performance of Fauré's *Requiem*. Both choirs were accompanied by the English Chamber Orchestra, and all profits were given to the Ely Cathedral Appeal Fund. July saw us singing an Anglican Evensong in Westminster Cathedral, followed by a Mass sung jointly by the Cathedral Choir and ourselves. The prayer after the Communion "Lord, may we never fail to praise you for the fulness of life and salvation you give us in this Eucharist" brought home to us most vividly the sadness of our own exclusion from the Sacrament.

We visited Derby Cathedral in July, and the fact that the concert was to be sponsored by the makers of Thornton's chocolates aroused mouth-watering expectations in the minds of us all—but, alas, in vain; and, perhaps as a judgment on our thoughts, most of the Choir suffered dreadfully with stomach pains on our return to Cambridge. The Cambridge Festival concert, described by the local critic as "serious but satisfying," consisted of music by Taverner, Couperin, Orr, Purcell, Franck and Finzi. The December concerts began with yet another visit to the Sheldonian Theatre, Oxford, to sing Mozart's *Requiem* and his *Solemn Vespers* (K339), and to the Chapel of Rugby School.

Bishop William Morgan, who had been an undergraduate at Saint John's, published the first complete translation of the Bible into Welsh in 1588, and it was to celebrate this event (largely responsible for the continued existence of the Welsh language) that the College sent the Choir to Wales in 1988 to give three concerts. These took place in Saint Mary's Church, Swansea; the Great Hall, University College, Aberystwyth; and Bangor Cathedral. British Gas were the joint sponsors, and the group of Welsh pieces were particularly well received.

We paid our second visit to Sweden and our first to Norway in June and July, giving concerts in Strömstad Church; Oslo Cathedral; Rygge Church; Stenkyrka Church;

Lysekils Church; Göteborg Cathedral; Martin Luther's Church, Halmstad; Varberg Church and Falkenburg Church. The usual Cambridge Festival concert was followed by a second journey to Saint Asaph Cathedral, Wales, to sing at the 17th North Wales Festival. The Festival was directed by William Mathias, and we included a performance of an anthem commissioned by the College from Mathias to celebrate the Morgan anniversary. This work, entitled *Y nefoedd sydd yn datgan gogoniant Duw* was the final item in a splendid concert, recorded by TVS4C, and those who were present will no doubt recall the nuisance of raindrops on the nave roof, especially during the quiet sections. Robert Morgan accompanied splendidly both in Sweden and in Wales.

The pre-Christmas tour was again to the Netherlands and Belgium. We sang in Schagen Church; the Dominican Church, Zwolle; Saint Catherine's Church, Maaseik (Belgium); Saint Martinus Church, Doesburg; Saint Petrus Church, Sittard; and Saint Laurenskerk, Rotterdam. This latter recital was memorable for the fact that incorrect timings had been given to us in respect of the ferry's departure from the Hook of Holland, and so, as the last chord died away, and with the large audience still clapping, we marched smartly out of the church through the rarely-opened west doors into our coach, standing outside with its engine running, and were driven at high speed and with a police escort of motor-bikes to the dockside, where we were just in time to board, and so reach home on Christmas Eve.

April 1989 provided me with my greatest disappointment. Our Choir was invited to sing before Queen Beatrix of the Netherlands and her family at the Noordeinde Palace in The Hague, as part of the celebrations to mark the 300th anniversary of the coronation which put William of Orange and Queen Mary on the throne of this country. Some fortnight before the performance I was told that a

Dutchman would be conducting our Choir, and this I was not prepared to accept. But to withdraw the Choir (which was contemplated at one stage) might have been taken as an insult to the Dutch Royal Family, and so I agreed to bear the insult myself; the fact that I subsequently received an apology from a Palace official went a very little way to compensating me for a disappointment which I shall always remember. The Choir flew in Dutch Air Force planes from Cambridge Airport, and, by all accounts, enjoyed themselves thoroughly.

The Cambridge Festival recital consisted of early French music, motets by Poulenc and Duruflé's *Requiem* (at which the baritone soloist—and former Chorister of Saint John's—was my son David Guest). We paid a short visit to Catalonia in August, giving concerts at the Monastery of Santes Creus, Llivia Church and for the International Festival at Torroella de Montgri, where our Organ Student, Andrew Nethsingha worked wonders on a totally inadequate instrument. We gave concerts in Saint Lambert's Church, Helmond, the Netherlands (the Vienna Boys Choir had appeared in the same Festival on the previous day), and in the Hall of Bedford School, before setting off for a very cold Canada on our pre-Christmas tour. It was indeed fortunate for us that Mrs Penny Gummer (wife of the then Minister of Agriculture and Fisheries, The Rt Hon John Gummer) was, with other parents, at the airport to say goodbye to her son Ben, because it turned out that one of the basses was hoping to cross the Atlantic and enter Canada on a temporary passport. When the unlikelihood of this happening was pointed out to him he was in despair, but, fortunately for us, Mrs Gummer took complete charge, and while we disappeared on to the aircraft, she accompanied the offender back to London where, by some miracle unknown to ordinary mortals, he was immediately issued with a full passport, and joined us in a very cold Port Hope on the following day. We then moved to Ottawa and experienced what was for us the coldest weather we had ever known. The streets were covered with hard-packed snow, and icicles over each doorway made entry into any building extremely dangerous. We sang in the Ottawa National Arts Centre and subsequently in the Roy Thomson Hall, Toronto, after which we made the by now customary trip to Niagara Falls, but this time, in the depths of winter, it presented a completely different picture, ice and snow everywhere, even at the edges of the fast-flowing river. It was indeed an unforgettable sight. We went on to give concerts in the Fisher Auditorium, Barrie; the 'Centre-in-the-Square', Kitchener-Waterloo; Saint George's Cathedral, Kingston; and Christ Church Cathedral, Montreal.

One of the most ancient of services in Saint Paul's Cathedral is that known as the Festival of the Sons of the Clergy. In 1990 the 336th such service was held, and it was a great pleasure to receive an invitation to take part, together with the Choirs of Liverpool and Salisbury Cathedrals. Unfortunately I had been taken ill a few days earlier and so missed the event, but our Choir was directed very capably by our Organ Student, Andrew Nethsingha. Later that year we took part in the Oundle Festival and gave a concert in Oundle School Chapel. The Cambridge Festival recital this year consisted of motets from the Italian 16th century School, and music by des Prés, Bruckner and John McCabe.

The last American tour under my direction followed in August and September, beginning with a concert in Garden City Cathedral, NY, and followed by recitals at Saint Peter's Church, Geneva, NY; Saint Joan of Arc Catholic Church, Indianapolis and Grace and Holy Trinity Cathedral, Kansas City. We stayed a night in Saint Louis, where the more intrepid members of the party ascended to the top of the Gateway Arch (though I was not amongst the number who braved the rather claustrophobic lift). We proceeded to sing in the very beautiful Denver Cathedral, Col. and were fortunate to be taken up into the Rockies and to experience their breathtaking beauty. Another first experience was to be grounded at Denver airport for over an hour before the presence of the very dangerous 'wind sheer' disappeared, and so made it safe for us to take off. We then sang in the enormous cathedral of Saint Paul, Minn.; Saint John's Church, Detroit; Saint Thomas Church, New York; Bridgewater College, Virginia; Saint Paul's Church, Philadelphia; and, finally, the National Cathedral, Washington, DC. This magnificent building was just about to be completed, and it is fervently to be hoped that the authorities will soon establish a choral tradition commensurate with its architectural magnificence.

December 1990 saw us breaking new ground in our tour of Brazil. We began in the near-tropical city of Recife, singing in the Teatro Santa Isabel, a fine old building but one whose acoustics were not nicely calculated to aid choral singing. From Recife we moved to the capital city, Brasilia, and its very modern Teatro Nacional Claudio Santora. The wide open spaces and the exciting architecture were indeed memorable. From there we moved to the enormous and extremely dangerous city of São Paulo. We were all warned not to leave our hotel under any circumstances; three of our party did, and, within a few yards of it, were mugged and relieved of their money—one of the three, a tenor, cheerfully boasted that he had now been mugged in Amsterdam, Barcelona and São Paulo! In many ways the city of Curitiba, so little-known in Europe, was the most interesting—we sang again in a theatre, the Teatro Guaira. Finally we travelled to Rio de Janeiro, and to the magnificent Copacabana Palace Hotel, situated right on the world-famous beach of that name. It was a great disappointment to us all to find that the beach itself was too dangerous on which to venture, but the facilities in the hotel, particularly the swimming-pool, more than compensated us. Another memory is of the breakfasts—exotic fruits of all descriptions abounded, together with every variety of bread that one could think of, and a multitude of hot dishes. Rio is, of course, famous for the enormous statue of Christ the Redeemer standing on top of the Corcovado Peak (2,297 feet in height), and we travelled up by train to enjoy the breath-taking views from the top. A slight hiccup in our travel arrangements occurred on our way home; Air France admitted that they had overbooked, and that some of our party would have to return to London by a later flight. This, of course, could not be allowed, so the airline asked if we would be prepared to accept four First Class seats, and a number of Club Class seats in lieu. We accepted this arrangement, and some of us enjoyed the most luxurious flight we had ever experienced! A few days after our return I entered hospital for a quadruple heart by-pass. This operation is now almost routine, and I left hospital after exactly a week, with strict instructions to watch my diet in the future.

I returned to the College to direct the Choir in the usual Ash Wednesday broadcast, and there followed an excellent concert in Lincoln Cathedral, and one given by the Choirs of Saint John's and King's Colleges and that of Saint Alban's Abbey in the Abbey. The three choirs sang separately in different parts of this vast building, before joining together under my direction to sing Duruflé's *Requiem Mass*. The Abbey was absolutely full, and the singing quite first-class.

We sang in two concerts in the 1991 Cambridge Festival. To mark my retirement it had been arranged to give a concert in Ely Cathedral featuring the Choirs of Winchester Cathedral (directed by David Hill), Saint Paul's Cathedral (directed by John Scott), King's College, Cambridge (directed by Stephen Cleobury), and Saint John's College. All of the four conductors had been at one time Organ Students of Saint John's College. Each choir contributed a section of the first half, and all joined together in the second half for a performance (again under my direction) of Duruflé's *Requiem Mass*, accompanied with his customary skill by Stephen Cleobury—a particularly happy event, when one recalled the same player's wonderful playing when, as our Organ Student many years ago, he accompanied our recording of the same work. The cathedral was completely full, and people made long journeys to attend. The evening was completed by a Reception given by the Lord Bishop of Ely, our former Dean.

Our second concert for the 1991 Cambridge Festival included three works written for Saint John's College Choir—Lennox Berkeley's *Three Latin Motets,* Howells' *Sequence for Saint Michael,* and a splendid setting of the *Evening Canticles* by the American composer Gerald Near. The Choir also sang Howells' *Requiem* and Tallis' *Missa Salve Intemerata Virgo,* and the Senior Organ Student, Alexander Martin, played works by Vivaldi/J. S. Bach and Dupré. So ended my long association with a most worthwhile and prestigious Festival; it is a great sadness that, in early 1993, it was decided, on financial grounds, to abandon it altogether.

My final overseas tour with the College Choir was to Australia and Hong Kong in August/September 1991. We began in the Concert Hall, Brisbane, and followed this with further concerts in the Lazenby Hall, Armidale; Saint Mary's Cathedral, Sydney; the Sydney Opera House, the Llewellyn Hall, Canberra; the Concert Hall, Melbourne; the Festival Centre, Adelaide; and the Concert Hall, Perth. We then flew to Hong Kong to give a concert (my last with the Choir) at the quite remarkable Cultural Centre Concert Hall. My wife Nan and I had the great pleasure of being invited to luncheon by the Governor and Lady Wilson at Government House, whilst the Choir was similarly entertained in the very spacious grounds. The concert itself, with Alexander Martin at the organ, was all I had wished it to be, and the South China Morning Post began its review with the words "If there will always be an England, there must undoubtedly always be a Saint John's College Choir." These are important words, for there is no mention of a Choir in our College Statutes (the opposite is true in the case of King's College Choir, and in the cases of New College Choir, Magdalen College Choir and Christ Church Cathedral Choir in Oxford) and an unsympathetic College Council or Governing Body, or too rigorous a body of Tutors could so easily bring a tradition of international fame and importance to an end. Our Choir has now, I believe, ceased to be purely of college concern—it is an organisation of national importance, indeed of international importance.

8

Broadcasting
and Recording

When lovely woman stoops to folly and
Paces about her room again, alone,
She smoothes her hair with automatic hand,
And puts a record on the gramophone.
                                    Thomas Stearns Eliot

It was not easy to get on to the BBC's books in the early
50s, and we were obliged to have an audition from Dr
George Thalben-Ball. He expressed himself as being happy
with what we had to offer, and so we became one of the
number of choirs broadcasting a weekly Evensong. In those
days the Third Programme also broadcast (or recorded for
future broadcast) concerts of church music and organ
recitals, and we were able to take a full share in these
events. It took many years to persuade the BBC to broadcast
our Ash Wednesday Evensong, but this has become a
regular feature since 1972—as has our Advent Carol Service
since 1981. In 1993 there was broadcast for the first time
our Lenten Carol Service; this service, built around

the Gospel account of the Crucifixion, and interspersed with suitable carols and other music, has quickly become popular throughout Cambridge and is nowadays to be heard in most college chapels.

Television programmes have been fewer, largely because of the difficulty of placing the cameras in our long, fairly narrow chapel, especially in the presence of a large congregation, but there have been a number of very successful programmes.

Our Choir has been recording since 1958. We began with a record which the Manchester Guardian called a programme of "ecclesiastical pop," and in the next 33 years produced some 60 records of all kinds, ending with the Nimbus record of 1991 entitled *The Sound of Saint John's*— the last under my direction. The full list of recordings (some now inevitably deleted) follows; all were conducted by myself:

1. 1958—Argo RG 152   *'Hear my prayer'*
    Alastair Roberts (treble); Peter White (organ)
    (a) A tender shoot (Goldschmidt)
    (b) Hear my prayer (Mendelssohn)
    (c) Jesu, joy of man's desiring (J. S. Bach)
    (d) Ave verum Corpus (Mozart)
    (e) I saw the Lord (Stainer)
    (f) Ye now are sorrowful (Brahms)
    (g) Sonata para organo con Trompeta Real (Lidon)
         George Guest (organ)

2. 1960—Argo RG 237-ZRG 5327
    Music by Tallis and Weelkes
    Peter White (organ)
    by Weelkes
    (a) Alleluia, I heard a voice
    (b) Nunc dimittis (9th Service)
    (c) Voluntary for organ
    (d) Voluntary for organ (Anon.)
    (e) Give ear, O Lord

(f)　When David heard
(g)　Hosanna to the Son of David
by Tallis
(a)　Te Deum (for 5 voices)
(b)　Iam lucis orto sidere (for organ)
(c)　Clarifica me, pater (for organ)
(d)　Fantasy (for organ)
(e)　In jejunio et fletu
(f)　Audivi vocem

3.　1961—Argo RG 320-ZRG 5320
　　The Crucifixion (John Stainer)
　　Richard Lewis (tenor); Owen Brannigan (bass); Brian Runnett (organ)

4.　1962—Disques Lumen—AMS 37-AMS 37 STE
　　The Golden Age of English Church Music
(a)　Quem vidistis pastores? (Dering)
(b)　Miserere mei (Byrd)
(c)　Christe Jesu, Pastor bone (Taverner)
(d)　Ne reminiscaris Domine (Philips)
(e)　Ad Te clamamus (Tye)
(f)　Haec dies (Byrd)
(g)　The Leroy Kyrie (Taverner)
(h)　Justorum animae (Byrd)
(i)　O nata lux (Tallis)
(j)　Cantantibus organis (Philips)
(k)　Salvator mundi (Tallis)
(l)　O bone Jesu (Dering)
(m)　Gaudent in coelis (Dering)
(n)　Laudibus in sanctis (Byrd)
(o)　In pace (Blytheman)

5.　1962—Argo RG 340-ZRG 5340
　　Twentieth Century Cathedral Music
　　Brian Runnett (organ)
(a)　Festival Te Deum (Britten)
(b)　Let all mortal flesh (Bairstow)

(c)	Like as the hart (Howells)
(d)	Lord, Thou hast been our refuge (Vaughan Williams)
(e)	Jubilate in C (Britten)
(f)	A Litany (Walton)
(g)	Greater love hath no man (Ireland)
(h)	They that put their trust (Orr)
(i)	A Hymn to the Virgin (Britten)
(j)	Magnificat and Nunc dimittis—Collegium Sancti Johannis Cantabrigiense (Tippett)

6.	1963—Argo RG 406-ZRG 5406
	English Cathedral Music (1770-1860)
	Brian Runnett (organ)
	(a)	Evening Canticles in D minor (Walmisley)
	(b)	The souls of the righteous (Nares)
	(c)	If we believe that Jesus died (Goss)
	(d)	In exitu Israel (S. Wesley)
	(e)	The Wilderness (S. S. Wesley)
	(f)	Thou wilt keep him (S. S. Wesley)
	(g)	Blessed be the God and Father (S. S. Wesley)

7.	1963—Argo RG 405-ZRG 5405
	Hymns for all Seasons
	Brian Runnett (organ)
	(a)	Praise my soul, the King of Heaven (Goss)
	(b)	Come, thou long-expected Jesus (Stainer)
	(c)	O, for a closer walk with God (Scottish Trad.)
	(d)	Behold, the great Creator makes (English Trad.)
	(e)	Brightest and best of the sons of the morning (German Trad.)
	(f)	Let all mortal flesh keep silence (French Trad.)
	(g)	The strife is o'er (Vulpius)
	(h)	When morning gilds the skies (Barnby)
	(i)	The Lord ascendeth up on high (Praetorius)
	(j)	Spirit of mercy, truth and love (Webbe)
	(k)	Lead us, Heavenly Father (Filitz)
	(l)	Give me the wings of faith (Gibbons)
	(m)	Immortal, invisible, God only wise (Welsh Trad.)

(n)   Jesu, lover of my soul (Joseph Parry)

8.   1964—Argo RG 444-ZRG 5444
Music for the Chapel Royal (Henry Purcell)
Inia te Wiata (bass); Christopher Keyte (bass); Christopher Bevan (baritone); Wilfred Brown (tenor); Robert Tear (tenor); Charles Brett (alto); Roger Parker (treble); Brian Runnett (organ); The Academy of Saint Martin-in-the-Fields (leader—Neville Marriner)
(a)   They that go down to the sea in ships
(b)   Jehovah, quam multi sunt hostes
(c)   My beloved spake
(d)   O sing unto the Lord
(e)   Lord, how long wilt Thou be angry?
(f)   Who hath believed our report?

9.   1964—Argo RG 440-ZRG 5440
Music by Benjamin Britten
Marisa Robles (harp); Forbes Robinson (bass); Robert Tear (tenor); Michael Pearce (alto); Roger Parker (treble); Benjamin Odom (treble); Peter Ball (treble); Brian Runnett (organ)
(a)   A Ceremony of Carols
(b)   Rejoice in the Lamb
(c)   Missa Brevis
"This is one of the finest records of Christmas music in the Catalogue."   *(Penguin Stereo Record Guide 1978)*

10.   1965—Argo RG 500-ZRG 5500
The Theresa Mass (Haydn)
Tom Krause (bass); John Mitchinson (tenor); Bernadette Greevy (contralto); Erna Spoorenberg (soprano); Brian Runnett (organ); The Academy of Saint Martin-in-the-Fields (leader—Neville Marriner)

11.   1965—Argo RG 494-ZRG 5494
       Music by Monteverdi
       Jonathan Bielby (organ); Gareth Keene (baritone);
       Peter Birts (tenor); Robert Bishop (tenor); Michael
       Turner (treble); Benjamin Odom (treble); Strings from
       the Academy of Saint Martin-in-the-Fields
       (a)   Mass for 4 voices (1651)
       (b)   Laudate pueri
       (c)   Ut queant laxis
       (d)   Mass for 4 voices (1640)

12.   1966—Argo RG 515-ZRG 5515
       Harmoniemesse (Haydn)
       Joseph Rouleau (bass); Alexander Young (tenor); Helen
       Watts (contralto); Erna Spoorenberg (soprano); Brian
       Runnett (organ); Academy of Saint Martin-in-the-Fields
       (leader—Neville Marriner)

13.   1967—Argo RG 542-ZRG 5542
       Heiligmesse (Haydn)
       Christopher Keyte (bass); Ian Partridge (tenor); Shirley
       Minty (contralto); April Cantelo (soprano); Jonathan
       Bielby (organ); Academy of Saint Martin-in-the-Fields
       (leader—Neville Marriner)

14.   1966—Argo RG 511-ZRG 5511
       Evensong on Ascension Day
       The Revd S. W. Sykes (Precentor)
       The Revd K. N. Sutton (1st Lesson)
       The Revd J. S. Bezzant (2nd Lesson)
       The Revd the Master (Prayers)
       Jonathan Bielby (organ accompaniment)
       George Guest (organ volantaries)
       The London Brass Players
       (a)   Voluntary (Henry Purcell)
       (b)   Psallite Domino (Byrd)

(c) Psalms 24, 47, 108
(d) Evening Canticles (Sumsion in G)
(e) O clap your hands (Vaughan Williams)
(f) The Lord ascendeth (Praetorius)
(g) Hymn: The head that once was crowned with thorns
(h) Chorale Prelude: "Heut triumphieret Gottes Söhn"
(J. S. Bach)

15. 1966 and 1967—Argo RG 570-ZRG 5570
Music by T. L. da Victoria I
Michael Turner (treble)
(a) Requiem Mass à six
(b) Gaudent in coelis
(c) O magnum mysterium
(d) Ave Maria
(e) Ascendens Christus in altum

16. 1966 and 1967—Argo RG 578-ZRG 5578
Music by Palestrina I
Michael Turner (treble)
(a) Motet and Mass Veni Sponsa Christi
(b) Hymnus in Adventus Domini
(c) Exultate Deo
(d) Jesus, Rex admirabilis
(e) Tua Jesu dilectio
(f) Magnificat (6th Tone)

17. 1967—Argo RG 550-ZRG 5550
A Meditation on Christ's Nativity
Michael Matthews, Martin Redfearn and Michael
Turner (trebles); William Squire (reader); Peter Birts
and Philip Pettifor (tenors); Jonathan Bielby (organ)
(a) Torches (Joubert)
(b) Adam lay y-bounden (Warlock)
(c) The Linden Tree Carol (arr. Jacques)
(d) There is no rose (Joubert)
(e) Tomorrow shall be my dancing day (arr. M. Shaw)
(f) Up! good Christen folk (arr. Woodward)

(g)   Rocking (arr. Willcocks)
(h)   Balulalow (Warlock)
(i)   The Seven Joys of Mary (arr. M. Shaw)
(j)   The Cherry Tree Carol (arr. M. Shaw)
(k)   Ding dong! merrily on high (Williamson)
(l)   Eastern monarchs (Peter Naylor)
(m)   King Jesus hath a garden (arr. C. Wood)
(n)   O come, all ye faithful (Descant by J. Roland Middleton)

18.   1968—Argo RG 598-ZRG 5598
      Schöpfungsmesse/Creation Mass (Haydn)
      Forbes Robinson (bass); Robert Tear (tenor); Helen
      Watts (contralto); April Cantelo (soprano); Stephen
      Cleobury (organ); Academy of Saint Martin-in-the-
      Fields (leader—Neville Marriner)

19.   1968—Argo ZRG 621
      Italian and English Church Music
      Andrew Brunt (treble); Stephen Cleobury (organ)
(a)   A Hymn of Saint Columba (Britten)
(b)   Thy Word is a lantern (H. Purcell)
(c)   Evening Canticles—Collegium Sancti Johannis
      Cantabrigiense (Howells)
(d)   Hymn to Saint Peter (Britten)
(e)   Angelus Domini (Casciolini)
(f)   Missa Brevis (A. Gabrieli)
(g)   O vos omnes (Gesualdo)
(h)   Omnes gentes plaudite manibus (Banchieri)

20.   1968—Argo ZRG 620
      Music by T. L. da Victoria II
(a)   Motet and Mass O quam gloriosum est regnum
(b)   Iste sanctus pro lege
(c)   Magnificat Primi Toni
(d)   Veni Sponsa Christi
(e)   Hic vir despiciens
(f)   Estote fortes in bello
(g)   Litaniae de Beata Virgine

21. 1969—Argo ZRG 634
    Paukenmesse (J. Haydn) *Salve Regina* (Michael Haydn)
    Barry McDaniel (bass); Robert Tear (tenor); Helen
    Watts (contralto); April Cantelo (soprano); Stephen
    Cleobury (organ); Academy of Saint Martin-in-the-
    Fields (leader—Neville Marriner)

22. 1969—Argo ZRG 662
    French Sacred Music of the 19th & 20th centuries
    Andrew Brunt (treble); Stephen Cleobury (organ)
    (a) Quatre Motets (Duruflé)
    (b) Messe basse (Fauré)
    (c) Messe Solennelle (Langlais)
    (d) O sacrum convivium (Messiaen)
    (e) Litanies à la Vierge Noire (Poulenc)
    As a result of this recording the following letter was
    received from Jean Langlais:

    > 26 Rue Duroc
    > 75007 Paris
    > 7 November 1973

    Dear Mr Guest,

    Please forgive me for to be so late thanking you
    about the splendid recording of my *Messe Solennelle*.
    I admire everything—the style, the tempi, the voices,
    the organist, and the conductor. Let me tell you of my
    deepest gratitude and admiration.

    > Very cordially yours,
    > Jean Langlais

23. 1971—Argo ZRG 690
    Music by Palestrina II
    Thomas Hunt (treble); John Tudhope (tenor)
    (a) Antiphon and Missa Assumpta est Maria
    (b) Missa Brevis

24.   1972—Argo SDD 841-846
       Decca Bargain Boxes—*The Six Great Masses* (Haydn)
       (a)   The Theresa Mass
       (b)   Harmoniemesse
       (c)   Heiligmesse
       (d)   Schöpfungsmesse
       (e)   Paukenmesse
       (The above recorded by Saint John's College Choir,
       conducted by George Guest)
       (f)   The Nelson Mass
             (Recorded by King's College Choir, conducted by David
             Willcocks)
       As a result of this recording the following letter was
       sent to the Dean of Saint John's (the Revd S. W. Sykes)
       by Robert Armstrong (Secretary to the Prime Minister):

                                   10 Downing Street
                                   Whitehall
                                   12 October 1972

       Dear Mr Dean,
           The Prime Minister has asked me to thank you for
       your letter of 11 October. The recordings of Haydn
       Masses which he gave to the Pope were the six recordings
       published by Argo; and, of course, as you know, the
       Saint John's College Choir are included in five of the
       six. The Prime Minister is glad to think that it may
       please the Choir to know that the sounds of their voices
       may well be echoing round the Vatican.

                                   Yours sincerely,
                                   Robert Armstrong

25.   1972—Abbey LPB 730
       Cathedral Music of Various Periods
       William Kendall (tenor); Andrew Downes and Philip
       Griffiths (altos); Lynton Atkinson, Simon Keenlyside,

Mark Tinkler and Paul Williams (trebles); Jonathan Rennert (organ)

(a) Missa super Frère Thibault (Lassus)
(b) O mysterium ineffabile (Lallouette)
(c) Locus iste a Deo factus est (Bruckner)
(d) Christus factus est pro nobis (Bruckner)
(e) Give ear, O Lord (Weelkes)
(f) Vox dicentes: Clama! (Edward Naylor)
(g) Evening Canticles—The Gloucester Service (Howells)

26. 1972—Argo ZRG 724
Ceremonial Music (Henry Purcell)
Forbes Robinson (bass); Ian Partridge (tenor); Charles Brett (ctr. tenor); James Bowman (ctr. tenor); Malcolm Creese, Simon Keenlyside, Robert King, Robert Smith, Paul Williams (trebles); Jane Ryan (viol); Stephen Cleobury (organ); Symphoniae Sacrae; English Chamber Orchestra

(a) Te Deum and Jubilate in D
(b) The complete Funeral Music

27. 1973—Argo ZRG 760
Music by Liszt and Bruckner
Richard Suart (bass); William Kendall (tenor); Christopher Royall (alto); Lynton Atkinson and Mark Tinkler (trebles); Stephen Cleobury (organ)

(a) Missa Choralis (Liszt)
(b) Afferentur regi virgines (Bruckner)
(c) Os justi meditabitur sapientiam (Bruckner)
(d) Inveni David (Bruckner)
(e) Pange lingua gloriosa (Bruckner)
(f) Ecce sacerdos magnus (Bruckner)

28. 1974—Argo SPA 300 Cassette KCS 300
The World of Saint John's
Peter White, Brian Runnett, Jonathan Bielby and Stephen Cleobury (organists)

    (a)   Alleluia, I heard a voice (Weelkes)
    (b)   Jehovah, quam multi sunt hostes (Purcell)
    (c)   Psalm 47
    (d)   Thou wilt keep him (S. S. Wesley)
    (e)   Like as the hart (Howells)
    (f)   O clap your hands (Vaughan Williams)
    (g)   Laudate pueri (Monteverdi)
    (h)   Omnes gentes plaudite manibus (Banchieri)
    (i)   Kyrie, from Paukenmesse (Haydn)
    (j)   O for the wings of a dove (Mendelssohn)
    (k)   O sacrum convivium (Messiaen)

29.   1973—Argo ZRG 739
    Mass in C (Beethoven)
    Christopher Keyte (bass); Robert Tear (tenor); Helen Watts (contralto); Felicity Palmer (soprano); Stephen Cleobury (organ); Academy of Saint Martin-in-the-Fields (leader—Alan Loveday)

30.   1973—Argo ZRG 782
    Christmas at Saint John's
    Stephen Cleobury (Organ)
    (a)   Ding dong! merrily on high (arr. C. Wood)
    (b)   O little town of Bethleham (arr. Armstrong)
    (c)   Born on earth (arr. Rutter)
    (d)   The Twelve Days of Christmas (arr. Rutter)
    (e)   Up, good Christen folk (arr. G. R. Woodward)
    (f)   Silent night (Gruber, arr. Ridout)
    (g)   Good King Wenceslas (Trad.English)
         [Richard Suart (bass); Simon Keenlyside (treble)]
    (h)   While shepherds watched (Este's Psalter, 1592)
    (i)   God rest you merry, gentlemen (arr. Willcocks)
    (j)   The Holly and the Ivy (arr. H. Walford Davies)
         [Robert King and Mark Tinkler (trebles); Anthony Dawson, Hugh Hetherington and William Kendall (tenors)]
    (k)   Away in a manger (arr. Willcocks)
         [Mark Tinkler (treble)]

(l) Shepherd's Pipe Carol (John Rutter)
(m) The First Nowell (arr. Willcocks)
(n) I saw three ships (arr. Willcocks)
(o) Suo-gân (arr. George Guest)
(p) Hark, the herald-angels sing (arr. Willcocks)

31. 1974—Argo ZRG 787
Music by Maurice Duruflé
Christopher Keyte (baritone); Robert King (treble); Derek
Simpson ('cello); Stephen Cleobury (organ)
(a) Requiem Mass
(b) Prélude et Fugue, for organ
We were all delighted that this recording received the
approbation of the composer, who wrote to me as
follows:

Paris 3 Avril 1978

Cher Monsieur,

La Direction de la firme 'Decca Records' a bien
voulu me communiquer votre adresse. Je suis heureux
de vous adresser mes remerciements et mes vives
félicitations pour l'excellent enregistrement que vous
avez bien voulu faire de mon *Requiem.* J'en ai beaucoup
apprécié les qualités d'exécution, d'intérprétation et de
prise de son.

Si vous avez la possibilité de diriger à nouveau mon
Requiem dans l'avenir, je me permettrai de vous informer
que je préfère que les solos de Baryton soient chantés
par toutes les basses et les seconds ténors. C'est une
erreur de ma part d'avoir confié ces quelques mesures
à un soliste.

Avec encore tous mes remerciements, veuillez agréer,
cher Monsieur, l'expression de mes meilleurs
sentiments.

M. Duruflé
6 Place du Panthéon
75005 Paris

Paris 3 April 1978

Dear Sir,

The management of Decca Records has been kind enough to give me your address. It gives me great pleasure to send you my thanks and my sincere congratulations for the excellent recording which you have been good enough to make of my *Requiem*. I greatly appreciate the qualities of execution, of interpretation and of the sound itself.

If you have occasion to direct my *Requiem* again in the future, can I tell you that I prefer that the Baritone solos be sung by all the basses and the second tenors. It is a mistake on my part to have entrusted these few bars to a soloist.

Again with all my thanks etc. etc.

M. Duruflé
6 Place du Panthéon
75005 Paris

32.   1974—Argo ZRG 825
     Mass in E flat (Schubert)
     Christopher Keyte (bass); Kenneth Bowen and Wynford Evans (tenors); Helen Watts (contralto); Felicity Palmer (soprano); Academy of Saint Martin-in-the-Fields

33.   1975—Argo ZRG 831
     Verse anthems (Henry Purcell)
     Stafford Dean (bass); Anthony Dawson and Ian Partridge (tenors); Paul Esswood (counter-tenor); Lynton Atkinson and Harry Gregson-Williams (trebles); John Scott (organ); A string orchestra (leader— Raymond Keenlyside)
     (a)   Behold, I bring you glad tidings
     (b)   In Thee, O Lord, do I put my trust
     (c)   I was glad when they said unto me
     (d)   O give thanks
     (e)   O Lord of hosts

34. 1975—Argo ZRG 841
    Music by Gabriel Fauré
    Benjamin Luxon (baritone); Jonathon Bond (treble);
    Stephen Cleobury (organ); Academy of Saint Martin-
    in-the-Fields
    (a) Requiem
    (b) Cantique de Jean Racine
    This recording was adjudged 'Record of the Month'
    in 'EMG Handmade Gramophones' review, printed in
    April 1976. The reviewer wrote "Sometimes it is hard
    to describe exactly why a performance comes up to
    perfection in a recording, and this is an instance where
    our breath was taken away by the solemn beauty and
    absolute 'rightness' of the vocal quality, orchestral
    playing, choice, registration and balance of the organ.
    . . . Here, at last, from no less than five versions of
    the Requiem in the last three years, we have what we
    consider to be the ideal performance."

35. 1976—Argo ZRG 855
    *Chapel Royal anthems by Matthew Locke, John Blow and
    Pelham Humfrey*
    Christopher Keyte (bass); Anthony Dawson and Robert
    Tear (tenors); James Bowman and Christopher Royall
    (counter-tenors); Jonathon Bond, Nicholas Evans-
    Pughe and Simon Shaw (trebles); John Scott (organ);
    Philomusica of London
    (a) Sing unto the Lord (Blow)
    (b) O give thanks unto the Lord (Humfrey)
    (c) Hear, O heavens (Humfrey)
    (d) By the waters of Babylon (Humfrey)
    (e) The King shall rejoice (Locke)
    (f) When the Son of man shall come (Locke)

36. 1976—Argo ZRG 869
    Mass in A flat (Schubert)

Christopher Keyte (bass); Wynford Evans (tenor); Bernadette Greevy (contralto); Wendy Eathorne (soprano); Academy of Saint Martin-in-the-Fields

37. 1977—Argo ZRG 850
Music by Bononcini, Caldara and Lotti
Christopher Keyte (bass); Philip Langridge (tenor); Paul Esswood (alto); Felicity Palmer (soprano); John Scott (organ); Philomusica of London
(a) Stabat Mater (Bononcini)
(b) Crucifixus etiam pro nobis—à 16 (Caldara)
(c) Crucifixus etiam pro nobis—à 8 (Lotti)

38. 1976—Argo ZRG 883
Music by Francis Poulenc and Flor Peeters
Jonathon Bond (treble); John Scott (organ)
(a) Mass in G (Poulenc)
(b) Exultate Deo (Poulenc)
(c) Salve Regina (Poulenc)
(d) Missa Festiva—Op.62 (Peeters)

39. 1977—Argo ZRG 867
Music by Haydn
Benjamin Luxon (baritone); Robert Tear (tenor); Helen Watts (contralto); Jennifer Smith (soprano); John Scott (organ); Academy of Saint Martin-in-the-Fields
(a) Missa Cellensis
(b) Clock pieces, for organ
(c) Missa brevis Saint Johannis de Deo

40. 1978—Decca D112 D3 (3 records)
A Choral Festival (of works taken from previous recordings)
(a) Te Deum (H. Purcell)
(b) In exitu Israel (S. Wesley)
(c) In jejunio et fletu (Tallis)
(d) Hosanna to the Son of David (Weelkes)

(e)   Exultate Deo (Palestrina)
(f)   Magnificat Tone 1 (Victoria)
(g)   O vos omnes (Gesualdo)
(h)   Laudate pueri (Monteverdi)

(a)   Jesu, joy of man's desiring (Bach)
(b)   Ave verum Corpus (Mozart)
(c)   Paukenmesse (Haydn)

(a)   Hear my prayer (Mendelssohn)
(b)   Ecce sacerdos magnus (Bruckner)
(c)   Quatre motets (Duruflé)
(d)   Cantique de Jean Racine (Fauré)
(e)   Lord, thou hast been our refuge (Vaughan Williams)
(f)   A Hymn to the Virgin (Britten)
(g)   Greater love hath no man (Ireland)
(h)   Missa Brevis (Britten)
(i)   O clap your hands (Vaughan Williams)

41.   1977—Argo ZRG 892
      Psalms of Consolation and Hope
      John Scott (organ)
      Psalms 139, 49, 67, 39, 96, 130, 150, 121, 42, 23, 90,
      69, 98.

42.   1978—Argo ZRG 903
      Saint Cecilia Mass (A. Scarlatti)
      Christopher Keyte (bass); Wynford Evans (tenor);
      Margaret Cable (contralto); Wendy Eathorne and
      Elizabeth Harwood (sopranos); The Wren Orchestra
      One of the 'Records of the Year' *(Daily Telegraph 15/
      12/80)*

43.   1979—Argo ZRG 913
      Music by Pergolesi
      Alfreda Hodgson (contralto); Felicity Palmer (soprano);
      David Hill (organ); The Argo Chamber Orchestra

(a)　Stabat Mater
(b)　Concerto Armonico No.2 in G

44.　1979—Argo ZRG 924
Music by Mozart
Stephen Roberts (bass); Philip Langridge (tenor); Margaret Cable (contralto); Felicity Palmer (soprano); David Hill (organ); The Wren Orchestra
(a)　Mass in C (Spaur Mass, K258)
(b)　Vesperae Solennes de Confessore (K.339)
This recording was adjudged 'Record of the Month' in 'EMG Handmade Gramophones' review, printed in February 1982.

45.　1980—Argo ZRG 933
Music by Mozart
Stephen Roberts (bass); Wynford Evans (tenor); Margaret Cable (contralto); Margaret Marshall (soprano); David Hill (organ); The Wren Orchestra
(a)　Vesperae de Dominica (K321)
(b)　Litaniae de Venerabili Altaris Sacramento (K243)

46.　1981—ASV DCA 511 ZCDCA 511
Music by Tallis and Shepherd
Angus Smith (tenor); Ian Shaw (organ)
(a)　Missa Salve Intemerata Virgo (Tallis)
(b)　Clarifica me Pater I, II & III for organ (Tallis)
(c)　Western Wind Mass (Shepherd)

47.　1982—Meridian E 4577052
Music by Des Prez and Titelouze
Hal Vernon (treble); Adrian Lucas (organ)
(a)　Missa Pange lingua (des Prez)
(b)　Versets for organ on Pange lingua (Titelouze)

48.　1981—Argo ZRDL 1006
Two Glorias (Vivaldi)

Kenneth Bowen (tenor); Anne Wilkins (mezzo-soprano); Patrizia Kwella and Lynda Russell (sopranos); Ian Shaw (organ); The Wren Orchestra
(a)   Gloria—RV 588
(b)   Gloria—RV 589

49.   1982—Meridian E 4577058
Music by Allegri
(a)   Miserere mei
(b)   Missa Vidi turbam magnam
(c)   Motet: Gustate et videte
'Certainly we have here the best version of the famous Miserere.' *(Monthly Guide to Recorded Music—April 1983)*

50.   1983—Meridian E 4577069
Music by Palestrina and his successors
Adrian Lucas (organ)
(a)   Exultate Deo (Palestrina)
(b)   O mors illa (Frescobaldi)
(c)   Omnes gentes plaudite manibus (Orgas)
(d)   Assumpta est Maria (Allegri)
(e)   Ego dormio (Quagliati)
(f)   Gaude Virgo (Agazzari)
(g)   Cogitavi dies antiquos (Antonelli)
(h)   In convertendo (Landi)
(i)   Jubilemus in arca Domini Dei (Anerio)
(j)   Pange lingua (Palestrina)

51.   1984—Meridian E 4577094
Music by Orlando Gibbons
Adrian Lucas (organ)
(a)   Almighty and everlasting God
(b)   O Thou, the central orb
(c)   Lift up your heads
(d)   See, the Word is incarnate
(e)   Hosanna to the Son of David
(f)   This is the record of John

(g)   Prelude, for organ
(h)   O Lord, in Thy wrath
(i)   Great Lord of Lords
(j)   Fantasia, for organ
(k)   O clap your hands
(l)   Fantasia, for organ

52.   1984—Meridian KE 77121
The Office of Compline (D. Massenzio)
Adrian Lucas (organ)

(a)   Organ Voluntary
(b)   Prayers and Responses
(c)   Psalms 4, 31, 91, 134.
(d)   Prayers and Responses
(e)   Hymn
(f)   Lesson
(g)   Nunc dimittis
(h)   Prayers and Responses
(i)   Hymn
(j)   Prayers and Blessing
(k)   Organ Voluntary

53.   1986—EMI EMX 2104 (MC: TC—EMX 2104)
Music by William Byrd

(a)   Mass for four voices
(b)   Mass for five voices

54.   1986—Chandos ABRD 1201 CHAN 8485
Carols from Saint John's
Paul Lindsell (baritone); Garth Bardsley and Andrew
Carwood (tenors); David Gould and Desmond O'Keeffe
(altos); Benjamin Beer and Alexander Hardy (trebles);
Philip Kenyon (organ)

(a)   Unto us a Boy is born (arr. G. Shaw)
(b)   Ding dong! merrily on high (arr. C. Wood)
(c)   Balulalow (Warlock)
(d)   The Holly and the Ivy (arr. Walford Davis)
(e)   In the bleak midwinter (Holst)

(f)   Sussex Carol (arr. Willcocks)

(g)   I sing of a maiden (Hadley)

(h)   Shepherds' Pipe Carol (Rutter)

(i)   Silent night (arr. Cashmore)

(j)   Hark, the herald-angels sing (arr. Willcocks)

(k)   O little town of Bethleham (arr. Vaughan Williams)

(l)   God rest you merry (arr. Willcocks)

(m)   Jesus Christ the apple-tree (Poston)

(n)   Good King Wenceslas (arr. Jacques)

(o)   There is no rose (Anon. ed. Stevens)

(p)   Dwy garol Gymraeg (Raymond Williams)
- (i) Greawdwr Nef a Daear lawr
- (ii) Pan fo'r stormydd garwa'n curo

(q)   Away in a manger (arr. Willcocks)

(r)   O come, all ye faithful (descants by Willcocks and J. R. Middleton)

55. 1987—Sain 1467 D

Welsh music

Jeremy Huw Williams (baritone); Marcus Polglase (tenor); James Turnbull (alto); Alistair Flutter a Benedict Perch (treblau); Andrew Nethsingha (organydd)

(a)   Codi fy llygaid wnaf (Dilys Elwyn-Edwards)

(b)   O Arglwydd, dal ni'n ddiogel (Bradwen Jones)

(c)   Dwy garol gynnar (tr. George Guest)
- (i) Ar fore Dydd Nadolig
- (ii) Myn Mair

(d)   Iesu, drud ddifyrrwch dynion (J. S. Bach)

(e)   Dwy garol Adfent (Raymond Williams)
- (i) Greawdwr Nef a Daear lawr
- (ii) Pan fo'r stormydd garw'n curo

(f)   Y Nefoedd sydd yn datgan gogoniant Duw (Mathias)

(g)   Yr Arglwydd yw fy Mugail (Dilys Elwyn-Edwards)

(h)   Pum cân gyfriniol (Vaughan Williams)
- (i) Y Pasg
- (ii) Mi roddais flodau
- (iii) "Croeso", medd Cariad
- (iv) Yr Alwad

    (v) Antiphon
(i) Dyrchafaf fy llygaid (T. Hopkin Evans)

56. 1987—Chandos CHAN 8574
Requiem K626 (Mozart)
David Wilson-Johnson (bass); William Kendall (tenor); Sarah Walker (contralto); Yvonne Kenny (soprano); English Chamber Orchestra

57. 1988—Chandos CHAN 8658
Music by Charpentier and Poulenc
Andrew Rupp (bass); Ben Cooper (tenor); James Turnbull (alto); Alistair Flutter and Allan Walker (trebles); City of London Sinfonia; Robert Huw Morgan (organ)
  (a) Messe de Minuit pour Noël (Charpentier)
  (b) Quatre Motets pour le temps de Noël (Poulenc)
      (i)   O magnum mysterium
      (ii)   Quem vidistis pastores?
      (iii) Videntes stellam
      (iv) Hodie Christus natus est
  (c) Salve Regina (Poulenc)
  (d) Quatre Motets pour un temps de pénitence (Poulenc)
      (i)   Timor et tremor
      (ii)   Vinea mea electa
      (iii) Tenebrae factae sunt
      (iv) Tristis est anima mea

58. 1988—EMI EMX 2155
Music by Taverner and Tallis
  (a) Missa Salve Intemerata Virgo (Tallis)
  (b) Western Wind Mass (Taverner)

59. 1990—EMI EMX 2180
Music by Allegri, Lassua and Palestrina
  (a) Miserere mei (Allegri)
  (b) Missa super Bell' Amfitrit' altera (Lassus)
  (c) Missa Veni Sponsa Christi (Palestrina)

60. 1991—Nimbus NI 5335

The Sound of Saint John's

Andrew Carwood (tenor); Alexander Martin (organ)

(a) Psalm 112—Beatus vir (Langlais)

(b) Songs of Zion (Robin Orr)

    (i)   Be gracious to me, O God

    (ii)   By the rivers of Babylon

    (iii) Sing to the Lord a new song

    (iv) Blessed be the Lord God of Israel

(c) Magnificat and Nunc dimittis—Collegium Sancti Johannis Cantabrigiense (Tippett)

(d) A Sequence for Saint Michael (Howells)

(e) Requiem (Howells)

(f) Three Advent Carols (Hoddinott)

    (i)   The Holy Son of God

    (ii)   The Coming of the Lord

    (iii) Saviour of the nations

(g) Magnificat and Nunc dimittis—Collegium Sancti Johannis Cantabrigiense (Howells)

9

The Organs of Saint John's College

> Whence hath the church so many organs and
> musicall instruments? To what purpose, I pray
> you, is that terrible blowing of belloes, expressing
> rather the crakes of thunder than the sweetnesse
> of a voyce?
>
> *Abbot Ethelred (12th century)*

It is clear that from the earliest times the College regarded the music of the Chapel as being of great importance and an organ is mentioned in a list of benefactions assembled in 1528. "Sondry and divers merchauntes in London gave emongist theyme Xli (£10) towardes the byeing of the newest Orgaynes." Nothing further is known of this instrument (if indeed it ever existed) but what is more certain is that an agreement was signed in 1634 between "Robert Dallam of the Citty of Westtminster, Organ Maker, and the Master of the Colledge of Saint John the Evangelist in the University of Cambridge, the ffellowes and schollars of the said Colledge to build one payre of organs, or Instrumentes, to conteyne six several stoppes of pipes, every stoppe conteyning forty nine pipes (viz) one diapason most part to stand in sight, one Principall of Tynne, one Recorder of Wood, one small Principall of Tynne, one two and twentieth of Tynne, with sound boords, Conveyances, Conducts, Roller boord, Carriages and Keyes, two bellowes and wind trunkes." Including carriage from London this instrument cost £185 and, although the bulk of this sum was donated by Mr Boothe, Fellow and Senior Dean, twenty-two pieces of college plate "growne old and uselesse" were also sold to defray part of the cost.

But disaster was hard at hand, and in the accounts of 1642-44 we read "Item payed by Mr Heron the Ju. Bursar for taking down the pictures and the organs and whiting the walls—£2-8-6." Not only was the instrument itself dispensed with, but even the case was taken away by someone referred to as "old Dowsy" (? old Dozy) who was paid 6/8d for perpetrating this vandalism. At the Restoration, and during the enlightened Mastership of Dr Peter Gunning, the organ (which had evidently been carefully preserved during the bleak days of the Commonwealth) was re-erected on a gallery at the west end of the Chapel. It was subsequently cared for by the organ-builder Thomas Thamer, of Cambridge and Peterborough, and during this period Thamer added a second manual—a chair (choir) organ. The organ at this time must have been a most colourful sight for in 1669 John Ivory was paid £2-0-0 for "painting the case of ye great organ and grounding ye pipes with blew and guilding the armes and balls at ye top, per bill."

Although there were minor alterations during the 18th century (Renatus Harris was paid £150 for general repairs and adding six stops—Humphrey Argent, of Cambridge, cleaned and repaired the instrument in 1777—Mr Henry Lincoln repaired the instrument in 1796) the organ remained *in situ* and largely unaltered until after T. A.

Walmisley's appointment in 1833. By this time, however, it clearly needed major work and the College decided to purchase a new organ. A contract was signed with the firm of William Hill for this instrument; the builders, in addition to the purchase price of £690, were to receive the old organ. The new organ, considerably larger than the one it replaced, was described as having "power far beyond the needs of the small chapel and choir." Details of the specification differ, but, according to W. L. Sumner, it was as follows:

GREAT		SWELL	
Open Diapason No. 1	8'	Open Diapason	8'
Open Diapason No. 2	8'	Stopped Diapason	8'
Stopped Diapason	8'	Dulciana	8'
Principal	4'	Principal	4'
Wald Principal	4'	Harmonica	4'
Flute	4'	Fifteenth	2'
Twelfth	2²/₃'	Sesquialtera	4 ranks
Fifteenth	2'	Oboe	8'
Sesquialtera	4 ranks	Horn	8'
Trumpet	8'	Clarion	4'
CHOIR		**PEDAL**	
Open Diapason	8'	Open Diapason	16'
Stopped Diapason	8'	**COUPLERS**	
Dulciana	8'	Great to Pedal	
Flute	4'	Choir to Pedal	
Principal	4'	Swell to Great	
Fifteenth	2'	Choir to Great	
Cremona	8'	Octave Swell to Great	
		COMPASSES	
		Great and Choir—FFF to F	
		Swell—FF to F	
		Pedal—FFF to C	

This instrument did duty until the building of the new Chapel, but was clearly unsuitable for its new surroundings. Unfortunately the two very elegant cases were given away, the Great organ case to Saint Mark's Church, Old Bilton,

Warwickshire and the Choir organ case to Brownsover Church, near Rugby, and the organ itself was completely rebuilt and enlarged. The contract, signed on 10 December 1867, again went to Messrs Hill and Son, and the work itself was completed in 1869 at a cost of £1191. For the first time hydraulic engines were added to blow the instrument, and these gave fitful service until they were superseded by an electric blower in 1931. The specification, drawn up by the Organist, Dr George Garrett, was of a much more adventurous nature, and the Pedal organ in particular, was very much in advance of its time. The stop-list was as follows:

GREAT

Double Open Diapason	16'
Open Diapason I	8'
Open Diapason II	8'
Stopped Diapason	8'
Cone Gamba	8'
Clarabella	8'
Quint	6'
Gemshorn	4'
Harmonic Flute	4'
Principal	4'
Twelfth	3'
Fifteenth	2'
Full Mixture	3 ranks
Sharp Mixture	4 ranks
Posaune	8'
Clarion	4'
4 Composition Pedals to Great	
2 Composition Pedals to Swell	
2 Composition Pedals to Pedal	

SWELL

Lieblich Gedackt	16'
Open Diapason	8'
Stopped Diapason	8'
Pierced Gamba	8'
Voix Céleste	8'
Suabe Flute	4'
Principal	4'
Fifteenth	2'
Mixture	4 ranks
Double Trumpet	16'
Hautboy	8'
Horn	8'
Clarion	4'

COUPLERS ETC.

Swell Octave
Swell to Great
Swell to Choir
Great to Pedal
Swell to Pedal
Choir to Pedal
Swell Tremulant

CHOIR

| Double Dulciana | 16' |
| Open Diapason | 8' |

PEDAL

| Great Stopped Bass | 32' |
| Great Bass | 16' |

Stopped Diapason	8′	Violon	16′
Dulciana	8′	Principal	8′
Viol de Gamba	8′	Flute Bass	8′
Stopped Flute	4′	Fifteenth	4′
Gedackt Flute	4′	Mixture	4 ranks
Principal	4′	Great Trombone	16′
Flageolet	2′	Trumpet	8′
Cremona	8′		

This, then, was the Chapel organ until 1889, when pneumatic action was fitted to the Great and Swell organs, and tubular pneumatic to the drawstops and the Pedal organ. A Dulciana 16′ was added to the Pedal organ, again by Messrs Hill.

One of the most predictable things relating to the Saint John's organ is that, whenever a new Organist is appointed, he, within a short space of time, expresses extreme dissatisfaction with the instrument and strongly recommends the College Council to sanction a rebuild. The appointment of Cyril Rootham in 1901 did not break this tradition, and there was indeed justification for his plea. The instrument had become extremely dirty, extremely noisy in its action, and increasingly unreliable, and on 12 May 1902 the College Council signed a contract with Messrs. Norman and Beard, at the very reasonable cost of £924, to install pneumatic action throughout the organ, to rebuild the console and to add thumb pistons and combination pedals. There was also to be considerable re-voicing—as Nicholas Thistlethwaite comments "all the pipework was re-voiced in the direction of that opaque smooth quality of tone which was then becoming fashionable." There were minor changes to the stop-list: on the Great the Cone Gamba became Open Diapason III and there was a new Hohl Flöte 8′—on the Swell the old Voix Céleste, which had two ranks of pipes, was divided into two stops, Echo Dulciana 8′ and Vox Angelica 8′; there was a new Hautboy 8′ and

the Choir and Swell 4' flutes were exchanged. A Lieblich
Bourdon 16' was added. The opening recital was given
on Tuesday, 4 November 1902 by Sir Walter Parratt, M.V.O.,
Mus.Doc., Master of the King's Musick and Organist of
Saint Georges's Chapel, Windsor. The programme was as
follows:

1. Andante religioso ....Liszt
2. Prelude and Fugue in C major.................J. S. Bach
3. Musette ....Dandrieu
4. Pastorale: "Nun danket alle Gott" .... Herzogenberg
5. Fantasia in G major .... Hubert Parry
6. Choral Vorspiel: .... Brahms
       "O Welt, ich muss dich lassen"
7. Fantasia and Toccata................ Professor Stanford

By 1920 the instrument was again in need of repair,
and the Durham firm of Harrison and Harrison was given
the contract. The work, costing £2020, was completed in
1922; a remodelled console was provided, together with
new drawstops and piston action. A number of the stops
were renamed, and there was thorough cleaning, together
with a re-arrangement of the Swell organ, which had
become almost inaccessible. The only tonal work was a
reconstitution of the Swell and Great Mixtures, and the
stop-list was as follows:

GREAT		SWELL	
Double Open Diapason	16'	Lieblich Bourdon	16'
Large Open Diapason	8'	Open Diapason	8'
Small Open Diapason	8'	Stopped Diapason	8'
Spitz Flute	8'	Echo Salicional	8'
Hohl Flute	8'	Echo Gamba	8'
Stopped Diapason	8'	Vox Angelica	8'
Harmonic Flute	4'	Flute	4'
Gemshorn	4'	Principal	4'

Octave	4'	Fifteenth	2'
Quint	5¹/₃'	Mixture	5 ranks
Octave Quint	2²/₃'	Double Trumpet	16'
Super Octave	2'	Horn	8'
Harmonics	5 ranks	Clarion	4'
Great Reeds on Choir		Oboe	8'
Trumpet	8'	Tremulant	
Octave Trumpet	4'		

CHOIR   **PEDAL**

Contra Dulciana	16'	Sub Bass	32'
Open Diapason	8'	Open Wood	16'
Dulciana	8'	Violone	16'
Stopped Diapason	8'	Dulciana	16'
Viola da Gamba	8'	Bourdon	16'
Suabe Flute	4'	Flute	8'
Lieblich Flute	4'	Principal	8'
Principal	4'	Fifteenth	4'
Flageolet	2'	Mixture	3 ranks
Clarinet	8'	Ophicleide	16'
		Posaune	8'

COUPLERS   **PISTONS**

Swell to Great   6 to Swell
Swell to Choir   6 to Great
Swell to Pedal   4 to Choir
Choir to Great   6 to Swell and Pedal
Choir to Pedal   6 to Great and Pedal
Great to Pedal   Full Pedal and Pedal cancel
                                        Reversible thumb pistons for Gt.-
                                        Ped., Sw.-Gt, Ch.-Ped. Reversible
                                        thumb pistons for Ped. Oph-
                                        icleide and Gt.Double Open
                                        Diapason

The opening recital was given on Wednesday, 8 November 1922 by H. G. Ley, M.A., Mus.Doc., Organist of Christ Church, Oxford. The programme was a follows:

1. Overture to Orlando............................Handel
   Adagio, Allegro-adagio, Allegretto.

2. (a) Largo from Golden Sonata ....Henry Purcell
   (b) Pavan ....William Byrd
3. Chorale in A minor (No.3)................César Franck
4. (a) Elegy ....Parry
      (composed for the funeral of the Earl of Pembroke)
   (b) Prelude on an Irish Melody ....Stanford
      (1st Set, No.6)
   (c) Sarabande from Phantasy ....Vaughan Williams
      Quintet for Strings
   (d) Psalm Prelude, No.3................Herbert Howells
         "Yea, tho' I walk through the valley of the shadow
      of death, I will fear no evil, for Thou art with me. Thy
      rod and Thy staff comfort me." -Ps. 23 v. 4.
5. Fantasia in F minor ....Mozart
      Adagio, Allegro, Adagio.
6. (a) Trio in C minor...........................J. S. Bach
      Adagio, Allegro, Adagio.
   (b) Choral Prelude ....J. S. Bach
      "O man, bewail thy heavy sin."
   (c) Passacaglia

I was appointed Organist in 1951 and, as the 50s
progressed, it became clear that the Chapel organ was once
more in need of urgent attention. The choice this time
fell on the now-amalgamated firm of Messrs Hill and
Norman & Beard, and the College in 1955 decided upon
a complete rebuild. Much of the internal mechanism of
the instrument was to be made good, a fourth manual was
to be added (which necessitated a new console), the manual
and pedal compasses were to be extended, the key and
pedal actions were to be electrified, and the whole tonal
range of the organ was to be re-designed. The result of
all this was an organ which W. L. Sumner described as
being "one of the most versatile and interesting in the
country." The stop-list was as follows:

GREAT		**SWELL**	
Double Open Diapason	16'	Lieblich Bourdon	16'
Open Diapason	8'	Open Diapason	8'
Geigen Principal	8'	Rohr Gedackt	8'
Spitz Principal	8'	Echo Salicional	8'
Stopped Diapason	8'	Vox Angelica	8'
Harmonic Flute	4'	Principal	4'
Octave	4'	Lieblich Flute	4'
Spitz Principal	4'	Fifteenth	2'
Octave Quint	2²/₃'	Larigot	1¹/₃'
Super Octave	2'	Mixture	4 ranks
Quint Mixture	3 ranks	Oboe	8'
Flute Cornet	3 ranks	Double Trumpet	16'
Trumpet	8'	Cornopean	8'
Clarion	4'	Clarion	4'
Great Reeds on Choir		Tremulant	
CHOIR		**PEDAL**	
Prinzipal	8'	Subbass	32'
Quintade	8'	Open Wood	16'
Glockengamba	8'	Violone	16'
Octav	4'	Bourdon	16'
Gemshorn	4'	Dulciana	16'
Nasat	2²/₃'	Lieblich Bourdon	16'
Blockflöte	2'	Principal	8'
Sifflöte	1'	Bass Flute	8'
Zimbel	3 ranks	Fifteenth	4'
		Nächthorn	4'
		Sifflöte	2'
		Quartane	2 ranks
		Ophicleide	16'
		Posaune	8'

PISTONS (thumb)	**PISTONS (toe)**
8 to Great, 8 to Swell	8 to Pedal
6 to Choir, 6 to Solo	4 Generals to all stops
8 Reversible acting on Couplers	4 Reversibles acting on
1 General cancel	Couplers, and on Full Organ
Capture setter piston	
Rocking Tablet to Manual	
Doubles off	

SOLO

Quintatön	16'
Hohl Flute	8'
Viola da Gamba	8'
Viole Céleste	8'
Lieblich Flute	4'
Harmonic Twelfth	2²/₃'
Piccolo	2'
Harmonic Tierce	1³/₅'
Clarinet	8'
Tremulant	
Trompeta Real	8'
(en chamade)	

WIND PRESSURES

Great Flutes	3½"
Great Reeds	4½"
Swell Organ	4"
Swell Reeds	8"
Choir Organ	2½"
Solo Organ	6"
Trompeta Real	7"
Pedal Organ	4 to 8"

COUPLERS

Great to Pedal
Swell to Pedal
Choir to Pedal
Solo to Pedal
Swell to Great
Choir to Great
Solo to Great
Swell to Choir
Solo to Choir
Swell Octave
Swell Sub-octave
Swell Octave to Pedal
Solo Octave
Solo Sub-octave
Solo Unison off
Great and Pedal pistons
   coupler
Full Organ

This scheme, which cost about £10,000, was drawn up by myself and by Hill, Norman and Beard's chief voicer, Mr Mark Fairhead. Organ recitals to mark the rebuilding of the organ were given as follows:

Monday 23 January 1956 at 8.30 pm. Alan Hemmings (Organ Student of Saint John's College)

1. Fanfare (Psalm 81, vv. 1-3) ....John Cook (1952)
2. Clock Pieces....................................Handel
   (a) Voluntary on a Flight of Angels
   (b) Minuet
   (c) Jig
3. Prelude and Fugue in G minor ....J. S. Bach
4. Fugue and Choral.....................Honegger (1920)

5. Concerto No.3 .... Hans Friedrich Micheelsen (1947)
6. Pastorale .... Milhaud (1941)
7. Sonata (Op. 92) .... Ernst Krenek (1942)
8. Episode.......................... Aaron Copland (1941)
9. Chorale No.1 in G .... Roger Sessions (1941)

Monday 6 February at 8.30 pm. Francis Jackson (Organist of York Minster)

1. Voluntary on the 100th Psalm Tune ...... Henry Purcell
2. Toccata and Fugue in the Dorian Mode....... J. S. Bach
3. Sonata in E flat .... Bairstow
4. Toccata in C .... Gordon Phillips
5. Rhapsody on a Ground............. Heathcote Statham
6. Variations on a Noël .... Dupré

Monday 20 February at 8.30 pm. George Guest (Organist of St John's College)

1. Ciacona in E minor .... Buxtehude
2. Passacaglia and Fugue in C minor............ J. S. Bach
3. Pastorale .... H. von Herzogenberg
4. Introduction and Passacaglia..................... Reger
5. Elegiac Rhapsody .... Rootham
6. Canzona (Sonata in C minor) .... Whitlock
7. Toccata alla Marcia.......................... Robin Orr

Wednesday 14 March at 8.30 pm. Fernando Germani (Rome)

1. Concerto in D minor .... A. Vivaldi
   (a) Allegro—Fugue
   (b) Largo Spiccato
   (c) Allegro
2. Prelude and Fugue in D .... J. S. Bach
3. Fantasie and Fugue .... F. Liszt
   on "Ad nos ad salutarem undam"

4. Sonata on Psalm 94 .... J. Reubke

Further work was done in 1974, during which time the Mixtures were remodelled and the opportunity was taken to exchange the Pedal Sifflöte 2′ for a Schalmei 4′, and to add a partly-derived Contra Posaune 32′ and a Cymbelstern.

Dr Nicolas Thistlethwaite, in his Report on the Chapel Organ (1988) offered "a tentative analysis of the origins of the various registers in the present organ," and I am extremely grateful to him for permission to quote from his findings. The following table shows the date of the original pipework, the maker, and known subsequent modifications. Where the nomenclature has changed, the original name of the stop is shown in brackets:

GREAT

Double Open Diapason	16′	Hill 1869, 1889
Open Diapason	8′	Hill 1869, 1889; re-scaled NB 1902
Geigen Diapason	8′	Hill 1869 (Open Diapason II) re-made 1955
Spitz Principal	8′	Hill 1869 (Cone Gamba)
Stopped Diapason	8′	Hill 1839; re-made
Octave	4′	Hill 1869 (Principal)
Spitz Principal	4′	Hill 1869 (Gemshorn)
Harmonic Flute	4′	Hill 1869
Octave Quint	2²/₃′	Hill 1839 (Twelfth)
Super Octave	2′	Hill 1869 (Quint)
Mixture	¾ ranks	Hill 1838, 1869 etc.
Flute Cornet	3 ranks	HN & B 1955
Trumpet	8′	Hill 1869; NB 1902; HN & B 1955
Clarion	4′	Hill 1869; NB 1902; HN & B 1955

CHOIR

Prinzipal	8′	Hill 1839 (Open Diapason)
Quintade	8′	Hill 1839 (Stopped Diapason); re-made 1956

Glockengamba	8'	Hill 1869 (Viol de Gamba)
Octav	4'	Hill 1839 (Principal)
Gemshorn	4'	HN & B 1955
Nasat	2²/₃'	HN & B 1955 (?)
Blockflöte	2'	HN & B 1955 (?)
Sifflöte	1'	HN & B 1955 (?)
Zimbel	3 ranks	HN & B 1955, 1974

SWELL

Lieblich Bourdon	16'	Hill 1869 (Lieblich Gedackt)
Open Diapason	8'	Hill 1839, 1869; NB 1902; HH 1922
Rohr Gedeckt	8'	Hill 1839, 1869 (Stopped Diapason); re-made NB 1902
Echo Salicional	8'	Hill 1869 (Voix Céleste II); NB 1902
Vox Angelica	8'	Hill 1869 (Voix Céleste II); NB 1902
Principal	4'	Hill 1839, 1869; re-scaled 1955
Lieblich Flute	4'	Hill 1839, 1869 (Choir Stopped Flute?); re-made
Fifteenth	2'	Hill 1839 (Great Fifteenth?); re-scaled 1956
Larigot	1¹/₃'	HN & B 1955
Mixture	4 ranks	HN & B 1974
Oboe	8'	NB 1902 (Hautboy)
Double Trumpet	16'	Hill 1839 (Great Trumpet), 1869; NB 1902; HN & B 1955
Cornopean	8'	HN & B 1955 (secondhand pipework)
Clarion	4'	Hill 1869; NB 1902; HN & B 1955

PEDAL

Sub Bass	32'	Hill 1869; HN & B 1955
Open Wood	16'	Hill 1869
Violone	16'	Hill 1869
Bourdon	16'	[from Sub Bass]
Dulciana	16'	Hill 1889
Lieblich Bourdon	16'	HN & B 1955
Principal	8'	Hill 1869 [1839]

Bass Flute	8'	[from Sub Bass]
Fifteenth	4'	Hill 1869 [1839]
Nächthorn	4'	HN & B 1955
Mixture	4 ranks	Hill 1869 [1839], etc.
Contra Posaune	32'	[from Ophicleide]
Ophicleide	16'	Hill 1869; NB 1902; HN & B 1955, 1974
Posaune	8'	Hill 1869
Schalmei	4'	HN & B 1974
SOLO		
Quintatön	16'	HN & B 1955
Hohl Flute	8'	NB 1902 (ex-Great Organ)
Viola da Gamba	8'	HN & B 1955
Viole Céleste	8'	HN & B 1955
Lieblich Flute	4'	Hill 1869 (Choir Gedackt Flute 4'); NB 1902
Harmonic Twelfth	$2^2/_3'$	HN & B 1955
Piccolo	2'	Hill 1869 (Choir Flageolet)
Harmonic Tierce	$1^3/_5'$	HN & B 1955
Clarinet	8'	Hill 1869; NB 1902 (ex-Choir Organ)
Trompeta Real	8'	HN & B 1955

By the time of my retirement in 1991 the instrument was again giving trouble and an Organ Committee, which included my successor Mr Christopher Robinson, recommended that major work was urgently necessary. Reports and estimates were sought from three builders, and expert advice taken from the Revd Dr Nicholas Thistlethwaite, before the College finally decided to invite the London organ builders, N. P. Mander Ltd to undertake the work. The old organ was dismantled early in January 1993, and, just as I was the first person to play it in 1955, I was also the last, for I made a private recording of Franck's *Prelude, Fugue and Variation* on the night before it was taken down.

The Organ Committee was adamant that the need for

a first-class accompanying organ should be borne in mind, and that the basic sound of the previous instrument should be retained, particularly as so few of its type now remain in Cambridge. However, it was soon discovered that much of the pipe-work had been so damaged over the years that, with the exception of much of the Pedal Organ, it had become necessary to install new work. The innards of the instrument, altered so much since the 1869 rebuild and now a jumble of little soundboards (consequent upon the increase in the manual and pedal compasses), were to be completely re-designed and re-built. The specification is as follows:

GREAT

Double Open Diapason	16′	Part in case, all new
Open Diapason I	8′	new
Open Diapason II	8′	new
Stopped Diapason	8′	wood, new
Principal	4′	new
Gemshorn	4′	new
Wald Flute	4′	tapered, new
Twelfth	$2^2/_3$′	new
Fifteenth	2′	new
Flageolet	2′	wood, new
Full Mixture (15-19-22)	3 ranks	new
Sharp Mixture (22-26-29)	3 ranks	new
Cornet (1-8-12-15-17)	5 ranks	Middle C, new
Trumpet	8′	new
Clarion	4′	new

CHOIR (all new)

Open Diapason	8′	lowest 5 stopped, part in case
Gedackt	8′	tapered, metal
Gamba	8′	metal, wood bass
Principal	4′	part in case
Flute	4′	metal, with chimneys
Nazard	$2^2/_3$′	

Fifteenth	2′	
Flautina	2′	
Tierce	1³/₅′	
Mixture (19-22)	2/3 ranks	
Cremona	8′	
Tremulant		

SOLO (enclosed)

Viola da Gamba	8′	new
Viola Céleste (tenor C)	8′	new
Hohl Flute	8′	new, metal
Flauto Traverso	4′	new, harmonic
Corno di Bassetto	8′	new
Cor Anglais	8′	new
Tremulant		
Tuba Mirabilis	8′	new, 12″ wind pressure
Trompeta Real	8′	original, 7¾″ wind pressure
Cymbelstern		

SWELL

Bourdon	16′	original, wood
Open Diapason	8′	new
Rohr Gedackt	8′	new, wood
Salicional	8′	original
Voix Céleste	8′	original
Principal	4′	new
Stopped Flute	4′	new, metal
Fifteenth	2′	new
Sesquialtera (17-19/12-17)	2 ranks	
Mixture (19-22-26-29)	4 ranks	
Oboe	8′	original
Vox Humana	8′	new
Double Trumpet	16′	new
Cornopean	8′	new
Clarion	4′	new
Tremulant		

PEDAL

Subbass	32′	original
Open Diapason (Wood)	16′	original

Open Diapason (Metal)	16′	new, partly in case
Dulciana	16′	original
Bourdon (ext. 32′)	16′	original
Principal	8′	original
Bass Flute	8′	from Great
Fifteenth	4′	original
Flute	4′	
Mixture (19-22-26-29)	4 ranks	original
Contra Trombone	32′	new, full length
Ophicleide	16′	original, wood
Fagotto	16′	from Swell
Posaune	8′	original
Clarion	4′	from Swell

COUPLERS

Choir to Pedal
Great to Pedal
Swell to Pedal
Solo to Pedal
Solo Octave to Pedal
Swell to Choir
Solo to Choir
Choir to Great
Swell to Great
Solo to Great
Solo to Swell

The Chapel also possesses a one-manual chamber organ, built in 1983 by E. J. Johnson, of Cambridge, to the following specification:

Gedackt Treble	8′
Gedackt Bass	8′
Flute Treble	4′
Flute Bass	4′
Principal	2′
Tierce	$1\frac{3}{5}$′
Mixture	2 ranks

10

Odds and Ends

When as a child I laughed and wept, time crept.
When as a youth I dreamed and talked, time walked.
When I became a full-grown man, time ran,
And later as I older grew, time flew.
Soon I shall find while travelling on, time gone.
Will Christ have saved my soul by then?
Anon. (from the Old Clock in Chester Cathedral)

Although I underwent a quadruple heart by-pass operation in early 1991, I was fortunate in making what has appeared to be a complete recovery, thanks to the devotion and technical brilliance of my surgeon, Mr Frank Wells. I came back to the Chapel to direct my last Ash Wednesday Evensong, and from then until my retirement on 30 September 1991 had an extremely busy few months. Meanwhile the College had been wise enough to appoint, as my successor, Mr Christopher Robinson, a native of Peterborough and Organist of Saint George's Chapel, Windsor. The transfer of direction was indeed smooth, and the College Choir has certainly prospered under its new Director.

It was a new experience for me to have free Sundays

and, if I wished, to go away from Cambridge for as long as I liked with impunity. Meanwhile, I had been made a Life Fellow, and so was able to continue the privilege of enjoying a college room. There was no lack of invitations, and I found myself adjudicating at a number of Musical Festivals, as well as directing choirs and lecturing abroad. There is a growing demand for this kind of work, especially in the United States, and in 1992 I made no less than four trips to that country. My first engagement was to take over Dr Gerre Hancock's excellent choir at Saint Thomas Church, Fifth Avenue, New York City for a long week-end, and to lecture to a course of choirmasters at the church. I then flew north to Buffalo to work with the Choir of Saint Paul's Cathedral in similar fashion. This in now under the direction of Dr Dale Adelmann, former Choral Student of Saint John's, and is already of an unusually high standard. There followed visits to Cincinnati, and to the Master Schola at the Community of Jesus, Orleans, Cape Cod. Finally I spent a long week-end in Washington D.C., taking part in the centenary celebrations of the birth of Herbert Howells, former Honorary Fellow of Saint John's, and Acting-Organist during World War II, when Robin Orr was away on war service.

Other work continued to come in, and in particular I enjoyed conducting youth choirs in Basel (what an extraordinary experience to take a tram for a few minutes down one street and find oneself in Germany, and a few minutes down another street and find oneself in France), Eindhoven and Ghent. But in many ways my most interesting experience was to find myself involved in a completely new form of music making.

The English composer Robert Pearsall (1795-1856) came of a wealthy family, was privately educated for the Bar, to which he was called in 1821. His health was never robust and he lived successively in Mainz, in Willsbridge (Glos.), in Karlsruhe, Munich and Vienna. In 1837 he bought the castle of Wartensee on Lake Constance where he subsequently died of apoplexy. Although chiefly known for his excellent arrangement of the carol *In dulci jubilo*, he wrote many other works, most of which remain in manuscript, many of them in the monastery of Einsiedeln, Switzerland. Included in these latter are some works for the original combination of military band and organ. These gathered dust on the monastery shelves until just a few years ago when they were brought to light by Father Theo Flury, Director of Music at Einsiedeln. It so happened that two officers of the Band of the Royal Yeomanary had become connected with Einsiedeln, and so a concert for these particular forces was arranged. In 1991 it was decided to hold a competition for works written for this combination of instruments, and the final stages (for which I was one of the two judges) took place in Saint John's Chapel. The more successful pieces were interesting, though it appeared that the composers had never really decided whether the organ was to be a solo instrument, or merely an accompanying instrument. The Band played extremely well, though in the very live acoustics of the Chapel, their volume was such as to make the two judges beat a hasty retreat to the Ante-Chapel.

No competition was held in 1992; instead a concert of works for this unusual combination was given in Einsiedeln. My job, not on the whole particularly onerous, was to advise the conductor of the Band of the Royal Yeomanry about questions of balance between the various instruments and the organ; it was indeed a pleasant long week-end! I seem to have always been similarly fortunate in my engagements in Switzerland—I recall being engaged to adjudicate at the Montreux Competitive Festival for Choirs. Because I anticipated a heavy schedule I advised Nan, my wife, that there would be no point in her coming. I was therefore highly embarrassed to be told on arrival that I would not be required before 8 pm. on any day! Neither written nor spoken adjudications were wanted, and the three adjudicators, sitting separately some twenty feet from one another, were, after each piece, given a piece of paper with the numbers 1 to 10 on it; we were required to ring the number which we felt appropriate to the performance!

I was University Organist from 1974 to 1991. The duties were minimal, largely because I was never able to play for a University Sermon service after the time of its starting changed from 8.30 pm. to 11 am., a time which of course clashed with the Sunday morning service at Saint John's. I did however inaugurate the custom of Saint John's and King's Choirs joining to sing appropriate music in the Senate House during the yearly Honorary Degree ceremony. This was always an occasion to which we looked forward; the proceedings customarily ended with 'God save the Queen', and two verses were usually sung. After one ceremony the Duke of Edinburgh asked me if I was aware that no less than some 35 verses were in existence, and could we please have a third verse next year? I found one which had to do with social justice, and included it the following year. Eyebrows however were later raised when a message came down to me to say that "the Duke of Edinburgh wishes to know why it is necessary to have as many as three verses in 'God save the Queen'."

Meanwhile I continued to give organ recitals. Lack of adequate practice time meant that I could never regard myself in any way as a virtuoso, but I enjoyed playing and have now given concerts in most English and Welsh cathedrals, as well as in the United States and Holland. The standard of organ-playing in general has improved to a remarkable degree of late and we have indeed now reached the situation where there are more good players than are jobs for them to fill; though it would be true to say that there are many more first-class organists than there are first-class choirmasters. I miss the daily work with Saint John's, but I have of late received an increasing number of invitations to 'take over', for a week-end, established cathedral choirs. These have included the Choirs of Liverpool Metropolitan Cathedral, Worcester Cathedral and Winchester Cathedral, and it has been a wonderful experience to work with such talented and friendly people. There is an indefinable bond between cathedral musicians, and one is conscious of an immediate rapport.

One of the sad events of 1992 was the untimely death of the composer William Mathias. William had a long connection with the College, and his music was widely sung in Cambridge, as it was in Britain, and indeed throughout the world. His very talented daughter Rhiannon was a member of Saint John's, and this meant that he visited the college from time to time, as well as inviting the College Choir to sing in the very successful Festival which he directed, the North Wales Festival, based in the tiny but ancient cathedral of Llanelwy/Saint Asaph. It is entirely appropriate to recall that one of Saint John's most distinguished sons, William Morgan, who first translated the Bible into Welsh in 1588, was Bishop of Llanelwy, and his statue, commemorating this event, stands in the cathedral grounds. There was a Memorial Service to William in Saint Paul's Cathedral, London on 20 November 1992, and I was honoured by being asked to speak of my old friend at it.

"We meet this morning," I began in the cathedral with which he was so closely connected, "to remember with gratitude the life and work of William Mathias. A giant amongst composers, a man whose music touched all hearts, whether in the cathedral, the church or the concert hall— a pianist of the very highest standard—a superb teacher and lecturer, whose tenure of the Chair of Music at the University College of North Wales brought an enviable distinction both to the Faculty and to the College.

"William Mathias' energy was all-embracing, and to lesser mortals quite astonishing, for, in addition to his Faculty duties and to the long hours which he devoted to composition, he found time to be a member of the Welsh Arts Council, to be a member of the British Council, and to be a Governor of both the National Museum of Wales and the National Youth Orchestra of Great Britain.

"And, as if all that was not enough for one person, however energetic, he readily made himself available to help and guide aspiring musicians of all ages. He was a person full of kindness and encouragement especially towards the young. William was essentially a humble man, one who wore his many distinctions lightly, and one who was always approachable. He never seemed to be in a hurry, largely because he organised his time so cleverly—which of course made him the ideal person to direct the North Wales Festival at Llanelwy/St. Asaph. This yearly event has been a conspicuous success since its inception in 1972, and, under William's inspired direction, it has become one of the major Festivals of Wales, one of the major Festivals of Europe. And it is indeed appropriate that his successor as Director should be a former colleague at Bangor and member of Saint John's, Geraint Lewis.

"William Mathias' list of compositions is immense, encompassing, as it does, an opera, large-scale works for choir and for orchestra, and concertos for clarinet, flute, harp, harpsichord, horn and organ—as well as three piano concertos. One of his last works was a splendidly virile violin concerto, which received its first performance (with György Pauk as soloist) earlier this year. Church and cathedral music have both been enriched by a long succession of works, many as a result of commissions, but all with that characteristic beauty which permeates all his music. His musical style was inimitable, personal and instantly recognisable—and derives, in part at least, from the influence of his first composition teacher, Lennox Berkeley, and from his love for the music of Stravinsky and Poulenc.

"The 17th-century writer Edmund Waller, just before his own death, wrote:

The soul's dark cottage, batter'd and decay'd,
Lets in new light through chinks that time has made
Stronger by weakness, wiser men become
As they draw near to their eternal home.

"It is, perhaps fortunately, given to few of us to know the precise date of our own death, and I have never really understood, or sympathised with, the plea of the psalmist who sang 'Lord, let me know mine end, and the number of my days, that I may be certified how long I have to live.' But, at the beginning of this year, that particular information was made known to William and his immediate reaction was characteristic—he lived the remaining seven months of his life to the full, and with conspicuous and unusual bravery. Just a fortnight before his death he wrote to me 'Work at home goes on apace, and I'm entirely up to schedule!'—and indeed it did, and he was! Two days before he died he sat composing until midnight, took to his bed on the following day, and died a few hours later, secure in the strong faith which had sustained him throughout a dark period.

" 'Sanctaidd yw'r gwir oleuni, a thra rhyfeddol, yn rhoddi disgleirdeb i'r rhai a ddioddefodd ym mhoethder y frwydr; etifeddiant gan Grist gartref na wywa ei ysblander, lle byddant yn gorfoleddu mewn llawenydd byth mwy.' [Holy is the true light, and passing wonderful, lending radiance to them that endured in the heat of the conflict: from Christ they shall inherit a house of unfading splendour, wherein they rejoice with gladness evermore.][1]

---

[1] from the Antiphon at First Vespers on the Feast of All Saints (Salisbury Diurnal)
Sanctum est verum lumen et admirabile,
Minstrans lucem hic qui permanserunt in agone certaminis;
Recipient a Christo splendorem sempiternum,
In quo assidue felices laetantur.

"So ended, prematurely, the life of a great composer. His interests, quite apart from music, were widespread, and especially did he care for that tender, but well-rooted bloom, the Welsh language. Indeed, his interest in both Welsh and English literature was considerable, and his detailed knowledge of both was an immense help to him in his choice of texts.

"William made his way through life with a noble dignity which never wavered, but he never lost an impish sense of humour. He was fun to be with, especially in his very beautiful home in Sir Fôn/Anglesey—and the fact that he was supported by a warm, happy home life was, of course, largely responsible for his genial and urbane nature. He became an internationally famous composer—but he never forgot his roots, and his boyhood in Hendy-gwyn ar Dâf/Whitland.

"In our yearly Commemoration of Benefactors service in Saint John's College Chapel we recite those well-known verses from Ecclesiasticus which were heard earlier this morning, and, because these words are so particularly apt today. I should like to end by reading some of them to you again, this time in the ancient language which was so much a part of William's life: 'Canmolwn yn awr y gŵyr enwog, a'n tadau a'n cenhedlodd ni. Hwy a geisiasant allan felystra cerdd, ac a draethasant ganiadau sgrifenedig. Y rhai hyn oll yn eu cenedlaethau a gawsant ogoniant, a gorfoledd yn eu dyddiau. Eu cyrff a gladdwyd mewn heddwch, ond y mae eu henw yn byw byth. Y bobl a fynegant eu doethineb hwy, a'r gynulleidfa a draetha eu clod hwynt.' [Let us now praise famous men, and our fathers that begat us. Such as found out musical tunes, and recited verses in writing. All these were honoured in their generations, and were the glory of their times. Their bodies are buried in peace, but their name liveth for evermore. The people will tell of their wisdom, and the congregation will show forth their praise.]

"Boed i'w enaid, ac eneidiau'r holl ymadawedig ffyddlon,

trwy drugaredd Duw, orffwys mewn tangnefedd, a chodi mewm gogoniant. [May his soul, and the souls of all the faithful departed, rest in peace, and rise in glory.] Amen."

Over the years a large number of works have been either commissioned by the College, or written especially for its Choir. And we are indeed fortunate to be able to use the sum of money given, with great generosity, by Mr Kenneth Webster for the purpose of commissioning pieces of sacred music for the use, in the first instance, of the College Choir. Works written for or commissioned for the Choir may be listed as follows:

1. Lennox Berkeley (1903-1989)—*Three Latin Motets* (1972)
2. Malcolm Boyle (1902-1976)—*O perfect love*
   Written for the wedding in Chapel of George and Nan Guest on 31/10/59
3. Dilys Elwyn Edwards (1923-   )—*Yr Arglwydd yw fy Mugail* (1987)
   The composer was formerly a pupil of Herbert Howells
4. Dilys Elwyn Edwards—*Codi fy llygaid wnaf* (1987)
5. George Guest (1924-   )—*The Lord at first did Adam make* (1993)
   For the Advent Carol Service 1993
6. Gerald Hendrie (1935-   )—*Evening Canticles (Coll. Sancti Johannis Cantabrigiense)*
7. Tony Hewitt-Jones (1926-1989)—*Evening Canticles (Coll. Sancti Johannis Cantabrigiense)*
8. Herbert Howells (1892-1983)—*Evening Canticles (Coll. Sancti Johannis Cantabrigiense*—1957)
   The story of how this particular work came to be written is worth relating. In the London *Times* of 25 May 1956 there was an article on The Church Music of Herbert Howells; I noted particularly the following passage: "The new [Westminster Abbey] Evening Service showed an acute sense of what boys' voices can do in a vaulted building, the sudden splendours of soaring, melismatic passages, the grave beauty of an organ pedal entry. His

services are conceived for Collegiate churches, as is
indicated in their designation not by keys but by places—
King's, Saint John's etc. . . . and it is in the ambience
of such buildings that the flexible, undulating vocal
lines, the glancing dissonance of the harmony, and
a texture that is often complex, come together to form
an incandescence of a distinctive personal kind." Now
I realised that, in mentioning Saint John's, the *Times*
had made an uncharacteristic error, for I knew that
no Saint John's Service existed. Nevertheless, I lost no
time in writing to Howells, apologising for never having
performed the supposed work, and indeed for being
ignorant of its very existence. Back came the reply three
days later "My dear Guest, it's an inspired error, that
reference to Saint John's. And it has roused my
conscience, too; for Saint John's ought to have been
next to Gloucester in these Services of mine." On 7
July 1957 he wrote "Time I let you know there's (at
last) a Saint John's Mag. and Nunc D. . . . so here
it is, and you can send it back and re-address it to
Wigan or Widdicombe if you don't like it!" It goes
without saying that we have liked it, and it is now sung
widely by cathedral choirs.

9. Herbert Howells—*A Sequence for Saint Michael* (1961)
    This was another work written for the Saint John's 450th
    anniversary celebrations. The composer wrote on 16
    January 1961 "My dear George, I've been slow to answer
    your letter: and I'm the world's slowest composer, and
    my honoured Publishers the slowest in Christendom
    (if C. includes Soho!). But if it comes to writing a new
    anthem or motet for beloved Saint John's College—
    I'd love to: if there's time. There will be, I expect.
    Anyway, tell whomsoever it may concern there's no
    question of my being commissioned. I'll do it for love,
    or not at all. . . . Yours ever, Herbert."

    By the 9th of August he was writing "The planned

noises for Saint J's C. November celebration are . . . done—a setting of Alcuin's *Sequence for Saint Michael*."

A week later he wrote "I hope (a) it isn't too long, (b) it isn't too difficult, (c) it may fit into your scheme, (d) there'll be no objection on account of Alcuin's addressing the poem to Charlemagne, that the altos in Chapel, once over their fright, will realise I've really had contraltos in mind, (f) that you'll put the whole thing aside (by registered post to me!) if you can't abide it." A few days later another letter arrived to say that it was by now in the hands of Novello & Co., and that he was "Stabat Matering day by day. And there's still the Coventry ditty[2] to do before I go back to the various grindstones next month."

The Sequence is a wonderfully successful work, from the tension created by the first impassioned cry of 'Michael!' (a name never far from Howells' mind) to the sublimely peaceful ending.

10. Alun Hoddinott (1929-)—*Three Advent Carols* (1991/2)
    (a) The Coming of the Lord
    (b) Saviour of the World
    (c) The Holy Son of God
11. Jean Langlais (1907-1991)—*Beatus vir qui timet Dominum* (1985)

    Langlais visited Saint John's and having heard his *Messe Solennelle* at the Sunday morning Sung Eucharist, was moved to write this for the College Choir with organ accompaniment.
12. William Mathias (1934-1992)—*Yr Nefoedd sydd yn datgan gogoniant Duw* (1988)

    This work was commissioned to mark the 400th centenary of the translation of the Bible into Welsh by Bishop William Morgan.

---

[2] Coventry Antiphon 'My house shall be called an house of prayer' 1962.

13. John McCabe (1939-)—*Solomon, where is thy throne?* (1979)

14. Gerald Near (1942-)—*Evening Canticles (Coll. Sancti Johannis Cantabrigiense)*

    Another disciple of Herbert Howells, this setting is written by one who is perhaps the leading American composer of the church music at the present time.

15. Robin Orr (1909-)—*Come and let yourselves be built as living stones* (1961)

    Commissioned by the College as part of the 450th anniversary celebrations.

16. Robin Orr—*O God, ruler of the world* (1982)

    A short piece commissioned by Professor Glyn Daniel, Fellow of Saint John's, and sung at his Memorial Service on 28 February 1987 in Chapel.

17. Robin Orr—*Jesu, sweet Son dear* (1989)

    An Advent carol/motet.

18. John Rutter (1945-)—*There is a flower* (1985)

    An Advent carol.

19. Robert Spearing (1950-)—*Jesu, Son most sweet and dear* (1988)

    An Advent Carol by a former pupil of Herbert Howells.

20. Michael Tippett (1905-)—*Evening Canticles (Coll. Sancti Johannis Cantabrigiense)* (1961)

    This extraordinary setting, quite revolutionary in design, was commissioned (for a paltry £100!) by the College as part of the celebrations for the 450th anniversary of the founding of Saint John's. The *Magnificat* makes great use of the famous *Trompeta Real* stop, and the organ part is boldly independent throughout. The *Gloria* is a great jumble of vocal and instrumental sound, leads enter asymmetrically, and the composer clearly had in mind the whole of mankind enunciating the words, some in tune, some out of tune, some quickly, some slowly. The *Nunc dimittis* has three elements—the low, strange chords which punctuate the verses are the realisation in the mind of old Simeon that he will shortly be called before the judgment seat to give an account of his life. The old man, in his physical weakness, can only utter (A T B) the word "Lord, Lord." His brain, though, is still active; he *thinks* the text, and his words are picked up by a descending angel and enunciated (in the setting by a solo treble). This work has over the years become popular throughout the world, and is still a unique conception of the text.

21. Stanley Vann (1910-   )—*There is no rose* (1988)
    An Advent carol.
22. George Guest/Gerald Hendrie/Gerald Near—*Sets of Responses and Preces*
23. *A Book of Descants* for use in Saint John's Chapel (various composers)

Finally, in this chapter of "Odds and Ends" I should like to record, with some pride, that the composer of the hymn-tune *Aberystwyth*, Joseph Parry, was a member of this college. His obituary appears in *The Eagle*[3] (June 1903) and reads as follows: "Although the tie between Dr Parry and the College is but slight, he appears both in the College and University Registers as a member of Saint John's. He was admitted to the College as a matter of form to enable him to take a degree in Music 28th November 1870, proceeding to his Mus.B. degree in 1871. He was again admitted 9 October 1877, and took the Mus.D. degree in 1878.

"Dr Parry was of humble Welsh parentage. His father, Daniel Parry, was a "finer," presumably some kind of workman, in the iron works at Merthyr Tydvil *[sic]*. Joseph Parry was born in Chapel Row, Merthyr Tydvil, co. Glamorgan, 21 May 1841. His mother, whose name was Elizabeth Richards, was a superior woman with much music in her nature. At an early age young Parry showed that

---

[3] The Saint John's College magazine.

he had real musical talent, but when only ten years old he was forced to go to the puddling furnaces and to stop education of any kind. In 1853 his father emigrated to the United States, and the family followed him a year after. After a few years in the United States, Parry returned home, and then received some instruction in music from John Abel Jones, of Merthyr, and John Price, of Rhymney [sic]. In 1862 he won prizes at the Llandudno Eisteddfod, and in 1865, while a second time in America, a prize was adjudged to him at the Swansea Eisteddfod for a harmonized hymn tune. The excellence of the latter attracted the attention of Mr Brinley Richards, one of the musical adjudicators of the meeting, and at his instance a fund was raised to enable Parry to return to England and to enter the Royal Academy of Music. The result of this appeal was that, in September 1868, Parry joined the Academy and studied under Sterndale Bennett, Garcia, and Steggall. He took a bronze medal in 1870, and a silver one in 1871, and an overture of his to *The Prodigal Son* was played at the Academy in 1871. He was appointed Professor of Music at the University College, Aberystwyth, and soon after took his Mus.Bac. degree at Cambridge, proceeding, in May 1878 to that of Mus.Doc. An opera of his, *Blodwen,* founded on an episode in early British history, was performed in Aberdare in 1878, and shortly afterwards at the Alexandra Palace. An oratorio, *Emmanuel,* was performed at Saint James's Hall in 1880. He also wrote several operas, the latest of which, *The Maid of Cefn Ydfa,* was recently produced at Cardiff.

"He published several cantatas, upwards of three hundred songs, glees, and anthems, some four hundred hymn tunes, and many male choruses.

"He was Professor of Music at the University College, Cardiff, and Director of the South Wales School of Music. He died at his residence, 'Cartref', Penarth on the 18 February 1903."

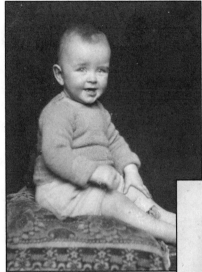

Dr George Guest at a very early age

George Guest's mother, Gwendolen Guest as a nurse in World War I

*18 Friars Avenue, Bangor, Wales
[George Guest born here 9/2/24]*

George Guest, his father Ernest Joseph Guest, his sister Gwendolen Guest 1933

George Guest a Chorister of Chester Cathedral c. 1937

The organ of Chester Cathedral (below). Malcolm Boyle (1902-1976), Organist of Chester Cathedral (1932-1949), George Guest's teacher (inset).

The Royal Air Force
1942

George Guest - 1942

The Football team - RAF Juhu (Bombay) 1945
(George Guest standing at extreme left)

Ascension Day 1954 on the Chapel Tower

Royal College of Music Senior Common Room
PRINCE CONSORT ROAD
SOUTH KENSINGTON
LONDON, S.W.7

Telegrams:
Initietrie, London, SW7

Telephone:
Kensington 3645 (5 lines)

25 October
1966

My dear George:
          Just like you to send me
that greeting about the Honorary
Fellowship: and it adds so
much to my happiness to
know that you and the Choir
share it.   It delights me to be
'one of you' at St. John's College.
I love the place, and it has
meant so much to me since
those two or three years, I was
in my about' it.   And your
own friendship warms my
ancient heart! Bless you and
the Choir and everybody concerned

in the new relationship that
has come about.
And I hope it won't be long
before I climb your stairs,
and hear the Choir and
wander about the precincts
minus any feeling of being
a stranger.
          Warmest greetings
          Yours ever
          Herbert.

*A letter from Herbert Howells
on his election as an Honorary Fellow of Saint John's
College in 1966.*

George Guest receiving the Lambeth Doctorate of Music from the Archbishop of Canterbury, The Most Revd Donald Coggan, in 1977 (Below)

The College Choir giving a concert at the Yehudi Menuhin Festival in Gstaad, Switzerland August 1972

Saint John's Chapel

George Guest at the organ of St Joseph's Parish Church (the Bamboo organ), Las Piñas, Manila, Philippines. February, 1980

George Guest with the Las Piñas Boys Choir Manila, Philippines. February, 1980. (Left)

In concert at Las Piñas, Manila. February, 1980 (Below)

*George Guest with the
Choristers on the Bridge
of Sighs, Saint John's
College. Spring, 1988*

Saint John's College Chapel

*At sea with the Choristers,
off the Swedish coast.
June, 1988*

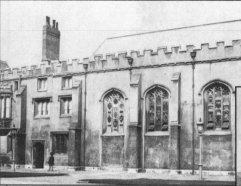

The exterior of the Old Chapel of Saint John's College

The Old Chapel - Saint John's College showing the organ as it was until 1868. The Great organ case was given to Brownsover Parish Church, near Rugby, and the Choir organ case to Saint Mark's Church, Old Bilton, Warwickshire.

The organ in Saint John's College Chapel, 1922 - 1955

Memorial to Miss Maria Hackett Saint Paul's Cathedral, London

TO THE MEMORY OF
MARIA HACKETT

TO WHOM THROUGH THE COURSE OF A LONG
LIFE THE WELFARE OF CATHEDRAL AND
COLLEGIATE CHORISTER-BOYS WAS THE
OBJECT OF DEEP AND UNFAILING INTEREST
AND WHO, AFTER DEVOTING HER TIME
AND SUBSTANCE TO EFFORTS, WHICH
NOTHING COULD DISCOURAGE, FOR THE
IMPROVEMENT OF THEIR CONDITION AND
EDUCATION, WAS ALLOWED TO SEE ON
ALL SIDES THE SUCCESS OF HER LABOURS
DIED NOV. 5 1874 IN HER 91ST YEAR.

From l to r: (below)
Elizabeth Guest (George's daughter),
David Guest (George's son),
Nan Guest,
Gwendolen Jorss (George's sister)

George and Nan Guest in
Paris, 1993

The corner of the organ-loft in Saint James'
Church, Medjugorje, where Our Lady is said to
appear daily to one or other of the young people
of the village.

George Guest and family outside
Buckingham Palace after the
Investiture, 3/11/87

Christopher Robinson, George Guest, Robin Orr

Seven former Organ Students of Saint John's College
From l to r: George Guest, John Scott (Saint Paul's Cathedral, London),
David Hill (Winchester Cathedral), Adrian Lucas (Portsmouth Cathe-
dral), Andrew Lumsden (Lichfield Cathedral), Andrew Nethsingha (Asst.
Wells Cathedral), Stephen Cleobury (King's College)

Sing we merrily unto God our strength: make a cheerful noise unto the God of Jacob. Take the psalm, bring hither the tabret: the merry harp with the lute. Blow up the trumpet in the new moon: even in the time appointed, and upon our solemn feast-day.

Psalm 81, vv. 1-3

Part II

11

An Approach to the Intangibles

The broad essentials of good choral singing were well put by an anonymous writer of the 15th century:
"Forth to high heaven" (he wrote) "let your praises ring
But yet with caution—*listen* while you sing,
    Let there be in you unity and peace,
    Begin together, and together cease.
No word or note should ever be begun
Before the former one is fitly done.
    Be careful not to cut or syncopate,
    Each syllable must have its proper weight.
For if you keep enunciation good
The words are rightly heard and understood.
When to the Lord you will your voices raise
These simple maxims shall perfect your praise:-
    Lift up your hearts to God in love and fear,
    Lift up your voices resonant and clear
    Lift up your minds by *thinking* what you say,
    Not noise, but prayerful music be your way.
The cry that to the ear of God doth dart
Is cry, not of the throat, but of the heart."

These few lines enshrine, simply but comprehensively, all that goes to make a memorable performance of a piece of choral music and, in many ways, the last two lines are the most important of all. Choir training is one of the most subtle and elusive of the arts; it is also, for those who practise it, one of the most frustrating, for the successful choir-trainer inevitably finds himself in the ambiguous position of aiming at his idea of the perfect performance, perfect in interpretation as well as in technique, but, at the same time, being forced to realise that this perfection is, in our imperfect world, always just out of his reach. The unsuccessful choir-trainer, on the other hand, is not able to imagine the perfect performance, particularly that as conceived by the composer, and the root cause of so many of the unsatisfactory performances we hear is the inability of the conductor to transmit to his choir the elements of speeds, tone-colours and phrasing as envisaged by the composer—and especially is this true of *speeds*.

It is often not realised that the margin between either too quick a speed or too slow a speed, and a wholly satisfactory and appropriate speed, is slim indeed. To a certain extent an acceptable tempo depends on the acoustic of the building concerned, and whether it is full of people or empty; but it depends much more on the nature of the music itself. How often, for example, does one hear Lutheran chorales or Welsh hymn tunes played or sung so quickly that they become mere jingles—for it is a truism that the simpler the melody the slower must be the tempo. And it is indeed odd that the crowds who burst into song, or into hymn-singing, during the second half of a rugby international at the National Stadium, Caerdydd (Cardiff), seem to understand this vitally important fact better than do most cathedral, chapel and church organists! Similarly, how often does one hear an Allegro, or even a Presto, sung as an Andante, thus destroying at a stroke something essential—the buoyancy of the phrases, and the whole rhythmic impetus of the piece itself. Speeds are seldom taught in choir training courses, and there is a tendency these days to take everything as quickly as possible. One has only to recall some recent recordings of Handel's *Messiah* to realise that over-quick tempi, especially in the choruses, can never be equated with the dignity and the nobility so essential for such a profound work. Excessive speed trivialises, whilst excessive slowness debilitates—the margin of difference between them is slight indeed.

Tone-colour, and its various possibilities, is a subject which has been almost completely neglected by choirmasters, and by those who write text-books on the subject. It is taken for granted that each singer has one voice, and one voice only. One hears such comments as "Hasn't that boy got a beautiful voice?", but when one considers the thousands of different sounds which can come out of any one human mouth, it should surely be possible to train any singer, whether boy or man, to sing with at least *two* distinct and quite different sounds. One thinks, in England, of the boys of King's College Choir, Cambridge and those of Westminster Cathedral. The treble sounds produced by each of these two choirs are of extreme beauty, but they are profoundly different from one another. In orchestral terms one might describe a similar difference between a flute and an oboe. "Which is the more beautiful sound?" is *not* a question; "which is the more historically correct in a given context?" *is*. And this latter point is also true for choral music, for it is surely valid for us to consider the kind of treble sound which Palestrina, Victoria and the other contrapuntal composers of the 16th century had in mind when composing their church music. It is reasonable to suppose that there has been a continuing tradition in this respect, and that the treble sound we hear today in Italy, Spain and Catalonia is part of that continuing tradition. Similarly, English church composers of this century had a more flute-like, less penetrating, often slightly breathy sound in mind—one thinks of such composers as Stanford, Charles Wood, William Harris and Howells—and it is surely equally reasonable to expect choirmasters to obtain from their trebles the kind of sound which these men had in mind when writing their music.

But how much more valuable is the chorister who can produce *both* kinds of sound thus, as it were, offering to his choirmaster an organ of *two* stops, rather than an instrument with just the one tone-colour; that is to say, *two* voices, either of which can be used at will, depending on whether the music is contrapuntal, or essentially homophonic? This has been the practice in Saint John's College Choir for many years, and there is a marked difference between the treble tone used at Saint John's for, say, a Mass by Palestrina or Victoria and an anthem by William Harris or Vaughan Williams. This difference is also a characteristic of the tenors and basses, who are encouraged to sing in a quasi-operatic and lyrical style in contrapuntal music, whilst reverting to a smoother and more intimate style in music which is predominantly homophonic.

Perhaps the most intangible and elusive quality of any musical performance is its phrasing. This is, of course, an intensely personal quality, and depends entirely on the musicianship and personality of the conductor, and on his ability to communicate his feelings to those directed by him. It is impossible to notate musical phrasing; it cannot be taught (except perhaps by example, by watching a supreme artist at work), and it most certainly cannot be learnt by recourse to text-books. For, even if every note is correctly sung, even if the balance and blend of a choir is almost without blemish, even if the composer's dynamic markings are followed assiduously, even if the tempo chosen is exactly right, the resulting performance, without musical phrasing, can easily be dead, something completely unmoving and barren.

It follows therefore that the musical notation of today

is not able to indicate a way of obtaining a living and vibrant performance. All it can do is to show which notes are to be sung, when they are to be sung and by whom and to what words, and it can give some general indication of the required dynamics. But beyond that it cannot go, and one of the chief reasons for the unsatisfactory nature of so much choral music we hear today is that the conductor (however skilled he may be in detecting wrong notes, and in guiding his choir through the complexities of modern rhythms) is unable to put into his performance those subtle elements which cannot be written down on paper, but which are vital to any performance.

'Speed' and 'tone' have already been mentioned, but I believe that 'phrasing' is the most important element of all. We sometimes read in text-books some such statement as 'a legato style of singing is always desirable', but what does this really mean? Let us take a very well-known example, C. V. Stanford's *Magnificat in B flat*. In a very bad choir one might hear every note thumped out, as follows:

Here there is no legato and each note receives an equal emphasis, therefore there can be no shape, no phrasing. In a slightly better choir one might hear:

Him, through - out __ all __ ge - ne - ra - tions.

There is certainly legato here, but each note receives an equal emphasis, therefore, once again, there is no shape, no coherent phrasing. Equally unsatisfactory is the choir which has been taught about accents on important syllables, but nothing else. From them one would hear:

And his mer-cy is on them that __ fear _____

him, through - out __ all __ ge - ne - ra - tions.

One comes therefore to the daunting realisation that *no two consecutive notes should ideally have the same degree of emphasis* (except, of course, for a special effect). But how can this possibly be put into practice, given an amateur choir and very limited rehearsal time? It is difficult initially to solve this problem, but one way which has not been unsuccessful is to tell the choir to 'aim' mentally at the accented syllable of the most important word in each phrase, and to think consciously of that syllable as a target *to be approached with increasing intensity*. I have used the word 'approached', and this is perhaps the most important element of all. The approach must be gradual but unrelenting, so that the accent is seen and taken as the summit of a mountain, and not as the crack of a whip. This mental attitude can become, with a little practice, part of every singer's musical equipment and, given an understanding and musical conductor—that is, one who can conduct with shapely and not jerky movements—can be put into practice in the music of all composers, from Byrd to Britten, from Tallis to Tippett. And it will be found that two birds will be killed by the one stone, phrasing will be coherent and musically satisfying, and legato singing will come of its own accord; and the extract from Stanford's *Magnificat* would sound as follows:

A similar problem is posed when one comes to perform such a work as Herbert Howells' *A Spotless Rose*. This work begins with no less than twenty-four consecutive quavers. So often does one hear a performance of this lovely piece with every quaver being given equal prominence, and with the tempo as relentless as that of a Sousa march. In many ways the most important direction given by the composer at the start is the exhortation 'With easeful movement'. That can only mean that he wished for some use of *rubato*. So, given the approach to phrasing which I have described above and a naturally relaxed tempo, and thinking of the three words which light up and give meaning to the text— the words 'spotless', 'blowing' and 'tender'—and bearing in mind that it is often desirable to have secondary accents in the middle of a general crescendo (taking due care not to allow the main phrase to sag) we might contemplate:

A spot-less rose _____ is blow - ing, _

sprung _ from a ten - der root. _____

So far, so good, but even with a diminuendo there is still the problem of how to interpret the second full bar with its upward phrase on the word 'blowing'. It is essential *not* to appear to have an accent on the second syllable and, at the time, perhaps to illustrate with subtlety the gentle movement of the Rose. A solution is to couple the diminuendo with a carefully contrived rubato, with the tiniest of secondary accents on the C sharp, and taking the last quaver of the bar, the note E, as quietly as possible. Each phrase should be shaped in this way according to the sense of the text. The words, and their general meaning in a particular context, should always govern the musical performance.

Phrasing in contrapuntal choral music of the 16th and 17th centuries poses different problems. Here accents do not necessarily coincide in each part, nor need any of them coincide with the first beat of the bar. The bar-line was not in general use at the time and is simply a later modern device which helps to keep the various parts under rhythmic control, especially when the texture is complicated. It does not, however, help in the matter of phrasing and so, given a sound technique on the part of the singers, unbarred separate part-books are almost always preferable to modern full scores for music of this kind. A sound rule of thumb in the performance of music of this period is for notes longer than their immediate neighbours to be thought of as 'summits of mountains', and for them to have a comparative accent; that is, the natural accent which will occur, or seem to occur, with a note that is longer than its immediate neighbours. A good example of this is the start of Part 2 of Christopher Tye's magnificent motet *Omnes gentes plaudite manibus*. The cross-accents bring the piece to life, and the whole motet is a perfect example of the complete rhythmic independence of each part, with the tactus (the 'beat') being maintained by the changes of harmony at regular intervals.

As the Renaissance period drew to its close the rhythmic independence of each part tended to become somewhat emasculated (one has only to compare the music of Fayrfax, Taverner, Tye and Tallis with that of Byrd, Morley, Weelkes and Gibbons to see the truth of that) and just about the only regular example of rhythmic independence in the music of the 18th century was the *hemiola,* so beloved at important cadences by J. S. Bach, Handel, and their contemporaries. In the music of English cathedral composers of the period, particularly that of Maurice Greene and his imitators, rhythms became even more stereotyped, and the four- and eight-bar phrase became an accepted ingredient in the large number of worthy but dull choral pieces which were the staple diet of cathedral choirs of the period.

And it is music of this period, perhaps more than that of any other, which needs a director who can first perceive, and then communicate to the choir members under his direction, those three elements of correct and fitting speeds, appropriate tone-colours, and musically inspired phrasing. It is always satisfying to bring what appears to be a dull and uninteresting piece to life, and never do such challenges more readily present themselves than in the church music of eighteenth-century England.

Some Basic Choral Techniques

R*easons briefly set down by the author* (William Byrd) *to persuade everyone to learn to sing:*

(a) First it is a knowledge easily taught, and quickly learned; where there is a good master, and an apt scholar.

(b) The exercise of singing is delightful to nature, and good to preserve health.

(c) It doth strengthen all parts of the breast, and doth open the pipes.

(d) It is a singular good remedy for a stuttering and stammering in the speech.

(e) It is the best means to procure a perfect pronunciation, and to make a good orator.

(f) It is the only way to know where Nature hath bestowed the benefit of a good voice; which gift is so rare, as there is not one among a thousand that hath it: and in many that excellent gift is lost, because they want art to express Nature.

(g) There is not any music of instruments whatsoever comparable to that which is made of the voices of men;

where the voices are good, and the same well sorted
or ordered.

(h) The better the voice is, the meeter it is to honour and
serve God therewith: and the voice of man is chiefly
to be employed to that end.

> Omnis spiritus laudet Dominum
> Since singing is so good a thing
> I wish all men would learn to sing.
> William Byrd (1543-1623)
> *Psalms, Sonnets and Songs of Sadness and Piety*

Good choral singing is a mixture of a variety of emotions
musically expressed and a fundamental and basically secure
technique. And it is a frustrating paradox that the more
one has of the one element the less one necessarily has
of the other. The texts of sacred music deal with the most
profound mysteries and I do not believe it right to sing,
for example, the words of the Agnus Dei with a 'stiff upper
lip' and always quietly—the generally preferred way of
Anglican composers and Anglican choirs. To the Roman
Catholic, however, the awe of the text seems to call for
a more elemental, a more emotional approach, well
exemplified in, for example, the *Messe Solennelle* by Jean
Langlais. I believe that every choir should strive for as large
a dynamic range as possible, and for the ability to warm
and colour tone through a judicious use of *tremolo* (which
should always be of the slow variety, and never even
approaching judder).

In a consideration of choral techniques it might, first
of all, be instructive to imagine a choir so bad that it
habitually sang with a large number of wrong notes, with
bad voice production, with inaudible diction, with sour and
insecure intonation, with disproportionate blend and
balance, with loose and imprecise ensemble, and with poor
rhythm. A performance by a body of singers with all of

these distressing characteristics would almost be beyond one's imagination, but there can be few choir directors who have not, at one time or another, been faced by some of them. Let us therefore take them in order:

Wrong Notes

Although there must often be the greatest temptation to do so, it is always counter-productive to teach correct notes parrot-fashion. At best that particular method can only lead to a tenuous and perhaps insecure performance, whilst at worst it can so easily lead to a complete breakdown of the kind that precludes any hope of recovery. A Probationer in a collegiate or cathedral choir can easily, in a few months, be taught (a) to recognise, and (b) to pitch, intervals within his compass, and also to learn about note-lengths and rests. That is all there is to it, and it is as simple to assimilate in Old Notation as it is in Tonic Sol-fa. For village church choirs a Rudiments Class held weekly will always pay handsome dividends and bring a new sense of security to the singing of those persons attending it.

The invariable rule at St. John's was, when a wrong note had been sung, it was first of all corrected, then it was sung incorrectly again, before being put right once more. The essential thing is that the person making the mistake should understand exactly what that mistake was, to see the difference between what was correct and what was incorrect. Reading at Sight is always taken very seriously at Choral Scholar Trials, and it needs to be, for our repertoire, consisting as it does of some 1500 items, is circumscribed not by what the Choir knows and is able to sing, but by what music there is in the Choir Library.

Bad Production

Most fundamental faults of production are tied up with the question of breathing; as that eminent choir-trainer Dr C. B. Rootham (Organist of Saint John's College 1901-

1938) wrote "good singing is impossible without a copious and well managed supply of breath. The most beautiful organ-pipe or orchestral wind instrument sounds feeble or grotesque if the wind supply that makes it speak be insufficient or fitful. Similarly, the human voice, by far the most expressive melodic instrument in existence, depends primarily on the supply of breath from the lungs for sustaining tone, for expression, and for phrasing ... breath should be taken into the body easily, but without raising the shoulders or stiffening the body."

This is sound advice and it includes the fundamentals of good tone production, but there are also two other important points worth mentioning. Firstly, it is essential to make singers concentrate on producing their voices *forward,* just behind the front teeth and secondly, it is vital to remember that the tongue, as far as possible, should lie flat in the mouth. Bad tone is so often caused solely by allowing the tongue to rise, thus interfering with the clear emission of tone from the mouth.

There is a simple way of getting vocally inexperienced boys to produce good tone. The thing should be taken in slow and patient stages, and first of all they should be asked to hum notes within their compass for a duration of between five and ten seconds (having taken a good, deep breath). In doing this they should be asked to notice the slight buzzing sensation which will occur between their top teeth and their nostrils. When they can do this easily and without strain they should be asked to hum again, then very gradually to open their mouths, gently and slowly, thus producing the syllable 'mah'. They should be asked to sustain this sound for some ten seconds' duration. It is of vital importance that (a) they should not open their mouths quickly and (b) that they should experience the same buzzing sensation between their top teeth and their nostrils which occurred when they were humming only. Finally, when they are quite familiar with this, they should move on to simple melodies sung to a variety of vowel sounds, but with exactly the same tone production.

It is perfectly possible for a boy to sing a three octave arpeggio, and such arpeggios at morning rehearsal were the staple diet of the Saint John's boys. A typical arpeggio sung to a continuous 'ah', 'oh' or 'oo' would be:

The extreme high notes are not of any practical value, but they are certainly within the average boy's range (if they are produced correctly), and the ability to pitch them does remove any fear that might otherwise be engendered by, say, a live broadcast of Allegri's *Miserere mei*. The extreme low notes are, of course, of immense value in an authentic performance of Italian, Spanish, Flemish or French choral music, and the development of this part of a boy's voice does give immense power in the lower register; it does also mean that a boy can sing alto in an emergency. Other 'warm-up' exercises at the beginning of morning practice included:

(a) **Andante**

To be sung to any vowel, with or without initial consonants of D, L or M before each note. For legato singing, and careful intonation.

(b) **Allegro**

Al - le - lu - ia,

Al - le - lu - ia

For agility; think in groups of 4 semiquavers.

(c) **Andante**

For accurate pitching of intervals: to be sung slowly to any vowel, preceded by initial consonants of D, L or M.

(d) **Allergetto**

For recognising the difference between Major and Minor Scales. To any vowel, preceded by initial consonants of D, L or M.

(e) **Andante e legato**

Also for recognising the difference between major and
minor keys.

(f)

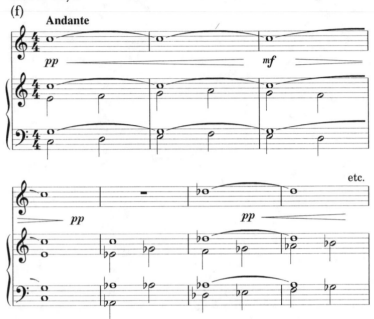

For becoming familiar with controlled *crescendi* and
diminuendi. To any vowel. Note that *diminuendi* are always
the more difficult to control.

Inaudible Diction

A fundamental question is: what is the use of singing
words at all if they are so distorted or mis-pronounced
that they cannot be distinguished or understood by those
listening? No one, I imagine, would seriously doubt that
in church music (or indeed in any choral music) the words
are more important than the music itself, and yet they often
receive scant attention. There are choirs which seem unable
to manage an initial or a final soft consonant, and there
are those who distort difficult vowels, especially on the
higher notes, in order, one presumes, to allow of an easier

production. How can what they sing possibly edify or help a congregation? It cannot be too strongly urged that initial and final consonants are of prime importance, especially words beginning and ending with the letters *b, d, f, l, m, n, p* and *v*. For words containing them to be heard clearly the pronunciation of these consonants must be exaggerated; indeed, one may go so far as to say that if they sound over-emphasised to the members of the choir themselves you can be certain that they will be 'just right' for the congregation or audience. For American choirs the letter *r* presents the most frightful problems. In pronouncing it their tongues are usually curled up, thus preventing proper emission of tone; in all other respects the curious thing is that the profound differences so evident between American and British speech are never apparent in singing. In order to make choirs aware of this problem of soft consonants the choirmaster might consider inventing such phrases as this cunning example by the late Dr C. B. Rootham, to be said or sung together by the whole choir in a recognisable rhythm, as for instance:

Diction in Wales, on the whole, is not markedly better than that in England or in the United States, and for Welsh choirs the following example, kindly provided by Dr Manon Williams, might be of value:

It will be noticed that many words end with the same sounding consonant with which the following word begins, and it is therefore very important to differentiate between the two of them. One more point: the consonants *s* and *t*, once enunciated, need no exaggeration, and especially is this true in the field of broadcasting and recording, where over-pronunciation of sibilants can often ruin an otherwise musical and moving performance. If, however, a choir can sing such sentences as those quoted above it is well on the way to achieving good diction.

One of the commonest faults in choral diction is the distortion of vowels, and especially is this likely to happen when the vowel sounds *ah* and *eh* (as in 'Amen') are sung to high notes. It is a fault which affects choirs of high renown, as well as amateur choirs, and can be put down basically to laziness in production. The word 'palaces' is the more easily sung to high notes as 'poloces', and 'Amen' as 'Amin', and so sometimes both choirs and their choirmasters take the easy way out. But it is perfectly possible to sing without distortion of vowels, and it is often a good plan to spend a little rehearsal time on them, especially when set to higher notes as, for instance in the phrase:

world with - out   end,   A - men

It might be useful to add a word here about the pronunciation of Ecclesiastical Latin. One of the commonest mistakes is the conversion of the last letter of a word ending with a vowel into a dipthong (eg 'Dominay-*ee*', instead of 'Domin*eh*', 'Fili*ow*' instead of 'Fili*oh*'). Church Latin should be pronounced as modern Italian; that is to say, Cs should always be hard (as in 'card', 'country') unless followed by an 'e' or an 'i', in which case they become soft (as in 'church', 'cheese'). Similarly with Gs; these are always hard (as in 'garden', 'grand') unless followed by an 'e' or an 'i', in which case they become soft (as in 'gentry', 'German').

Sour and Insecure Intonation

This is a common bugbear to all choirmasters, and because there is such a variety of causes it is often difficult, but never, I believe, impossible to cure. Flat singing is probably more common than sharp singing, but both are equally painful to the listener. Boredom, either with the music or with the choirmaster, is often responsible, but bad production (especially incorrect breathing) and/or a defective ear are usually the main causes—especially the latter. If a singer cannot recognise, when the fact is pointed out to him, that he is singing flat, or if he cannot pitch in tune a note given to him on the organ, piano or pitch-pipe, then his case is probably hopeless. Certain intervals commonly cause difficulty, especially the Major Third of a chord and, even more commonly, a series of downward semitones, which are so often made too large, thus producing continuous flat singing. A common instance occurs in the tenor part of a Plagal Cadence 'Amen',

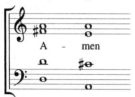

but, in the great majority of cases, if the breathing is correct and the ear accurate, there should be no flat singing. All choir members should be encouraged to *listen* keenly, and one exercise which always amused (and indeed helped) the Saint John's boys, both Choristers and Probationers, was to play them a note in the lower part of the piano, and get them to distinguish the upper harmonics thus

created. For example the note C  will, at the same

time, produce the following upper harmonics,

and an ear which can pick these out is indeed a keen one.

Sharp singing is certainly less common, but infinitely more difficult to cure. it usually springs from an inaccurate ear, over-excitement, and/or forcing too much breath through the larynx, just as over-blowing a wind instrument raises its pitch. Sharp singing is usually at its worst in the upper register, and for some reason sopranos (not trebles) and tenors seem more prone to sing sharp than are contraltos and basses, but if it persists over a length of time, and all appeals to sing quieter have been disregarded, the offender should be asked to resign, or to take up another office within the church—nothing can be done for him or her, except perhaps to check that upward semitones are not being made too large. A final point: loud and high final chords marked with a crescendo commonly go sharp. It is vitally important to keep choral discipline even when singing in a high state of excitement!

There are a few other more general points which have a bearing on this problem. See that the church or practice-room is both well-lit and well-ventilated; all should be able to see clearly the words and notes they are required to sing, and they should be able to breathe pure, unadulterated air, free from the smell of both incense and stale cassocks. And, finally, *the louder the singing, the more likely it is to go out of tune, either one way or the other.*

Disproportionate Blend and Balance

Of all the aspects of choral technique so far discussed these are perhaps the most elusive and difficult of solution, for they are intimately connected with differing tone-colours, with phrasing, and with interpretation. There can be few choirs who have not, from time to time, experienced the booming, ultra-loud (especially around middle C) type of bass, the over-powering shrillness of the goat-like tenor, or the foghorn type of alto. They usually are supreme individualists, having little interest in the general musical well-being of their choirs apart from their own contributions, and possessing the utter conviction that, but for them, the choir would fall to pieces. It would perhaps be truer to say that, *because* of them, their choir is often on the point of falling to pieces! One should never tire of pointing out to offenders of this kind that a choir is *one* instrument, and that it is the conductor who plays on that instrument. In many ways the analogy of driving a car is apt; the driver must have full control of every aspect of it, and must adjust where necessary the steering, the speed, the gear-changes etc. In exactly the same way the conductor should and must be able to adjust the relative strengths of the voices as the performance proceeds, and also the particular tone quality.

Perhaps the ideal solution to the problem would be for the choirmaster to take a tape-recording of the choir (with the microphones cunningly placed!) and play it back to the offender, on the principle of 'actions speaking louder than words', but few churches can afford either the time or the money to do that, so the only practical solution appears to be a direct appeal to the culprit to sing quieter but, given good-will on both sides, and very carefully-chosen words, it could just turn out to be one of the easiest choral problems to solve.

Loose and Imprecise Ensemble

There is the story of a performance, incompetently directed, of J. S. Bach's church cantata *God's time is the best.* "Aye," said a disgruntled member of the choir, "and I wish he'd come down to conduct it!"

This is a fault to be found to a greater or lesser degree in all concerted music. One hears ragged untidiness from the most famous orchestras and secular choirs, as well as from collegiate, cathedral and church choirs. The chief causes of this are (a) a basically imperfect sense of rhythm, and (b) an inability or disinclination to watch the conductor—or, in the case of the church choir, an unwillingness to watch one another, especially from the one side to the other. It is often difficult to persuade members of an amateur church choir of the absolute necessity of *watching* wherever possible, indeed some may go so far as to suggest that their choral experience is so lengthy that it entitles them to bury their heads permanently in their copies, and to sing without reference either to their colleagues or to their conductor. But if members of a choir do *not* watch each other closely (but always with one eye on the conductor), especially at beginnings and ends of phrases, and especially at changes of tempo, their singing will always sound ragged and untidy.

Poor Rhythm

All choral music tends, at times, to suffer from this, and the end product of unrhythmical singing is a flabby and characterless performance—yet many singers and choirmasters seem quite unaware of this problem. And so it persists, and is perhaps at its worst in hymns. In parish churches the congregation requires to be led, not followed, and if one wants to improve one's own rhythmic sense (and therefore that of the choir one directs also) the first thing to do is to acquire the ability to maintain a constant and steady tempo in one's own conducting or playing. It is surprising how few church choirs can sing even a verse of a hymn without slowing down. Getting this right is quite fundamental and will, without any question, improve congregational singing to a marked degree. Two suggestions are (a) do not neglect the use at rehearsal of that valuable invention the metronome and (b) try rehearsing sometimes without conductor and without accompaniment.

Common rhythmic faults include an inability to keep the notes of smaller values from hurrying as, for instance,

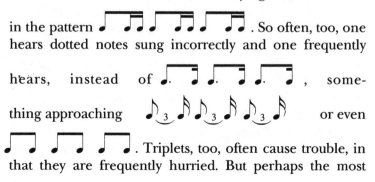

in the pattern   . So often, too, one hears dotted notes sung incorrectly and one frequently hears, instead of   , something approaching   or even   . Triplets, too, often cause trouble, in that they are frequently hurried. But perhaps the most common of all rhythmic faults is the tendency on the part of unrhythmic choirmasters to hurry over the bar-line on to the following strong beat. This maddening and irritating habit rightly infuriates all orchestral musicians, and destroys any underlying rhythmic impulse which the choir might otherwise have.

In most cases the blame for rhythmic faults in choirs can fairly be laid at the choirmaster's door. So many are horrified at wrong notes, whilst condoning loose and imprecise rhythm—but it could reasonably be asserted that a sprinkling of wrong notes, coupled with good, strong rhythm, is always preferable to the reverse.

All choral music is a mixture of technique and emotion. We strive for the technically perfect performance which we will never achieve in this imperfect world, and, at the same time, attempt to impart the basic human emotions of sorrow, joy, excitement, even scorn, into our singing. The paradox, as I mentioned earlier, is that the more we have of the one element, the less we have of the other. Some choirs take the easy way out and concentrate solely on technique, regarding 'emotion' in church music as being somehow foreign to the average Englishman's view of religion. At best these are choirs which one *admires,* but one is not *moved* by them. Other choirs, of which Saint John's has long been one, take the view that a good basic technique is obviously necessary, but that a wide dynamic range, effective phrasing and careful accentuation are the elements which can bring to life some of the transcendental truths embodied in the words we sing. Think, for example, of the literal meaning of the Agnus Dei—not only *our* sins are being taken away, not only those of our *neighbours and friends,* but those of the *world* "qui tollis peccata mundi." Could there be a more tremendous conception of a religious truth? Could there be a more truly emotional prayer? The difference between our leading choirs is accounted for by the relative importance each attaches to 'technique' and to 'emotion'.

The Pointing of the Psalms

Every musical performance of every psalm should, ideally, be given in such a way as to enhance the *meaning* of the text. Purely musical considerations should always occupy a subsidiary position by comparison with this fundamental and all-important concept. It follows, therefore, that the elements of vocal technique mentioned earlier in this chapter should become second nature in order that the choir, when approaching the Psalms, can concentrate on the words and their meaning.

Most of these questions of interpretation are connected with *speeds* and as a general proposition, it is true to say that, in bad and insensitive pointing, the words before the bar-line are sung *too quickly,* and the words after it are sung *too slowly.* It is still quite common to hear the recitation gabbled, only for the listener to be brought up almost to a full stop at the first bar-line. One of the difficulties of pointing has always been that of thinking of each verse as an *entity,* rather than as a number of ill-defined sections.

The important thing is to decide on the most important syllable of the most important word in each verse and mentally to aim at that syllable whether it appears at the beginning, the middle or at the end of the verse. If this is done conscientiously, and each verse would need to be considered with this in view, the problems of speed would largely disappear; in other words, the overall speed would be uniform throughout the verse. The words 'overall speed' are used because it is important to realise that the rhythmic relationship between chords should, of course, be free; unimportant words such as 'and', 'but', 'the', 'in' etc. should be sung lightly and without accent. The relationship of one word to another, and one accent to another, should be the same in good pointing as in good speech. This concept of the relationship between good speech and good psalm-singing is quite fundamental and its neglect *always* produces stilted and exaggerated pointing.

In any consideration of musical interpretation *expression* is of vital importance, and here again there is a close relationship between expression and speed. By and large there is a tendency to sing psalms too quickly, thus often making it impossible for the words to make their full impact. Such a psalm, for instance, as 139 ("O Lord, Thou hast searched me out and known me") should be sung quite slowly, *nobilmente,* and with the utmost gravity and dignity; so should the various sections of Psalm 119, and indeed all psalms except those which are clearly psalms of praise. It should also be a cardinal rule that "the more elaborate the music, the slower should be the *tempo.*"

An aspect of interpretation which is frequently misunderstood is *accentuation.* There are those who only know of one type of accent—a dynamic accent—forgetting that a note which is even slightly longer than its immediate neighbours will appear to be emphasised. There are, in fact, two types of accents—the dynamic accent and the rhythmic accent. Both are useful but, in the Psalms, a judicious use of the latter can often shed light and meaning on a whole passage. Take, for instance, these verses of Psalm 139:

6.   Whither shall I go then/from thy/spirit:
     or whither shall I/go then/from thy/presence?
7.   If I climb up into heaven/thou art/there:
     if I go down to/hell . thou art/there—/also.
8.   If I take the /wings of . the/morning:
     and remain in the/utter -most/parts of . the/sea:
9.   Even **there** also shall/thy hand/lead me:
     and/thy right/hand shall/hold me.

If the length of the second word of verse 9 is doubled, but without any feeling of a dynamic accent, the meaning of the whole passage is made crystal clear. There are many similar examples, of which just a few follow:

Psalm 7, verse 7
And so shall the congregation of the people/come a-/bout thee:
for **their** sakes therefore lift/up thy-/self a-/gain.

Psalm 24, verse 7
Lift up your heads O ye gates, and be **ye** lift up ye ever/last-ing/doors:
and the King of/glo-ry/shall come/in.

Psalm 48, verse 13
For **this** God is **our** God for/ever . and/ever:
he shall be our/guide/un-to/death.

It is not difficult for a good choir to make any Psalter sound convincing and, conversely, a bad choir can make even the best Psalter sound quite wretched. That being so, those choirs who still use the Old Cathedral Psalter should not despair, for it is perfectly possible to achieve a musical result from it. It is also possible, though much more difficult (and one may ask oneself if the effort is really worthwhile) to obtain a passable result from those psalters which advocate placing the first bar-line as early as possible, thus leaving a large number of syllables to be fitted into the remaining chords. But generally, the simpler the pointing the better will be the result and, of those Psalters which adopt a simple method of pointing, the Parish Psalter is undoubtedly the best for a number of reasons. Sir Sydney Nicholson, at the end of an Evensong in King's College Chapel, is said to have complimented Boris Ord on selecting the Parish Psalter for use in King's. "Yes," said Boris in his characteristically amiable way "we bought it because it is the easiest to alter!"

13

Assembling a Choir

That no wine be given to the Choir boys at any of the College anniversaries. That after singing the second grace they do not wait for dessert as heretofore, but that each have a gift of fruit to take home with them.

Dean's Order Book, 27 April 1894

Towards the end of the year parents of boys between the ages of 7 and 9 start to think of the possibility of their son's joining a collegiate or cathedral choir, and the period October to February is the season of Voice Trials—though, in addition, most choirmasters are nowadays willing to audition boys throughout the year. There is still considerable competition for these places, because not only are the financial rewards very considerable (a Probationer or Chorister at Saint John's College, for instance, receives a remission of two-thirds the yearly fee), but choristers in a top-class choir learn, unconsciously, lessons which many, perhaps even most, adults never learn. By the nature and discipline of their duties they learn (a) to take, at an early age, responsibility. The Senior Chorister is responsible to the Choirmaster for the clean appearance

170

and conduct of his juniors. In an emergency he will himself take the rehearsal; he is the Choirmaster's right-hand man in every way. The other choristers have no less important responsibilities in connection with the assembling of the required music for the rehearsal or for the service, with the finding of the requisite books for the clergy, the lighting of candles etc. In addition to this, choristers learn (b) to make the most of very limited time; choir duties can often account for two hours of the working day and there is school-work to fit in, as well as private music practice (almost all choristers learn two or three instruments), games and leisure time. A chorister therefore learns to plan his day with care. He learns also (c) to work at and polish a piece of music for its own sake, and not with the expectation of monetary or other reward. There are those who are in favour of awarding badges, certificates and the like to successful choristers, though many choristers regard this as a kind of adult patronage, and resent it. A final point (d) is that collegiate and cathedral choristers listen to some of the best prose in existence (though the quality of the reading sometimes leaves something to be desired), and they take part in some of the best music of its kind.

It is essential that every potential chorister has a good ear, a nicely-produced and attractive voice, and is able to read English prose (this latter is a *sine qua non* for anyone who is required to read the Psalms). The most important part, therefore, of any Voice-trial is to ascertain, first, that the candidate can pitch accurately and instantly any note within his compass on hearing it played on the piano. If successful at that, he should be given two-part and even three-part chords and asked to pitch any note contained in them. Given practice, the ear of a seven-year-old boy can be as good as, or even better, than that of an adult.

Whilst most boys can be taught to produce their voices properly, it is clearly an advantage if a choir applicant can already sing easily and naturally up two octaves from middle

C. Arpeggios, both Major and Minor, are very suitable for this purpose, and they should be sung to a continuous 'ah' (*not* 'lah, lah, lah' etc.). There should be a light and simple accompaniment, as for example:

or

No boy is of real use in any choir unless he can read reasonably simple prose, and so it is absolutely essential to make sure that the reading of any candidate is commensurate with the average for his age. Psalm 15, 'Lord, who shall dwell in thy tabernacle?' is ideal for this purpose containing, as it does, few words which do not occur in everyday speech. One should listen, not only to the actual pronunciation of the words, but also to the general sound of the reading. A few mistakes could well be disregarded, as long as the overall reading was pleasant to listen to, and intelligible—a boy who later became an outstanding soloist at Saint John's gave a unique version of verse 3 of Psalm 15 at his voice trial. "He that hath used no deceit in his tongue," he read, "and hath not slandered his navel"!

Parents and teachers often act unwisely in the matter

of choosing a solo piece to be sung by a small boy at his voice trial. Elaborate arias are sometimes prepared, pieces which are, technically, above the candidate's ability and, more importantly, which call for a lung-power which no small boy can have developed. Nervousness at the voice trial itself brings on breathing difficulties, with the result that the longer phrases begin to break down, the performance begins to disintegrate, and all ends in disappointment, and sometimes in tears. It is always better on these occasions to sing a simple hymn accurately and with good diction and musical shape, rather than to attempt a showy aria which is clearly beyond the capability of the singer.

The ability to play a musical instrument or instruments has not yet been mentioned, but clearly this is of great advantage to a prospective chorister and most applicants are able to play the piano a little, and also a stringed or wood-wind instrument. The advantages of being able to do this are great, for it generally follows that basic rudiments have therefore already been learnt, as well as the concept of rhythm, and perhaps a start will have been made on recognising and pitching intervals.

Finally, in order that a boy may take his Choristership in his stride, a general academic test should be given, in order to make sure that the chorister can take his place in class with boys of his own age, without feeling mentally strained in any way.

These are the bare bones of a typical Voice Trial, and it is probably true to say that the boys probably enjoy the experience rather more than do the parents! But, at the end of the day, when the awards are made, some three or four boys are launched on a career which can, and often does, shape the whole of their future life. They begin as Probationers, with skilled musical instruction given almost individually. Probationers at Saint John's do not attend every service, but are introduced into the system gradually and are required to attend just two services a week, though they are sometimes asked to "stand in" if one of the 16 Choristers happen to be ill. When a Chorister leaves to move on to his next school the best Probationer is elected in his place, and then his duties multiply. He is required to attend seven choral services in each week of University Full Term, as well as to take part in broadcasts, recordings and outside recitals. Foreign tours are an integral part of a Chorister's life and, instead of staying in international hotels, which are largely the same throughout the world, they stay with very carefully selected families where some English is understood. And, in doing so, they unconsciously learn further lessons—they see how people in other countries live and eat, they observe their customs, they see the way they furnish their houses.

In a top-class choir choristers rehearse daily, preferably early in the morning when they are fresh and at their brightest and most receptive. The repertoires are usually very large; at Saint John's it consists of some 1500 items, including over 80 Latin Masses, and contains music from all periods, from the 13th-century to the present day, with an especial emphasis on contemporary music. It follows, therefore, that a high standard of sight-reading is necessary, and this is encouraged and developed from the moment a boy enters the Choir.

No choir can be successful without discipline, and the best kind of discipline is that easy, internal discipline which exists, apparently effortlessly, in the best choirs. The special role of the Senior Chorister has already been mentioned, and he is indeed worth his weight in gold if he can exert his authority without recourse to bullying. The system, however, does not find favour in all countries and, in Sweden in particular, the idea of boys being anything less than equal in rank with each other is anathema—but it has been a well-tried system for many years in England, and is a continuing one.

Alto, Tenor and Bass parts are taken in University choirs

largely by Choral Scholars ('Choral Students' in Saint John's). These are undergraduates, often former boy choristers themselves, who are successful in the yearly Choral Scholars' Voice Trial. In addition to their musical and vocal prowess, they have to satisfy the college authorities that they are capable of obtaining an Honours degree; the academic requirements for Choral Scholar entrants, however, are usually a little less demanding than those required for other entrants. The Trial itself is very similar in essence to that undergone by the boys, with great emphasis being placed on an accurate ear, and on fluent sight-reading.

Involvement with choirs also provides a unique training for would-be cathedral organists, and it is a particular form of instruction which is not available in any of the large colleges of music, nor is it available in its entirety in the Royal School of Church Music. Organ Scholars (Organ Students) have the opportunity of (a) working with an extremely large and comprehensive repertoire of music and, in doing so, learning about styles and about methods of performance. They are also (b) able to rehearse a responsive body of men and boys regularly, and to conduct them in performance. And in doing that (c) they learn to project their own personalities into the pieces they perform. At Saint John's and King's Colleges in Cambridge, and at New College, Magdalen and Christ Church in Oxford, the Organ Scholar acts as Assistant to the Organist, whilst in a number of the other colleges he directs the music himself and is encouraged to build up an amateur choir, consisting of a mixture of Choral Scholars (both male and female) and Volunteers. The duties in these colleges are much less onerous but equally rewarding, and provide vital training in assembling and keeping, largely by force of personality alone, a choir of decent standard.

Many Cambridge men, in addition to those from Saint John's who were mentioned earlier, have become Cathedral or Collegiate organists. From King's there have been a number: David Briggs (Truro and Gloucester Cathedrals), Francis Grier (Christ Church, Oxford), Douglas Guest (Salisbury and Worcester Cathedrals, Westminster Abbey), James Lancelot (Durham Cathedral), Philip Ledger (Chelmsford Cathedral and King's College, Cambridge), Lucian Nethsingha (Exeter Cathedral), Richard Popplewell (H.M. Chapel Royal), Simon Preston (Christ Church, Oxford and Westminster Abbey), Andrew Seivewright (Carlisle Cathedral), and Sir David Willcocks (Salisbury and Worcester Cathedrals, Kings's College Cambridge). From Gonville and Cauis College came Martin Neary (Winchester Cathedral and Westminster Abbey) and John Sanders (Chester and Gloucester Cathedrals)—from Peterhouse came Barry Ferguson (Rochester Cathedral)—from Emmanuel came Christopher Brayne (Bristol Cathedral), John Jordan (Chelmsford Cathedral) and Peter Wright (Southwark Cathedral)—from Saint Catherine's came Hugh Davies (St. Asaph Cathedral) and Bernard Rose (Magdalen College, Oxford). Richard Seal (Salisbury Cathedral) was at Christ's, Edward Higginbottom (New College, Oxford) was at Corpus Christi, Andrew Millington (Guildford Cathedral) at Downing, and Sir David Lumsden (Southwell Minster and New College, Oxford) at Selwyn and Saint John's.

14

Seating a Choir, Conducting It, and Accompanying It

All in their scarlet cloaks and surplices
Of linen, go the chanting choristers.
                                    David Herbert Lawrence

There are many schools of thought about the most advantageous way of seating a choir, but whatever method is adopted it should be taken as axiomatic that each boy occupies the same position in relation to the others in service as he does at rehearsal. The old terms *Decani* (the Dean's side) and *Cantoris* (the Precentor's side) are still in use in college chapels and in cathedrals, and great care should be taken that the two sides are balanced in volume and in musicianship as nearly as possible. Some choirs prefer to have their more senior boys at ends; others (and I do feel that this is the better plan) would have the two senior boys on each side in the middle, so as to provide

a strong lead on either side of them. A suggested plan
in a choir of 16 choristers and 14 men might be:

Altar

Bass	Boy 4	⎫	⎧	Boy 4	Bass
Bass	Boy 6	⎬	⎨	Boy 6	Bass
Bass	Boy 2	⎭	⎩	Boy 2	Bass
Tenor	Boy 8	⎫	⎧	Boy 8	Tenor
Tenor	Boy 1	⎬	⎨	Boy 1	Tenor
Alto	Boy 7	⎭	⎩	Boy 7	Alto
Alto	Boy 5	⎫	⎧	Boy 5	Alto
	Boy 3	⎭	⎩	Boy 3	
	Conductor			Conductor	
	if L-handed			if R-handed	

This has the value of compactness, and also enables
the very junior (and therefore inexperienced) boys to learn
by standing near the most senior choristers. The brackets
in the table above represent the number of boys sharing
a particular copy; I have never found it helpful to give
each boy, whether senior or junior, a separate copy.

There is a growing tendency these days for the choir
to be conducted in all it does, and there is no doubt but
that a much better performance is usually, but not always,
obtained when someone directs the music. But, at the same
time, too florid or flamboyant conducting is a distraction
and an irritation to the congregation. In order to counteract
this in Liverpool Cathedral shortly after World War II a
large high-backed chair was placed midway between the
two widely separated sides; in it sat the conductor
throughout the service, directing the music. This has now
been discontinued, as has the system formerly in use in
Ripon Cathedral, where a wooden hand, complete with
fingers and even finger nails, was affixed to the east side

of the organ loft, and animated by the organist by means of a lever, in order to bring in, and maintain in precise rhythm, unaccompanied music without the organist being obliged to go down into the choir to conduct it—it was, of course, incapable of shaping a performance!

In most cathedrals and collegiate chapels the Psalms these days are "conducted" by a tenor on either side, using the second and third fingers of each hand and a very flexible wrist in order to secure unanimity of attack and release. The more complex pieces, however, are usually directed by the organist, standing near one of the sides and facing east. In order to avoid undue flapping, to the distraction of the congregation, it is suggested that conducting in service is best done across one's body, so left-handed conductors should stand on *Cantoris* and right-hand conductors on *Decani*.

Conducting a small mixed choir is in itself a work of art calling for a technique quite different from that necessary to control a symphony orchestra. Excessive head and body movement is usually counter-productive, and the choir should be trained to watch the conductor's eyes, as well as his hands. Too many conductors use a stiff right wrist when directing, and wonder why they can never achieve a satisfactory legato and a musical shape in their performances. The overall shape and the phrasing of the choir depends, to a very large degree, on that which is indicated to them by the gestures of the conductor, and a jerky beat will always result in a jerky performance.

In particular is this true in the performance of an early sixteenth-century piece where the accents in the various parts are not regular, nor do they necessarily coincide with one another. As long as the singers can be relied upon to put a comparative accent on 'notes longer than their immediate neighbours', and usually on melodic peaks, the conductor's role is simply to indicate the *tactus* (or 'the beat') with his right hand, reserving the left hand for bringing in difficult leads, and for giving a general indication of the dynamic. In music of later periods, with its much more regular rhythms, one can beat two, three or four in the bar in the conventional way—but still avoiding, as much as possible, bodily movement—there is nothing which is more distracting to the worshipper than to see a multi-coloured Mus.Doc. hood flapping about wildly in, say, the last chorus of S. S. Wesley's *Blessed be the God and Father*. Finally, one should never forget the truism that the more restrained the conducting, the greater will be the concentration of the choir—a concentration forced on them by the sheer necessity of watching intently a conductor of economical movements.

Conducting plainsong calls for yet another technique. Here one simply needs to indicate the accents, and to convey the structure of the melodic phrases by the *shape* of one's beat—bearing in mind always that each phrase should start and end softly, with a slight, subtly graded *crescendo* in the middle—and that there should be a slight (again well-graded) *accelerando* to the main accent, and a corresponding *ritard* thence to the final note of the phrase. Finally, one should say that any attempt to reduce plainsong to a metrical performance destroys its soul, so does a performance without dynamic variation. To hear plainsong at its best one needs to travel to France, and to the monastery of Solesmes, near Le Mans, situated in idyllic surroundings overlooking the River Sarthe. For many years a special study of plainsong has been made here; one can attend classes and seminars on the subject but, best of all, one can hear their ideas put into practice in the Chapel at the full daily round of Masses and Offices. The singing of these monks, mostly untrained musically and sometimes with an idiosyncratic attitude to intonation, is nevertheless of supreme beauty and is a model for all who aspire to perform plainsong. There are those, a few scholars amongst them, who hold other views, but there is no denying the utter

fitness of the music at Solesmes to be an adornment of
the liturgy.

The organ accompaniment of the church service is a
branch of the art which, almost more than any other aspect
of the organist's work, shows up the difference between
the artist and the unmusical technician. Accompaniment
can be divided into two kinds—the *leading* which is
necessary for the accompaniment of congregational
singing, and the *accompaniment*, or adornment which, at
its best, so enhances the professional choir's contribution.
In the former, a completely secure, rock-like sense of rhythm
is absolutely essential—the lack of it can reduce hymn-
singing by a congregation of some hundreds to complete
chaos. Care should also be given to registration; a bright
sound, with plenty of upper work and mixtures, is always
more helpful than a thick sound, made up largely of 8
and 16 foot Diapasons. Tempi should be very carefully
calculated, and should always err on the side of slowness,
rather than the reverse. Congregations almost always try
to slow up at ends of lines, and the organist should resist
this by keeping the tone bright rather than over-powering,
and perhaps by sometimes playing detached chords on the
manuals, with a legato pedal.

Accompanying a professional choir is, however, a
completely different matter. The object here is to add a
further dimension of the meaning of the words being sung,
and nowhere is this more desirable than in the accompaniment of the Psalms. Perhaps the first point to make
is that each psalm, or each recognisably different portion
of it, is an entity, a whole. One of the chief functions of
the organ accompaniment is therefore to provide, as it were,
the musical cement between the verses, in order to link
then together. This is true especially in those buildings
with a dry acoustic, and in these situations there is nothing
worse than having gaps in between each verse, with the
accompaniment ending precisely with the choir at the end

of each verse.

Registration should always be chosen with the general meaning of the particular psalm in mind and seldom, if ever, to illustrate a particular word; it is not appropriate to illustrate, for example, the 'poison of asps' by recourse to an Orchestral Oboe, played an octave lower than written; on the other hand 'with trumpets and shawms' may well call for the use of the Swell Cornopean, whilst such verses as 'I will wash my hands in innocency, O Lord' would seem to demand a soft, white, fluty sound. The use of pedals needs great care and it can never be a good plan to use them unvaryingly throughout a psalm. Examine the possibility of manual only accompaniment, sometimes at pitch, sometimes an octave higher than written. Investigate the possibility of the use of melody only, again sometimes played an octave higher than written, and perhaps of improvising a melodic descant based on the alto and tenor parts—but beware of improvising a descant which results in either consecutive fifths or consecutive octaves with the bass part. On larger organs the atmospheric properties of a quiet 32 foot pedal stop should not be overlooked, nor should the possibility of leaving a few verses (or indeed a whole psalm) unaccompanied. This latter is particularly effective in the more reflective and introspective psalms, such as Nos. 23 and 43. Above all, psalm accompaniment should be subtle but unobtrusive.

The accompaniment of anthems and canticles often calls for a considerable technique. Works like Stanford's *Magnificat in G*, the *Magnificat* of Tippett's *Saint John's Service* and Britten's *Missa Brevis* require not only rock-steady rhythm and clarity of registration, but also absolute accuracy of notes. Further problems are posed when it is necessary to condense an orchestral score into a version for organ (eg. the Bach *Passions*, Handel's *Messiah*, Mendelssohn's *Elijah*, the *Requiems* of Brahms and Fauré). It is *not* necessary to reproduce every note in the full score; what is required is that the significant melodies, the important rhythmic figures and the basic harmony should be translated into organ terms. Pedals should be used sparingly, and there should be an attempt to imitate the orchestral colours as shown in the full score (which should, of course, always be consulted beforehand) before deciding upon an organ version.

There is a growing tendency to use small orchestras to accompany Masses by such composers as Haydn, Mozart and Schubert, and also in many of the large-scale Restoration anthems by Locke, Wise, Purcell and Blow. This is a welcome development, but the very clarity of texture demanded by the music of these composers demands not only accuracy but a thorough knowledge of styles. Notation (particularly that of dotted notes) and the bowing of string parts should be gone into in detail and, especially in the works of Restoration composers, the terraced dynamics should be precisely calculated. Care should be taken with ornamentation, and in this connection valuable and scholarly advice is offered in the late Professor Thurston Dart's book *The Interpretation of Music*. Above all, adequate rehearsal time should be insisted upon.

It is difficult to write objectively about the use of guitars in churches. To some its use is an indispensable aid to eternal salvation—to others it is an abomination, a distraction which keeps as many *from* a church service as are attracted to church *by* it. I will simply comment that young people resent being patronised, and my recent experience at Cambridge has convinced me that there is a most definite reaction on the part of young people to the trivial in worship. In an ever-changing and often frightening world they look increasingly for dignity, for tradition. For many people the harmonium ("Never" the late Dean Bezzant used to delight in saying, "was an instrument more inappropriately named!") is equally abhorrent but, given an instrument in reasonable condition and an adequate technique on the part of the player (especially in the steady manipulation of the pedals supplying the wind) the harmonium still has a part to play in those places of worship which do not possess an organ.

15

Repertoire

> Agreed that the Organist be requested to prepare
> a Scheme of services, including anthems and
> hymns, for each Quarter in sufficient time to issue
> it in printed form before the end of the pre-
> ceeding term.
>
> *Dean's Order Book, 26 January 1877*

The amount of sacred music suitable for liturgical use is so great that no choir can hope to perform more than a very small percentage of that available in print, and it can only be regretted that so much bad music has been printed, and is continuing to be printed—particularly when there is so much left unpublished which is liturgically apt and sound musically, and so much of which has gone out of print. Latin (except in the more blinkered Anglican establishments and in some Roman Catholic churches) is now widely permitted, and the sheer number of Masses by Palestrina, Victoria, Lassus, Guerrero, Morales and Monteverdi is, to say the least, daunting. Add to that the grossly neglected masterpieces in this form by Tye, Taverner, Tallis, and by many minor composers, and it becomes impossible to do more than offer token representation to one of the truly great fields of liturgical music. In recent years the 3, 4 and 5 part Masses of William Byrd have become popular, especially in England, though performances are often less than ideal, especially in tempi, accentuation and tone-colours. The settings of the Holy Communion service in English by composers of the late 19th and 20th centuries are, by comparison, generally dull and often derivative. Stanford's many settings are perhaps the best, though they lack the Benedictus and Agnus Dei, the composer being of Irish Protestant stock. But later in life, perhaps at the urgent request of his publishers, he composed a Benedictus and Agnus Dei, separately, in F major, thus making them tonally appropriate for his settings in A major, B flat major and C major.

A welcome modern trend has been a revival in the popularity of Masses by Haydn and Mozart. These call for orchestral as well as organ accompaniment, and are both short and tuneful. A reliable orchestra is, of course, required, and skilled soloists, but otherwise they are within the range of most choirs. Given a competent player they can be accompanied, if need be, on the organ alone.

One of the main disadvantages of performing most Latin Masses liturgically is their length, and, in an increasing number of Anglican establishments, the Kyrie and Credo are being sung to the traditional plainsong found in the *Liber Usualis*. These lovely settings, very regrettably, have been almost completely discarded by the Roman Catholic Church, but are being used increasingly in the Anglican Church. They are short, tend to be repetitive (especially in the Credo settings), and are easy to sing, given an adequate plainsong technique. The melodies themselves are beautifully supple and exquisitely shaped and, it goes without saying, are absolutely fitting in the context of the Mass. An appropriate organ accompaniment is published by L'Abbaye de Saint Pierre, Solesmes, Sarthe, France.

Finally, a word should be said about 20th-century settings

of the Latin Mass. Vaughan Williams' setting in G minor, though it poses many problems of intonation, is deservedly popular, and Edmund Rubbra's *Missa Sancti Dominici* has kept a place in the repertory. There have been notable contributions from France, including Masses for choir, organ and brass by Widor (which were, at one time, a regular feature of Sunday morning Eucharists at Chichester Cathedral), an exciting *Messe Solennelle* by Vierne, a number by Jean Langlais (perhaps the best known being his under the same title as that by Vierne), and a remarkably individual setting by Francis Poulenc. The wanton destruction of cathedral choirs (many of them of considerable antiquity) in France has, no doubt, been responsible for the fact that virtually nothing has been written during the last quarter of a century. Flor Peeters, in Belgium, has composed some Latin Mass settings (especially successful is his *Missa Festiva*), but one of the most remarkable, original, effective and moving was that written in 1948 by Stravinsky for SATB choir and double wind quintet. Stravinsky, with his Russian Orthodox background, approached the text in an extremely individual way, and the result is a composition which owes almost nothing to the past, but which sheds new light and meaning on the familiar words of the Ordinary.

Music suitable for an Anglican Evensong is available in very large quantities, and here it may be convenient to divide it up into the three main sections of Responses and Preces, Canticle-settings, and Anthems.

According to the late Professor E. C. Ratcliff, who was an international authority on liturgical matters and Regius Professor of Divinity at Cambridge University, it is more correct to apply the term 'Responses' to the section 'O Lord, open Thou our lips' to 'The Lord's name be praised'. Can 'Praise ye the Lord!' properly be regarded as a 'little prayer', he argued? On the other hand, there is no doubt but that those immediately following the Lesser Litany (eg. 'O Lord, shew Thy mercy upon us', 'O Lord, save the Queen' etc.)

are Preces, or Prayers. Be that as it may, there is a small group of settings from the 16th and early 17th centuries, all of which are perfectly fitting and do much to illustrate the inner meaning of the text. The simplest is that by Tallis, but there are also sets by Byrd, Morley, Tomkins (one version in the Peterhouse MS, another in Musica Deo Sacra) and Ayleward; Gibbons, Amner (two settings) and Marson composed only the Responses. Later sets include those by John Ebdon (unique in that they are written in a minor key, and therefore particularly suitable for Advent and Lent) and John Reading. No sets from the 19th century are extant, but since World War II a number of modern settings have been written. Deservedly popular is that by Bernard Rose (which includes an exquisite setting of the Lord's Prayer), and there are examples by Gerald Hendrie and Gerald Near (both of which were composed for use in Saint John's Chapel), but most others are, also, either too complicated or too discordant to provide a fitting complement to the words, which are always simple and direct. Indeed, given the sheer complexity of many of them, they tend to hinder, or even prevent, the illustration of the text, rather than to enhance its meaning. They are therefore, however skilled musically, liturgically unsuitable.

Full Choral Matins has, as a Sunday service, greatly decreased in popularity in the face of the almost universal move to a Sung Eucharist. There are still some cathedrals where both services are usually held, but few, if any, where Matins is the only Sunday morning choral service and, as a consequence, the Te Deum (except for special occasions), the Benedictus and the Jubilate Deo are no longer an attraction to composers. Disregarding the large-scale setting in D by Henry Purcell (which calls for an orchestra and extremely skilled soloists) the repertoire consists of a number of *a capella* settings from the 16th and 17th centuries, chief amongst which are those by Tallis, Byrd, Tomkins and Gibbons. There are some dull settings from the 18th centuries, typical examples of which are Boyce in C, and Boyce in A. S. S. Wesley contributed some rather more exciting pieces, his *Morning Service in E major* being noteworthy in spite of its somewhat incohesive character. The many settings by Stanford pointed the way to better things, and notable landmarks were the contributions of Vaughan Williams, Herbert Howells, Benjamin Britten (two settings of the *Te Deum* and two of the *Jubilate Deo,* Robin Orr (a *Festival Te Deum* and a setting of the *Morning Canticles in C*), and William Mathias (a splendid *Festival Te Deum*).

In England and Wales however, it is the Evening Canticles which have remained popular, and the necessity in many cathedral and collegiate chapels of providing an almost daily change of setting has led to a large repertoire of some hundreds of compositions, many, alas, of doubtful artistic value, but also many gems, worthy to stand comparison with the best musical miniatures.

There are numerous settings from the 16th and early 17th centuries, most, but not all, without separate organ accompaniment, though it is clear from the surviving organ part-books that they were almost invariably accompanied. The two main forms were the Short Service, usually a simple mixture of homophony and polyphony; and the Verse Service, a large-scale setting with alternating solo and full sections, and, to a certain degree, an independent organ part. Byrd's *Second Service* is a typical example, but equally noteworthy are the settings by Morley, Gibbons, Tomkins and John Ward. It should be remembered, too, that many Evening Canticles have been lost, or exist in such a fragmentary form as to make their performance impossible; the many settings by Weelkes have suffered greatly in this respect.

The middle of the 17th century saw the introduction of a new style, and composers such as Michael Wise and Pelham Humfrey wrote their settings with a marked emphasis on melody and an increased tendency towards the polarity of outer parts in their harmony. Henry Purcell wrote two Verse Services (in B flat and in G minor) which have remained popular through the years, and he shows in them a mastery of both the old contrapuntal and the new melodic styles. But, in some ways, the lonely figure of William Child is of equal interest. Child was 17 years of age when William Byrd died, and survived long enough to see the birth of J. S. Bach, Handel and Maurice Greene. He adapted to the new style, and it is quite extraordinary that so little of his music is performed nowadays, and virtually nothing is published. Of the many Services he wrote two stand out—his *Verse Service in E minor* (which might well have been a model for the Restoration Verse Services), and a quite unique setting for 4 treble soloists and chorus.

The 18th century, with the exception of a notable example by Maurice Greene, was a barren period in which intolerable dullness coupled with inept inventiveness were sad characteristics. It was left to T. A. Walmisley and S. S. Wesley to rejuvenate the form, and the former's famous setting in D minor is thought to have been the first to have a separate organ part since the appearance of Gibbons' *Second Service*; of equal interest are the settings in D major and the splendid double-choir setting in B flat major. Wesley's monumental *Service in E major* contains some superbly exciting moments and, as always, the harmony is bold in the extreme, but the work as a whole lacks continuity, cohesion and formal shape.

Walmisley and Wesley undoubtedly provided a spur to Stanford and to Charles Wood who each wrote a large number of worthwhile, acceptable and sometimes inspired settings. Especially beautiful is the former's setting of the *Evening Canticles in G,* written largely for a treble soloist, with a running organ accompaniment, and said to be an illustration of the old legend that Our Lady sang the words of the Magnificat whilst working at a spinning wheel. Be that as it may, the works of both composers are a cornerstone of the repertoire, and remain deservedly popular everywhere. From this period, too, came the very effective eight-part setting of the Evening Canticles based on plainsong themes (in itself very much an innovation) by Edward Naylor.

Of post-World War II compositions the many contributions of Herbert Howells stand out, and there can be few choral establishments in the English cathedrals which have not had a setting of the Evening Canticles written for them by Howells. He invariably wrote with the particular acoustic of the building for which he was writing in mind, and, with few exceptions, they have become an almost indispensable part of the repertoire. Others of the same period who have written settings of the Evening Canticles (the remarkable work by Michael Tippett has been mentioned already) include Lennox Berkeley, William Mathias (two settings, written for Jesus College, Cambridge and for Saint David's Cathedral, Wales), Herbert Murrill, the American composer Gerald Near, Robin Orr, John Tavener (a remarkably effective and completely original setting, written for King's College, Cambridge), William Walton and Sydney Watson.

The thousands of anthems which have been written, and which continue to be written, make any detailed discussion impossible in these few pages. All one can do is to offer some general principles which might guide choice, and to refer to works which deserve recognition but have so far not found it.

Perhaps the first comment to make is that English Cathedral Music does *not* begin with the works of Thomas Tallis (1505-1585), and one wonders how much the tag of 'Father of English Cathedral Music' attached to him has been responsible for the scant respect shown to the many fine works of an earlier generation—the Masses and motets of Robert Fayrfax (1464-1521), for example, the Masses and motets of John Taverner (c. 1495-1545), and those of Christopher Tye (c. 1500-1573). It is an odd fact that, for some unknown reason, one composer can dominate completely the works of his contemporaries; it was thus in Italy with Palestrina, in Spain with Victoria, in the 18th century in England with Handel. Yet the works of such Italian composers as Gregorio Allegri (1582-1652), whose setting of the *Miserere mei* was *not* his only work, Felice Anerio (1560-1614), Giovanni Anerio (1567-1630), Paolo Agostini (1593-1625), Agostino Agazzari (1578-1640), Abondio Antonelli (b. late 16th cent.), Giovanni Asola (c. 1540-1609), Adriano Banchieri (1567-1634), Giovanni Bassano (17th cent.), Giovanni Croce (1557-1607), Alessandro Constantini (16th cent.), Antonio Caldara (1670-1736), Claudio Casciolini (17th—18th cent.), Giovanni Casali (c. 1715-1792), Costanzo Festa (c. 1480-1545), Girolamo Frescobaldi (1583-1643), Carlo Gesualdo (1560-1613), Andrea Gabrieli (c. 1510-1586), Giovanni Gabrieli (1557-1612), Alessandro Grandi (d. 1630), Marc Antonio Ingegneri (c. 1545-1592), Antonio Lotti (c. 1667-1740), Stefano Landi (c. 1590—c.1655), Luca Marenzio (c. 1553-1599), Domenico Mazzenzio (d. 1650), Giovanni Nanini (c. 1543-1607), Costanzo Porta (1529-1601), Paulo Quagliati (c. 1555-1628), Francesco Soriano (1549-1621), and Ludovico da Viadana (c. 1564-1645) are of the highest quality. Many have been transcribed, and published in the series entitled *The Chester Books of Motets* (Books 1, 8, 10 and 14).

The early French School has been almost completely forgotten. Yet, again in *The Chester Books of Motets* (Book 8), are splendid examples by such composers as Jean Conseil (1498-1535), Couillart (early 16th cent.), François Dulot (early 16th cent.), Mathieu Gascogne (early 16th cent.), Claude Goudimel (c. 1514-1572), Jachet of Mantua (mid 16th cent.), Jean Lhéritier (early 16th cent.), Antoine de Lonqueval (early 16th cent.), Jean Mouton (1459-1522), Passerau (early 16th cent.) and Claudin de Sermisy (1495-

1562). From the 20th century has come the splendid series of motets by Poulenc and Villette, and the solitary one by Messiaen.

Spain, too, has produced a number of very good but unknown composers. The works of Francisco Guerrero (1528-1599) and of Cristobal Morales (c. 1500-1553) have become increasingly popular of late, but those of Juan Esquivel (late 16th cent.), Diego Ortiz (mid 16th cent.), Martin de Rivafrecha (d. 1528) and Juan Perez (1548-1612) would still be completely unknown were it not for *The Chester Books of Motets* (Books 3 and 10). The motets of the internationally famous 'cellist, Pablo Casals (1876-1973) are becoming popular—passionate in the extreme, they reflect exactly the ambience of Spanish pre-war Catholicism.

Similarly with the German School (Books 4 and 11). Although the works of Jacob Handl (1550-1591) and Hans Leo Hassler (1564-1612) often appear on cathedral service lists, those of Gregor Aichinger (1564-1628), Blasius Amon (1560-1590), Michael Praetorius (1571-1621), Andreas Raselius (c. 1562-1602), Ludwig Senfl (c. 1499-c.1555), and Johann Walter (1496-1570) do not. The splendid motets of Anton Bruckner now have a deserved place in the repertoire.

Of the large number of sacred works emanating from England, the following, which certainly deserve many more performances than they get, may be listed alphabetically: *Jubilate Deo in E flat*—1934 (Britten), *Three Latin Motets* (Lennox Berkeley), *'Twas in the year that King Uzziah died* (George Benjamin), William Child's setting of the *Evening Canticles in E minor,* published by Paraclete Press, U.S.A. Adrian Cruft has written a setting of the *Evening Canticles for AATTBB,* as has Stephen Cleobury for ATB and organ (Paraclete Press). The works of John Dunstable (d. 1453) are of high merit; the *Magnificat* and the Whit motet *Veni Sancte Spiritus* are especially beautiful (*Musica Britannica* Vol. VIII). Elgar's *Ave verum Corpus* is deservedly well-known, but there are a number of other, equally effective anthems, both in Latin and in English, by him. All have that very characteristic melodic and harmonic style, so typical of the composer. Tastes change over the years, and whereas in the thirties the church music of Alan Gray (1855-1935) has rather fallen under a cloud, there is much that well deserves a hearing. Of the Evening Canticles the best is surely the splendid eight-part setting for unaccompanied voices in F minor, and there some extremely effective large-scale anthems. It may surprise some to find the name of Herbert Howells included in this list. His Mass in the Dorian Mode, written when he was only 20 years old, has recently been published by the Church Music Society, and is well worth revival. There are no less than 19 settings of the Magnificat and Nunc dimittis, of which only some four or five are in general use, as well as a large body of anthems.

Patrick Hadley (1899-1973) wrote very few works for the church, but his unpublished Lenten Cantata contains movements of rare beauty, especially the movements *I sing of a maiden* (for boys' voices) and *My song is love unknown* (for tenor solo and chorus). A gem, for use perhaps as an introit at a Sung Eucharist, is Julius Harrison's (1885-1963) unaccompanied piece *Open Thy gates to him who, weeping, waits.* Another composer, who is increasingly writing music for church use is Alun Hoddinott (b. 1929), whose *Three Advent Carols* for chorus and organ, and published by Lengnick, are of striking originality. The many anthems of Matthew Locke (c. 1630-1677) are for a great variety of textures; some, like *Sing unto the Lord,* are scored for strings, woodwind, organ continuo, chorus and soloists—others, like *Lord, let me know mine end,* are on a smaller scale—but all show that subtlety of word-setting which was a characteristic of English church composers from Gibbons to Blow. Hubert Middleton (1890-1957) wrote disappointingly little, but a tiny piece which most certainly deserves a place in the repertoire is his canonic motet *Let my prayer be set forth.*

Much of William Mathias' work was written to commission, and there is perhaps a lack of variety at times, but two notable peaks are *Ave Rex* (a sequence of carols) and the *Rex Gloriae* (Four Latin Motets). Each can be performed as a complete work, or the movements can be sung separately. In his earlier days John Merbecke wrote a number of works to Latin words, an especially beautiful example of which is *A Virgin and Mother.*

Of the many American composers perhaps the most distinguished is Gerald Near (b. 1942) a disciple and great admirer of Herbert Howells. His two settings of the *Evening Canticles,* and his anthems and carols are all of consummate beauty and skilled craftsmanship (they can be obtained through the Paraclete Press). The music of Robin Orr (b. 1909) makes no concessions to immediate popularity. His style is often stern, but there is distinction in every bar; characteristic pieces are the *Festival Te Deum* (1951), the unaccompanied anthem *I was glad* and, perhaps the most affecting and moving work of all, the *Songs of Zion,* a collection of four unaccompanied pieces.

Hubert Parry's (1848-1918) *The Great Service* deserves to be better known, as does Cyril Rootham's (1875-1938) setting of the *Evening Canticles in E minor.* A gem, for those of an operatic turn of mind, is Rossini's *O Salutaris Hostia.*

The fact that the music of John Shepherd (d. c. 1563) is not much more widely known has always struck me as being astonishing. His *Western Wind Mass,* although in many ways simpler than those of Taverner and Tye, is nevertheless attractive and interesting to sing. His Latin motets are of the highest quality, too. Two single works which deserve mention are *Hear my prayer* by Charles Stroud (c. 1705-1726), and *Veni, Sancte Spiritus,* a splendid unaccompanied motet for Whit by H. C. Stewart (1868-1942).

The works of John Tavener (b. 1944) are rapidly coming

into favour. His style is quite unique and of characteristic beauty. Perhaps the most immediately attractive of the anthems are the *Hymn to the Mother of God, The Lamb,* and *The Tiger,* but all deserve to be much better known. T. A. Walmisley (1814-1856) is widely known for his setting of the *Evening Canticles in D minor;* equally well-written is the setting for *Double Choir in B flat.* Finally, the many beautiful works of Michael Wise deserve recognition; especially fine are the Verse-anthems *Blessed is he that considereth the poor and needy,* and for Lent, *The ways of Zion do mourn.*

The Evangelist St. John my patron was:
Three Gothic courts are his, and in the first
Was my abiding place, a nook obscure;
Right underneath, the College kitchens made
A humming sound, less tuneable than bees.
But hardly less industrious; with shrill notes
Of sharp command and scolding intermixed.

William Wordsworth (1770-1850)

Part III

16

The Choral Services in Saint John's Chapel

... this man sings a base, that a [thin alto], another a treble, a fourth divides and cuts asunder, as it were, certain middle notes. Sometimes the voyce is strained, sometimes it is [relaxed], now it is dashed, and then againe it is inlarged with a lowder sound. Sometimes, which is a shame to speak, it is enforced into a horse's neighings; sometimes, the masculine vigour being laid aside, it is sharpened into the shrillness of a woman's voice; now and then it is writhed and retorted with a certain ridiculous circumvolution. Sometimes thou may'st see a man with an open mouth, not to sing but, as it were, to breathe out his last [breath] and, by a certain ridiculous interception of his voyce, as it were to threaten silence and now, againe, to imitate the agonies of a dying man, or the extasies of such as suffer. In the meantime, the common people standing by, trembling and astonished, admire ... the harmony.

Abbot Ethelred (12th century)

George Mursell Garrett was Organist of Saint John's College from the last day of 1856 until 1897. He contributed the following account of the Chapel Services to the College magazine, *The Eagle,* in 1890 (Vol. 16, No. 92).

"It is reasonable to suppose that the Chapel Services have been to some extent Choral for more than three centuries. The note in Mr Torry's *Founders and Benefactors* (p. 104) shews that the Chapel has contained an Organ since the year 1528; and in the same book (p. 51) will be found an account of various endowments for the support of a Choir; but it is doubtful whether the most patient research would yield any information concerning the nature and extent of the Choral Services. Even within the present century it was the habit to enter in the College Books 'Organist and Choir' as a single item: and although the name of the bellows-blower appears, the name of the Organist does not. There are entries in the Conclusion Book during the Mastership of Dr John Newcombe (1736-1765) of certain appointments of Organists, singing men and singing boys. In 1737 the appointment of one Turner to teach the Choir-boys is named. In 1741 the Organist received three guineas for entering the Anthems in the College books.

The name of the Revd Dr Jenkin, Master, appears in the list of Subscribers in the original edition (1724) of Dr W. Croft's *Thirty Anthems.* If the copy was for the use of the Chapel, it is probably the one still in the music room. The College also subscribed to the first edition of Dr M. Greene's *Anthems* (1743) and to the *Collection of Cathedral Music* edited by Dr Boyce (1790) and to its successor, edited by Dr S. Arnold (1790). All these volumes are still in use.

In 1777 Mr Tireman was elected Organist, and was succeeded, later in the same year, by Mr Jonathan Sharpe . . . the tenure of office of Jonathan Sharpe is worthy of remembrance. There is a College Order (June 9 1777) that proper music-books be purchased for the use of the Chapel, and that the pitch of the organ be altered under the direction of Mr Argent. He would appear to be a local organ-builder who had charge of the College Organ. His name appears for such a long series of years in the College [records] that it was probably a case in which the business descended from father to son. The [music-books] then purchased are still in constant use; and Mr Sharpe's handwriting, which is singularly beautiful, covers many of their early pages. They are 16 in number, and each volume contains from fifty to sixty pages of Sharpe's MS. Some idea may be formed from the kind of service in use from their contents. The service books, for example, contain nine settings of the evening service *Canticles,* and only two of the morning. It is thus probable, at least, that the order of service was nearly the same as that described below to have been found in existence by Walmisley on his appointment, 40 years later, and remaining practically unaltered during his tenure of office.

In 1796 the College voted a sum of 60 guineas for the repair of the organ, and this would seem to be the last money spent on the old instrument. In 1837 a new Organ was erected.

Of the remaining Organists, Dr Clarke-Whitfeld's name is still well-known. He was a voluminous writer, in his day very popular; and some of his Church Music still survives. S. Matthews, Mus.Bac., was a pupil of and assistant to Dr Chard, sometime Organist of Winchester Cathedral. During his residence in Cambridge he 'adapted' to words from the Psalms certain movements from the Masses of Haydn and Mozart; in doing so he set a fashion which has, unhappily, not yet quite expired. It is remarkable that two of the chief 'adapters' should have been Cambridge organists. John Pratt, for many years Organist to the University and of King's College (1799-1855), owed his reputation entirely to his labours in this direction. *Plead thou my cause* was, perhaps, the key-stone of that reputation; and it is significant that the collection in which it is found is called *Pratt's Anthems,* though neither of the volumes contains a single note of his own composition. A very devotional and meritorious setting of the words *Teach me, O Lord, the way of thy statutes,* in MS in our Choir books, would seem to shew that Matthews was capable of better work than 'adapting.' Dr Walmisley was in every respect in the very front rank of musicians in his time. He had great invention as a composer, and great power as a performer. If he had done greater justice to himself he might have left behind him a reputation second to that of no English musician. But he was, like his distinguished contemporary Sir John Goss, easily discouraged. The comparative inattention with which his early compositions were received disinclined him to further effort, and his early death prevented him from receiving that public recognition which, as in the case of Sir John Goss, would no doubt have stimulated and rewarded his continued labours. At Dr Walmisley's accession to office the state of musical matters at Saint John's was this. The same Lay-Clerks sang at King's, Trinity and Saint John's; the eight Senior Choir-boys of Trinity sang also at Saint John's. A Choir School was not in existence, but the boys were sent, at the joint expense of Trinity and Saint John's, to a private school in Downing Terrace, kept by a Mr Denny. Subsequently they went to the school of Mr Barber in Prospect Row. I am indebted for much of this information to my friend Mr W. Amps, of Peterhouse, who was a chorister in the Trinity and Saint John's Choir from 1831 to 1840, and subsequently a pupil of Professor Walmisley.[1] They were examined periodically by the Deans of each College. The College Chapel Services were held at 9:15 am. and at 5 pm. on Sundays; and later on there was a Choral Service

---

[1] He was later Organist of King's College from 1855 to 1876.

on Wednesday evening. The only Sunday mornings on which there was a Choral Service were Easter Day, Whit-Sunday, and Trinity Sunday. There was also Choral Service on the morning and evening of Christmas Day, but none on Holy Thursday, nor on any Saint's Day. The note-books of Dr Walmisley, from March 1840 to December 1853, give the Service Music and Anthem for each service, and shew that during that period the type of service known as 'Cathedral' was followed. The Responses were monotoned, until Dr Walmisley arranged the Tallis *Responses* in the form in which he published them in his *Cambridge Chant Book;* and from that time they were used in Chapel. The Priest's part of the Service was always read, not sung. This custom has lasted until the present day.

When the new organ was erected in 1837 some improvements were made in the Choral arrangements. It was then, for example, that the weekly Wednesday evening service was established, partly as a set-off for the non-observance of Saints' Days. The fact that the same men sang in all the three Choirs, and the same boys at two of them, had, as might be expected, a very prejudicial effect on the Saint John's Chapel music. Brevity was inevitable. But even the desire for brevity can scarcely justify the fact that some of Handel's finest *Messiah* Choruses were curtailed for Johnian use. Our Choir books contain shortened versions of *Lift up your heads; Worthy is the Lamb*; and *But thanks be to God.* The first chorus is reduced by 25 bars, the second by 12, and the last, which occupies 50 bars in the score is 'boiled down' to 22 in the M.S.

I have been unable to identify the writing in the Choir-books. It is certainly, to all appearance, as modern as that of Clarke-Whitfeld; and certainly not that of Walmisley. But 'that which is written remains'; there are the Choruses in the Choir-books.

It was not only, however, in such ways that a perusal of Walmisley's note-books proves that in the curious musical partnership which existed, Saint John's was always treated as the junior member of the firm. Not once on any Christmas Day was the appropriate anthem, *There were shepherds* sung in Chapel. Easter Day, Advent, Whit-Sunday, were either left unnoticed, or had such anthems assigned to them as *I have set God* (Blake), *Prepare ye the way* (Wise),[2] or other short and simple settings of more or less appropriate words. Dr Walmisley's note-book is merely a record of music performed. There is a note, however, on Sunday, Dec. 9 1843, which is amusing. A Funeral Anthem had been sung 'for H. M. The Queen Dowager.' N. B. The Dean would not suspend the Choral Service, as was done at Trinity and King's. On Nov.23, 1851, no such sarcastic note was possible. Choral Service was suspended, 'in consequence of the death of the King of Hanover.'

The Chapel Services were continued almost all the year round. Sometimes there was not a 'vacation' Sunday even in September. And from the fact that the musical part of the service was quite as elaborate in what are now Easter and Christmas vacations as in full Term, it seems probable that there was a full congregation in Chapel even at those seasons.

Upon the death of Dr Walmisley (1856) the Choirs were finally divided. For some years longer the same Lay-Clerks continued to sing at both King's and Trinity, but Saint John's has since October 1856 maintained an independent Choir. The number of Lay-Clerks was originally six, and of boys eight. Choral Services were held on Sundays, and on all Festivals and their eves. The first Organist of the College under the new *régime* was Mr Alfred Bennett, a pupil of Dr S. S. Wesley. He retained office, however, only from June to December 1856. On December 31, 1856 a new Organist entered on his duties."   G. M. Garrett.

---

[2] [a more appropriate anthem than *Prepare ye the way* (Wise) for Advent Sunday could hardly have been chosen! G.H.G.]

The original Chapel of the Hospital of Saint John, later to become the College Chapel from 1511 until its destruction in 1869, was built in the late 13th century, its outline still remains in First Court. The present Chapel was built in the 1860s, and consecrated on Wednesday, 12 May 1869. The following account is taken from the *Eagle* (June 1869):

Invitations to the Consecration had been issued by the Master and Fellows three months before hand to all non-resident members of the college whose names were on the boards and addresses known, and to all subscribers to the Chapel fund. to each of those who accepted the invitation, 600 in number, was sent a card of admission to the Consecration, and also a card of invitation and admission to a collation. Some, as was to be expected amongst so many, were, at the last, prevented from coming; but, as far as could be ascertained, there were present at the Consecration, residents included, some 900 members of our own body. Many non-residents arrived before the day. The Music Society of the college had provided for them a hearty welcome in a Concert, which they gave in the large room of the Guildhall on the evening of May 11th, Dr Garrett conducting. To all who had accepted the College invitation to the Consecration, invitations to the Concert had been sent for themselves and for any number of friends. The response shewed how well the greeting was appreciated, and the delight of the audience, which filled the room, how much the musical treat was enjoyed.

The weather on the 12th, the day of Consecration, was genial in its sunshine and temperature. A special train from London brought large numbers in the morning: a return special train had been provided for the evening also.

Morning Prayer and Litany were said in the Old Chapel as usual, at 7 am., a throng of old members of the College being present to join in the last service that would be held within its walls.

After the service in the Old Chapel, the day was a Surplice Day. 11.15 am. was the time appointed for the service of Consecration; but the Great Door of the New Chapel was opened half an hour beforehand to admit the Vice-Chancellor, the Members of Parliament for the University, Heads of Houses, Proctors, the Mayor of Cambridge, and any others that desired to take their places before the entrance of the procession; Fellows of the College being in attendance to marshal to their places both those who entered before the procession, and those who entered in it.

The Choir for the day consisted, men and boys included, of 48 persons.

Twelve were Undergraduates of the College:

Carver, T. G.	Madge, F. T.
Cook, C. H. H.	Norris, L. C. C. R.
Drew, C. E.	Pate, H. W.
Evans, L. H.	Pierson, C. H.
Hanbury, W. F. J.	Roberts, F. P.
Macmeikan, J. A.	Savage, F.

To Dr Garrett, who conducted, and to all who composed the Choir, the College is very greatly indebted for careful preparation, and effective and reverential execution of the musical part of the day's services. Dr Garrett had practised the Choir with his accustomed painstaking and skill, seconded by the able and heartily rendered assistance of Mr Frederic Smith, one of the permanent College Choir, and master of the Choir-boys' school. Of the effect of the New Organ in the Chapel nothing more needs be said, than that the acoustic properties of the Chapel are good, that the instrument is magnificent, and that Dr Garrett played it.

The order of the Procession was as follows:

1. The Choir, led by Dr Garrett, the Organist of the College.

2. Undergraduate Members of the Foundation.

3. Scholars, B.A.

4. Fellows.

5. The Master, accompanied by the Bishop of Ely, who was to consecrate the Chapel; Dr Selwyn, Bishop of Lichfield, Honorary Fellow and formerly Fellow, who was to be the preacher for the day; Dr Ellicott, Bishop of Gloucester and Bristol, formerly Fellow; Dr Atlay, Bishop of Hereford, formerly Fellow and Tutor; and the Bishops of Oxford and Rochester, both of the University of Oxford; His Grace the Duke of Devonshire, Chancellor of the University; the Earl of Powis, High Steward; the Dean of Hereford; Hon R. C. Herbert; Sir Thomas Watson, Honorary Fellow and formerly Fellow; and many old members of the College.

The Bishop of Ely was attended by his chaplain the Revd S. G. Phear, B.D., Fellow and Tutor of Emmanuel College.

6. Graduates above the degree of B.A.

7. B.A.s.

8. Undergraduates in order of seniority.

The Choir and the members of the Foundation assembled within the old Chapel, and the Procession passed, two in each line, along the South side of the old Chapel, then towards the College gates, down the middle of the first court, through the Hall screens, along the South half of the East side of the second court, along its South and West sides and the West half of its North side, then through the North side of the second court to the North side of the New Chapel, along this North side, round the Apse, and down the South side, to the Great Door.

The processional hymn was Ps. 84, New Version, sung to the tune of "Winchester." It was conducted by Dr Garrett till he arrived at the door under the Organ Chamber, and from that point by Mr Smith. With the long procession of surpliced hundreds, it was one of the most thrilling parts of the day's solemnity. As the procession wound its way, the hymn was, by those within and those without the Chapel, sometimes heard, sometimes lost, sometimes faintly caught in the distance, till, as the Choir entered the Great Door, the burst of sound filled the Ante-Chapel, and all that had assembled within the Chapel rose, and a volume of voices joined in the hymn. The hymn was continued, whilst those that preceded the Bishop of Ely in the procession were taking their places, the Scholars on the basement of the Choir on each side, below the stalls of the Master and the President, and eastward. When the Bishop entered within the screen, the Organ pealed, and Psalm xxiv was chanted, as the Bishop advanced to the East end of the Chapel. The Bishops of Ely, Oxford, and Rochester, took their places on the North side of the Altar; the Bishops of Lichfield, Gloucester, and Hereford, on the South. Chairs placed in the sacrarium were occupied by the clergy. There had been placed, in addition to the permanent accommo-dation in the Chapel, four lines of forms extending, from west to east, from the screen to the places provided next to the sacrarium for the Choir: and the Ante-Chapel was filled with lines of chairs. The Bishops being seated, Dr Reyner, Bursar of the college, presented to the Bishop of Ely the Petition for Consecration, from the Master, Fellows, and Scholars, under the College Seal, and from the Incumbents of the parishes of All Saints, Saint Clement, and the Holy Sepulchre, within which the New Chapel is situated, under their hands. The Bishop received the Petition, and delivered it to H. R. Evans, Esq., Deputy Registrar of the Diocese, to be read. The Bishop then proceeded with the service, according to the form used in the Diocese of Ely. After the prayers of Consecration, the Revd Canon Sparke, M.A., of Saint John's college, Canon of Ely, acting for the Chancellor of the Diocese, read the Sentence of Consecration, which the Bishop signed, and delivered to H. R. Evans, Esq. Deputy Registrar of the Diocese, commanding it to be recorded and registered, together with the Petition, among the muniments of the

Diocese of Ely. Then followed Psalm 100, New Version, sung by the whole congregation; the lesson, I Kings viii.22-62 inclusive, read by Professor Selwyn, from a stall in the middle of the South side of the Choir; and the *Te Deum* sung to a service in A, composed by Mr E. J. Hopkins, organist of the Temple Church, London. The Bishop of Ely then commenced the office for Holy Communion, the Bishop of Hereford reading the Commandments. The *Kyrie* was from Dr Garrett's service in D. Dr Reyner, Senior Fellow, read the Epistle, and Dr Parkinson, Senior Fellow and President, the Gospel. The *Credo* was from Dr Garrett's service in D. After the Creed, the Bishop of Lichfield was conducted to a stall in the middle of the North side of the Choir, and preached the Sermon, taking for his text Saint John xxi.22, 23. An Anthem followed, composed for the Consecration by Dr Sterndale Bennett, of Saint John's College, Professor of Music in the University. The following were the words:

Now, my God, let, I beseech Thee, Thine eyes be open, and let Thine ears be attent unto the prayer that is made in this place.

Arise, O Lord God, into Thy resting place, Thou and the ark of Thy strength: let Thy priests, O Lord God, be clothed with salvation, and let Thy saints rejoice in goodness. 2 Chron. vi.40, 41.

So we Thy people and sheep of Thy pasture will give Thee thanks for ever: we will shew forth Thy praise to all generations. Psalm lxxix.13.

And I heard a voice out of heaven, saying,

Behold the tabernacle of God is with men, and He will dwell with them. And they shall be His people, and God Himself shall be with them and be their God. Rev. xxi.3.

The Bishop of Gloucester read the Offertory Sentences; and the Alms, for the further decoration of the Chapel, were placed upon the Altar by the Bishop of Ely, who proceeded with the office, assisted by the Master. The *Ter Sanctus* was from the late Professor Walmisley's service in B flat. In the administration all the Bishops present took part. The *Gloria in Excelsis* was from Dr Garrett's service in D. Handel's *Hallelujah Chorus* was sung before the Bishop of Ely gave the final blessing.

And so ended this spirit-stirring service, with which we have set apart our beautiful and now holy House for Almighty God, to be His dwelling place amongst us in our College.

A Collation

was served at 4 pm., in the Hall, the Combination Room, and the two Racket Courts which had been kindly placed by the Managers at the disposal of the College; B.A.s and Undergraduates being in the Racket Routs. There were four lines of tables in the Hall below the table on the dais, two lines in the Combination Room, and four in each Racket Court. The accommodation in the Hall was for 302 persons; in the Combination Room for 180; and in the Racket Courts for 415. Doctors were in scarlet. The Master presided in the Hall, supported by His Grace the Duke of Devonshire, Chancellor of the University; the Earl of Powis, High Steward; the Bishops of Ely, Lichfield, Gloucester, Rochester, and Hereford; Lord Lyttelton; the Right Hon S. H. Walpole, and A. J. B. Beresford-Hope, Esq., M.P.'s for the University; Sir Thomas Watson; the Master of Clare College, Vice-Chancellor; the Masters of Sidney, and Saint Peter's; the Mayor of Cambridge; Dr Parkinson, President of the College; Dr Reyner, Senior Fellow.

Fellows presided over the tables below the dais, and over those in the Combination Room, and in the Racket Courts.

Places in the Hall and in the Combination Room had been so assigned that guests of the same Academic standing were near each other: and many were the recognitions, and cordial the greetings, between old friends who had not met for twenty, thirty, and forty years, and now lived their College days over again.

It had been arranged by the Master and Seniors that there should be but one toast proposed, "Prosperity to Saint John's College." But in the Hall the enthusiasm could not be restrained; and speech followed speech nearly till the time of the Evening Service.

Evening Prayer

was said at 7.30, the Chapel being completely filled, and the Choir being lighted with the lines of gas jets within the sill of each window, the effect of which was very beautiful. The Anthem of the morning was repeated.

And thus this happy day was brought to its close.

17

Organ Students and Organists of Saint John's College

Oft in danger, oft in woe,
Church musicians come and go,
Undismayed by petty strife,
Guardians of a way of life.

Gordon Reynolds

Organ Students of Saint John's College

1947	George Howell Guest
1951	William Bennett
1952	David James Lumsden (Assistant Organist)
1953	Alan Stephen Hemmings
1956	Peter Gilbert White
1960	Henry Brian Runnett
1963	Jonathan Leonard Bielby
1967	Stephen John Cleobury
1971	Jonathan Rennert

1974　John Gavin Scott
1976　David Neil Hill
1978　Ian Christopher Shaw
1980　Adrian Paul Lucas
1981　Andrew Michael Lumsden
1983　James William Cryer
1984　Philip Charles Kenyon
1985　Robert Huw Morgan
1987　Andrew Mark Nethsingha
1988　Alexander Philip Martin
1990　Philip Neville Scriven
1991　James Benedict Martin
1993　Allan James Walker
1994　Peter Davis

Organists of Saint John's College

> The Chapel Clerk, having lighted and prepared the Organ Loft, shall lock the door of the Staircase, and keep possession of the key. During service [he is] to keep the door locked during the whole time, except for admitting the Organist and others.
>
> *Dean's Order Book, 2 March 1839*

H. Watkins Shaw, in his splendid volume *The Succession of Organists* (O.U.P.), notes that, unlike those of King's College, there is no mention in the Saint John's statutes (1530 and 1545) of either choristers, lay-clerks or organists; though there was a choir by inference, in that a Precentor and 'Rectores chori', appointed by the Deans, had the duty of compelling members of the college to sing in Chapel. There was clearly some kind of choral establishment before the Civil War, for in the Will of Peter Gunning (the 22nd Master, and subsequently Bishop of Ely) provision was made for six choristers, and also for "more voices for the Choir." Of equal importance, in 1681 John Ambrose (Senior Fellow) bequeathed part of the tithes of Addingham, Cumberland "to be and remain for and towards the maintenance of a Quire in the chapel of the college." It is important to note, therefore that the Choral Services have been properly endowed.

No record has yet come to light of any 16th-century Organists of the College, and the first name noted by Watkins Shaw is that of **James Dunkin** (1638-1642). An equally shadowy figure is **Gibbons** (1642-1643), clearly a member of the very distinguished Cambridge family of that name, of which the best-known was Orlando Gibbons. It is thought that the **Loosemore,** mentioned in the College rentals for 1661, might have been the George Loosemore who was also Organist of Trinity College. He was paid for 'learning the choristers' and as Organist from 1661 to an unknown date. An additional complication is that the College records show that a **John Brimble** was Organist of Saint John's. He was a native of Peterborough and matriculated in Saint John's on 13 July 1668. He died, aged 19, and is buried in Peterborough Cathedral. There is a broken stone slab to his memory in the north aisle of the cathedral with the inscription "Johannes Brimble, Col. D. Johannis Cant. Alumnus & Organista, Musis et Musicae devotissimus, Ad Coelestem exectus Academiam 25 Julij, An. Dom: 1670, Aetat 19." Musical standards were probably not very high at this time, and clearly Peter Gunning, the 22nd Master, was disturbed by the music of the College Chapel. In his Will dated 25 August 1679 there appears the following bequest "Item I bequeath to Saint John's College where I was with all their good will and affection chosen Master, and there continued so about nine years or more, the sum of £100 more to be joined to that poor provision for a Quire there, which I have (under the College seal) assured for the maintenance of some singing Youths and others upon £300 given them by. . . . Dr John Barwick of pious memory, and upon my own £300 heretofore given, and Dr Turner's, Dean of Canterbury £150, and Dr Turner the present Master's £50. To all which I say I now desire to add my other £100 for the better provision of more voices for the Quire, whereby God's service may be more solemnly performed and decently sung upon the Lord's Days and other Holy-days, and their Eves, and their commemorations, by what way my very Reverend Friends the Master of the College and Dr Humphry *[sic]* Gower and the Senior Fellows shall contrive."[1] And, perhaps encouraged by the munificent example of Peter Gunning, John Ambrose (Senior Fellow) in his Will dated 18 January 1681, declared that half the Tithes of Addingham Rectory, Cumberland, "should be and remain for and towards the maintenance of a Quire in the Chapel of the College or to be disposed of for the greatest good and benefit and advantage of the said College as the Master Fellows and Scholars shall think fit."

James Hawkins was a Chorister at Saint John's, becoming Organist in 1681. He held this post for just a year, before becoming Organist of Ely Cathedral from 1682 until his death in 1729, though it is evident that he did not entirely sever connections with the college; his anthem *Behold, O God, our defender* was dedicated "to the very Revd Mr Tomkinson and the rest of the great, good and just non-jurors of Saint John's College in Cambridge by Ja: Hawkins, organist of Ely."

His successor was **Thomas Williams** (1682-1729); he combined his duties as Organist of Saint John's with singing in the choirs of King's and Trinity Colleges, and is recorded in the College Rentals as having been "paid a stipend for teaching the Quire from 1682 to 1729." He was followed

---

[1] *History of Saint John's College Cambridge,* by Thomas Baker, 1869 (Vol. 2, p. 658, line 29).

by a **Bernard Turner** in 1729; Turner, of whom nothing is known, held office for an indeterminate period. Not every Organist during this time gave satisfaction, or led a blameless life, and the next Saint John's Organist, **William Tireman,** held office for just one month, from February to March 1777. But Tireman had long been active in Cambridge music; he was appointed Organist of Trinity College in 1741, after having held a similar position at Doncaster Parish Church, though his service did not always give satisfaction to the college. He was admonished on 9 October 1762 in the following terms, "Whereas Mr Tireman, our organist, has several times received order from the Master in relation to playing the organ and accompanying the voices in the choir, and has repeatedly neglected them, the Master has summoned the Seniors on this occasion, who are come to this determination; that he shall be dismissed from their service if he does not observe the orders given him for the future." **Professor John Randall,** Organist of King's was appointed joint Organist with Tireman in 1762, but this arrangement only lasted for six years, and in 1768 Tireman became sole organist at Trinity once more. He died in Cambridge on 16 March 1777, after the briefest of all tenures of the position of Organist of Saint John's College.

Tireman was followed by **Jonathan Sharpe,** who was Organist from 1777 to 1794. Little is known of him as a musician, but G. M. Garrett commends the beauty of his handwriting, and he seems to have done a great deal to put the choir library in order.

John Clarke (later to be styled as John Clarke-Whitfeld) was born in Gloucester in 1770. He matriculated at Magdalen College, Oxford on 30 May 1793, when already Organist of Ludlow Parish Church, Shropshire, and subsequently moved to Ireland, becoming Organist of Armagh Cathedral from 1794 to 1797 and of Christ Church and Saint Patrick's Cathedrals, Dublin from 1797 to 1798. He became joint Organist of Saint John's and Trinity

Colleges, Cambridge in 1799, before moving to Hereford Cathedral in 1820. In the meantime he had been appointed Professor of Music at Cambridge, a position which he held until his death on 22 February 1836. His work at Hereford did not, however, meet with universal acclaim, for the Chapter on 16 June 1832 passed the following minute, "In consequence of the long and increasing deterioration in the choral services of the Cathedral, proceeding as they are aware from Dr Whitfeld's infirm state of health which has for a long period experienced the forbearance of the Chapter; the Dean and Chapter now feel it to be their indispensable duty to communicate to him their decision that the office of organist will be vacant at Midsummer next. Should it be a matter of convenience to Dr Whitfeld to be relieved from his responsibility at any earlier period the Dean and Chapter will be ready to concur in any suitable arrangement."

Another very short-lived appointment was that of **William Beale**, a Cornishman who had been a chorister at Westminster Abbey under both Samuel Arnold and Robert Cooke. He was appointed a Gentleman of the Chapel Royal at the age of 32, in 1816, and moved to Cambridge to become joint Organist of Saint John's and Trinity Colleges in 1820. But he retained these positions for little more than a year, before moving back to London to become, firstly, Organist of Wandsworth Parish Church and, subsequently, Organist of Saint John's Church, Clapham Rise.

A former chorister of the joint Saint John's and Trinity Choirs, William Glover, describes something of their life in the early part of the 19th century. "The organist was Mr Samuel Matthews, a pupil of Dr Chard, of Winchester. He was a kindly man in private, but a regular martinet during 'office hours'. We practised every morning the necessary chapel music; and then we went to school during the morning and afternoon. After school, we had another daily practice of music for the 'Camus' society, held at Tutor

Higman's rooms, in Neville's Court, near, I dare-say, the apartments occupied by our youthful prince. There was also a town choral society in which we were the only trebles employed. At this society I first heard the great works of Handel, Beethoven, and Mozart performed with band accompaniments. Such a society is an invaluable institution in any town. We attended service at chapel on Sundays and 'surplice days', that is, on Saints' Days and the evening previous. On Sunday, we went to chapel at eight am.; breakfasted; went to Trinity Church generally at eleven; then to Saint John's at five, and finally to Trinity Chapel service at six. I am wrong. I said 'finally', but it is an actual and maniacal fact that our friends positively desired our presence, unofficially, at Saint Mary's late service!"

Matthews was followed by one of the great names of English cathedral music, **Thomas Attwood Walmisley**. Walmisley, a godson of Mozart's pupil, Thomas Attwood, was born in Westminster on 21 January 1814. He grew up in a musical family, and his father, Thomas Forbes Walmisley, Organist of Croydon Parish Church, encouraged the boy to a broad education. At the very early age of 19 he succeeded to the joint appointment to Saint John's and Trinity Colleges, taking up his duties in 1833. Unusually for an organist, Walmisley took the Mathematical Tripos and, although taking his BA in 1838, he had already been appointed to the Chair of Music two years previously! He died on 17 January 1856, and how much his early death was accounted for by his enormous work-load on Sundays can only be conjectured. J. S. Bumpus' *A History of Cathedral Music* lists his duties as follows (in addition to his duties at Saint John's and Trinity he deputized for John Pratt at King's College and at the University Church Great Saint Mary's):

Saint John's College	7.15 am.
Trinity College	8 am.
King's College	9.30 am.

Great Saint Mary's	10.30 am.
University Sermon	2 pm.
(Great Saint Mary's)	
King's College	3.15 pm.
Saint John's College	5 pm.
Trinity College	6.15 pm.

John E. West suggests that "his death was hastened by an unwise indulgence in lethal remedies, taken as a sedative to an active brain and over-sensitive mind." A more outspoken comment on this grossly overworked organist was given by C. V. Stanford "Walmisley unfortunately, 'he wrote' like some others of his time, was a victim of four o'clock dinners in Hall, and long symposiums in the Combination Room after; and being a somewhat lonely bachelor, the excellent port of the College cellars was, at times, more his master than his servant. One catastrophe gave occasion for an admirable witticism of his bosom friend, W. G. Clark, the editor of *Shakespeare*. There was once such a crash of sound in the organ-loft at evening Chapel, that popular imagination pictured Walmisley sitting on the keys and playing on the seat. For this anticipation of Schönberg he was summoned to appear next day before the Seniority. In the morning Clark, who lived close by, came in to comfort and cheer him. He found the dejected organist sitting gloomily by a table on which was a tell-tale empty bottle, in a thick atmosphere of tobacco.

WALMISLEY: "Oh, what am I to say to them, Clark, what am I to say to them?"

CLARK: "Nothing easier, my dear fellow. Say 'I am become like a bottle in the smoke, yet I do not forget thy statutes'."

Alfred Bennett's tenure of the office of Organist was almost as short as that of William Tireman, lasting only from 24 June to 27 December 1856. Bennett's father had been Organist of New College, Oxford, and the son became a pupil of S. S. Wesley. He resigned from Saint John's in order to take up a position as Organist of Saint John's Church, Calcutta. He was followed on 31 December 1856 by **George Mursell Garrett.** Garrett was born on 8 June 1834, near Winchester. His father was a Lay-clerk at Winchester Cathedral, whilst he himself received his early training a chorister of New College, Oxford. After short periods as organist of two Winchester churches, he was appointed to Madras Cathedral where he stayed for two years, prior to his return to England, and to over forty years as Organist of Saint John's. Garrett was appointed University Organist in 1873, and died in Cambridge on 8 April 1897.

He was succeeded by **Edward Thomas Sweeting,** who was born in Cheshire on 16 September 1863. He held positions as Organist of Saint Mary's, Kensington, and later as Director of Music at Rossall School, Lancashire where he taught the future Sir Thomas Beecham. Sweeting was Organist of Saint John's from 1897 to 1901, when he was appointed Organist of Winchester College. He died on 8 July 1930.

The Rootham family had a long connection with Cambridge music: Daniel Rootham had been a pupil of Walmisley's, and had served as a chorister in both Saint John's and Trinity choirs. Daniel's father had been a bass singer from 1815 to 1852 in the two choirs. Small wonder then that Daniel's son, **Cyril Bradley Rootham,** followed in their footsteps and was Organist of Saint John's from 1901 to 1938. C. B. Rootham was born in Bristol on 5 October 1875 and was an undergraduate at Saint John's, reading for the Classical Tripos. He later studied at the Royal College of Music, London, and succeeded H. Walford Davies as Organist of Christ Church, Hampstead, London in 1898. In 1901 he became Organist of Saint Asaph Cathedral, Wales, before returning to Saint John's later that same year. Rootham was a University Lecturer in Music, and was elected a Fellow of the College in 1914; he died in Cambridge on 18 March 1938.

Robin Orr (Robert Kemsley Orr) was born on 2 June 1909 in Brechin, Scotland. He studied at the Royal College of Music, London, and was Organ Scholar at Pembroke College, Cambridge, subsequently receiving lessons in composition from Alfredo Casella and Nadia Boulanger. He became Organist of Saint John's in 1938, and was a University Lecturer in Music from 1947 to 1956. He resigned from Saint John's in 1951 on his appointment as Professor of Music at Glasgow University, but returned to Cambridge in 1965 to take up the Chair of Music, which he retained until his retirement in 1976. He is an Honorary Fellow of the College.

Robin Orr served in the Royal Air Force during World War II and, during his absence, **Herbert Norman Howells** (1892-1983) was appointed Acting-Organist. After his retirement from the post of Organist, Orr was succeeded by his Organ Student, **George Howell Guest,** who served as Organist of Saint John's College from 1951 to 1991. On his retirement the College appointed **Christopher John Robinson** as his successor. Robinson's experience has been comprehensive, having been a chorister at Saint Michael's College, Tenbury; Organ Scholar at Christ Church, Oxford; Music Master at Oundle School; Organist of Worcester Cathedral, and Organist of Saint George's Chapel, Windsor.

18

A Sermon at Saint John's College

A Sermon preached in Saint John's Chapel at the service for the Commemoration of Benefactors on 5 May, 1985 by G.H.G.

The first verse of Psalm 41, "Blessed is he that considereth the poor and needy: the Lord shall deliver him in the time of trouble."

Just over 400 years ago, on 15 October 1584 (during the Mastership of Richard Howland) a former undergraduate of this college, Richard Gwyn, was dragged through the streets of Wrecsam to the Beastmarket, now a busy bus and coach station, but then a place of execution. He had refused an offer of freedom if he would but acknowledge the Queen as Head of the Church. On this last grim journey he gently chided those who wept for him, saying "Weep not for me, for I do but pay my rent before the rent-day." He was sentenced to "hang half-dead, and so be cut down alive, his members to be cast into the fire, his body ripped unto the breast, his bowels, liver, lungs and heart likewise thrown into the fire, his head cut off, his body parted into

222

four quarters." To which Gwyn replied "What is all this, is it *more* than *one* death?"

To us, sitting in this Chapel in somewhat less immediately threatening times, those barbaric days seem far off indeed: and perhaps, at first sight, they might appear to have little connection with our annual service for the Commemoration of our Benefactors. We meet at this time each year to remember those who, over the centuries, have given money, land, or other possessions to the college. And rightly so; and we may rejoice in their good fortune in inheriting or otherwise acquiring their wealth in the first place—and also in their generosity in passing it on to enable the work of this college to continue over the centuries.

But benefactions need not be *material* benefactions only—and indeed the true definition of a benefactor is simply "one who confers a benefit," or "a doer of good to others"; and that, clearly, includes doing good by example—the example of piety, of compassion, of kindness, of bravery. Into *this* category of Johnian benefactors go an un-numbered and sometimes un-remembered host of men. One thinks of all those killed and maimed in a long succession of wars, some perhaps just wars, many unjust, some perhaps necessary, most unnecessary—and of all martyrs, and particularly this morning let us think of that sadly-forgotten Johnian Saint Richard Gwyn. By his shining example of courage and steadfastness in the face of appalling personal danger, this early member of Saint John's was and is a benefactor to us all. He was one of the first in a long line of Johnian benefactors to humanity itself—indeed, a man whose life and death should, many might feel, be commemorated in some permanent way in our Chapel.

Equally distinguished are two who already have memorials in this place—the two 'Williams', William Wilberforce and William Morgan, both benefactors almost without parallel in the scale of their benefactions.

The 150th anniversary of Wilberforce's death was marked in 1983, and can there have been *any* other member of this college who has possessed in equal measure his compassion, his determination, and ultimately his influence for good on the lives of so many people? Wilberforce's own life and work illustrates the truth that communities and human beings are always more important than financial or political considerations—this world, this country, this college all consist primarily of *individuals,* and any government (whether international, national, local, or even collegiate) ignores this at its peril. All of us need reminding from time to time, particularly those whose duty or inclination leads them to become formulators of rules or drafters of laws, of Saint Paul's words in the 2nd Epistle to the Corinthians "the letter killeth, but the spirit giveth life." Wilberforce's benefaction was a *humanitarian* benefaction—as was the benefaction of William Morgan, who came up to Saint John's in 1565, some 19 years before the martyrdom of Saint Richard Gwyn.

In 1988, we shall be celebrating the 400th anniversary of the first complete translation of the Bible into Welsh, that by William Morgan. Could there possibly have been a more needful gift, a more acceptable benefaction, to a nation going through a period of imposed spiritual deprivation? This great work had (and still has) an immense influence on the lives of his countrymen, and his name (as familiar in Wales as are those of Francis Drake, Nelson and Churchill in England) is rightly venerated. An associate in this work was his friend and contemporary Edmwnd Prys, who took his BA from Saint John's in 1567, and who is also rightly renowned for his metrical version of the Psalms. Morgan subsequently became Bishop of Llandaf, and later of Llanelwy[1]—but he is remembered throughout Wales with affection for the accuracy of his translation,

---

[1] i.e. Saint Asaph

and for the beauty and clarity of his prose. There is a copy of this Bible in the College Library, and it is used at the wholly appropriate and now, happily, customary bilingual Evensong held in this Chapel on Saint David's Day, March 1st, each year.

One's train of thought leads on easily from this to our Chapel Services in general, and also to the Chapel. And here one can, with truth, regard the College itself as a benefactor, and this particular part of "the work of this college which is called by the name of Thy beloved disciple" as a continuing gift, primarily to those who are members of Saint John's, but also to the thousands of visitors from all parts of the world who visit Cambridge throughout the year. To some the emphasis on music (and especially on choral music) is a blessing, to others a distraction. But many forget that *all* music in churches and chapels is or ought to be regarded as an *adornment of the liturgy,* not as an end in itself, not as a concert or recital. The proper function of such music is two-fold; it is essentially an *offering,* on behalf of the whole congregation, but it also serves to elevate the mind, and to illustrate the words (or, more importantly, the *meaning* of the words). I think in this connection especially of the *In Paradisum* from Fauré's *Requiem,* of Bach's *Saint Matthew Passion,* of the plainsong which we now traditionally sing in the Ante-Chapel at a Memorial Service as prime illustrations of that profound truth. We try always to remember that the *words* (and this will perhaps sound strange coming from a musician) are *always* more important than the music.

All of the music heard in this chapel, both choral and instrumental, consists of two main elements—technique (that is correctness of notes, correctness of intonation, good rhythm, good balance and chording, good diction, and so on), and *emotion* (the putting into a performance all those subtle elements of phrasing and expression too numerous to be notated). And if one further puts forth the general theory that (except perhaps for a special effect) no two consecutive chords in choral music should ever be of exactly the same dynamic, the immensity of the task facing every top-class choir becomes immediately apparent. From the conductor's point of view there is the added frustration that, although one *imagines* the perfect performance, it is never, in the event, even approached.

Every performance is a mixture of technique and emotion, and the very vexing thing is that the more one has of the one element, the less one necessarily has of the other. It is in this relative proportion between the two that is found the difference in style between choirs. In this Chapel we have always taken the view that it is important for people to be *moved* by the music they hear, rather than for them simply to admire pretty sounds and a sure technique—and that necessarily means an absolute identity between the words and their meaning on the one hand, and the music on the other. The aim, as I say, is to illustrate the liturgy even though, as with sermons, the sounds uttered are transient and passing.

Our Chapel services are impossible to quantify; they supply a need to young and to old; they have been responsible for changing the whole course of people's lives. They affect everyone in the College, for those absent are drawn into them by the prayers of those who are present. We pray as a College, always (one hopes) putting first things first—praying for sound learning, and at the same time encouraging ambition, but always recalling the one inevitable fact of *life,* which is *death.* "We brought nothing into this world, and it is certain we can carry nothing out"— sombre words for all benefactors, or would-be benefactors. There are some splendid lines in this connection from an unknown source, though they might well have been written by a wise College Tutor:

"Saint Philip Neri, as old readings say
Met a young stranger in Rome's streets one day.

And, ever being courteously inclined to give
   young men a sober turn of mind,
The dialogue they held comes down to us.

N. Tell me, what brings you, gentle youth, to Rome?

S. To make myself a scholar, sir, I come.

N. And when you *are* one, what do you intend?

S. I hope to be a priest, sir, in the end.

N. Suppose it *is* so, what have you next in view?

S. That I may come to be a Canon, too.

N. Assume it so.

S. Were it too bold to say that I a Bishop might become
some day?

N. What then?

S. Why, Cardinal's a high degree, and yet my lot it possibly
may be.

N. A Cardinal! What then?

S. Why, who shall say but I've a chance of being Pope
one day.

N. Well, having worn the triple crown and hat, and held
the keys, what follows after that?

S. Why, having held an ordinance so high as long as heaven
shall please, then I must die.

N. What, *must* you die, fair youth, and at the best but wish
and hope, and may be all the rest? Take my advice,
whatever may betide, for that which *must be* first provide;
then think of that which *may be,* and, indeed when well
prepared, who knows what may succeed."

For "that which *must be* first provide." That is the particular
benefaction offered by this Chapel to the members of this
college and to its visitors. We think today of our good fortune
at being here—of the munificence of our benefactors
through the centuries—of the College itself as a benefactor—and we think especially of those thousands, millions,
of unfortunate people in East Africa, whose desperate need
is for benefactors in sufficient numbers, and for material

benefactions of sufficient size, to enable them to receive the one meal a day they need to remain alive.

Let us pray for grace to be *true* benefactors, and for the ability to live as a caring society, so that we too may help those *in real need,* for the commonsense to distinguish the important from the trivial, for understanding and warmth so that our College may be a real *Society,* in every sense of the word.

Now to God the Father, God the Son, and God the Holy Ghost, be ascribed all praise, might, dominion and glory now and for ever.

19

Fifty Years of Church Music

Excerpts from "Fifty Years of Church Music," by the Revd W. E. Dickson (1894)

> Every undergraduate is required to attend Chapel during the first three years of his residence, if in College *nine* times, if in lodgings *seven* times a week.
>
> *Dean's Order Book, September, 1839.*

"When I arrived at Cambridge, and found myself the happy possessor of a set of rooms in the old court of Corpus Christi College, I needed no introduction to a considerable number of the compositions in use in the college chapels which maintained a choral service.

These chapels were three, and only three, namely those of King's, Trinity, and Saint John's Colleges, though Peterhouse indulged its men with a little music of a humble kind on Sunday evenings. At all the other colleges the daily prayers (which the men were compelled to attend), were dreary in the extreme, being simply read in parson-and-clerk fashion. Although there were three chapels with choral foundations, the provision made for the maintenance of the musical services was most meagre and insufficient. There was really but one choir of lay-clerks, and those only six in number, and some of them elderly; they hastened from chapel to chapel, taking part, on Sundays, in no fewer than six repetitions of the Morning and Evening Service. A single organist had shared with them this almost incredible drudgery.

Those were days in which an education of a liberal or even of a reasonably useful kind was not to be had in the school maintained for the boys; and as the choristers were employed as assistant waiters at the daily dinner in the Hall, it was not likely that the College could attract recruits for its choir among the children of tradesmen, still less of musicians or of other professional men; but I am bound to declare that the lads, though rough in their manners, were honest and truthful, and anxious to please their masters.

Greatly desiring to convey to my readers a faithful impression of the state of Church Music at Cambridge in 1843, I must declare that a very imperfect and inferior rendering of the musical services was the natural result of such mismanagement of the choristers. coming straight from the Abbey and from Saint Paul's, innumerable shortcomings of the choir at King's College were most painfully apparent to me. I am guilty of no exaggeration when I say that not one boy in the choir of sixteen could read his part at sight, or had an acquaintance with rules for the production of the voice, or had ever heard of phrasing, or was ever told to attend to marks of Expression.

A very different account can be given of the choral Service at Trinity College. Thomas Attwood Walmisley had been elected in 1833, when only nineteen years of age, organist of Trinity and of Saint John's colleges. In 1836 he had become Professor of Music in the University, and he graduated afterwards as B.A. and M.A. in the regular course, giving proof in his examinations of much intellectual power.

My references to him will be facilitated if I mention here that I had had the honour of an introduction to him at the rooms of my friend John Sutton, of Jesus College. Mr Sutton possessed a very curious and interesting chamber-organ by Schmidt, quite unaltered, and in perfect repair. It had two manuals, so peculiarly constructed that a player unaccustomed to them might find his fingers *under* the keys instead of pressing on them: the lower key-board commanded three sets of pipes in oak, of most refined tone; the upper row had three metal stops, and the six sets of pipes, united on this manual by a coupler, formed a miniature "Great Organ" of surprizing brilliancy and sprightliness. It was necessary to stand while playing this quaint old organ, and to supply the wind by the foot. Mr Sutton led the life of a recluse; but occasionally he invited a few of us to little concerts in his rooms, and it was at one of these that I was introduced to Walmisley. Two or three boys, and two or three men of the Trinity choir were present,—one of these was Machin, afterwards well-known as a good bass vocalist; the Professor had brought under his arm some copies of Spohr's *Last Judgment,* then little known in England, the English translation, by Edward Taylor, of Norwich, having been but recently printed. Every musician who glances at these pages will appreciate the difficulty of accompanying the voices in Spohr's music on the little quaint organ described above: more than one of my readers, perhaps, would have recoiled from the attempt. Probably the Professor regretted the absence of a piano-forte, but he was one of those gifted men to whom victory over difficulties is in itself, and for its own sake, the highest of enjoyments, and not a word of complaint did he utter as he stood at the instrument, manipulating the curious keys with the most perfect smoothness and skill. I had never before heard a note of Spohr's music; the impression made upon me now by this quiet rehearsal of it is quite indescribable. The heavenly beauty of some of the movements haunted me for many days afterwards, sweetly and accurately sung, as they were, I believe, at sight, by the small choir, and since that evening I have never ceased to be an ardent admirer of that most sacred and solemn work. After the oratorio, the Professor, still full of energy, extemporized for some time, delighting us all by his clever imitations of the Fantasies of Bull and Gibbons, and ending with a fugue. At the subsequent supper, he was a charming companion, full of anecdote and lively repartee.

My position as an undergraduate in his first year did not entitle me to hope for intimate friendship with Walmisley: now and then, however, I found myself in the organ-loft at Trinity. The instrument had been built by Schmidt, in 1708, but finished and voiced after his death by his son-in-law Schreider; it had been greatly altered, however, in 1834, by Gray, who had carried out the suggestions, and perhaps here and there the whimsical fancies of the young organist.[1] It had a pedal-board of two octaves, from CCC to tenor C; the Swell had been carried down to G-gamut: the wind-pressure had been increased, and the pipes revoiced to it; hence it had entirely lost the sweet quality of Schreider's organ at Westminster, though it had gained an addition of volume and power. The chapel, ceiled with a flat roof of wood, had but little resonance; and when it was filled by some 500 men in

---

[1] Among these was a coupler which united the pedals with the *upper octaves* of the choir-organ. It was said that Walmisley introduced this for the sole purpose of playing the melody of the National Anthem in his godfather Attwood's fine composition written for the Coronation of K. George IV. "I was glad, etc."

surplices—a very remarkable sight, especially as seen from the organ-loft—the sound of the few voices of the choir was much deadened. The selection of the music rested with the Professor. One of his predecessors, Samuel Matthews, like Pratt, had adapted English words to movements from the great German composers, and these were occasionally heard at Trinity; but Walmisley's own leanings were towards the Anglican school of Cathedral music, as represented by Boyce, Croft, Greene, Hayes, and perhaps Kent; and he himself was the author of four or more complete Services, and of several anthems of great excellence, worthy rivals of those produced by his contemporary, Wesley. Among these may be specially mentioned the Service in B flat, and the anthem *If the Lord Himself*, with the beautiful quartett, *Our soul is escaped even as a bird, etc.* I had the good fortune to be present at an evening service in Trinity when his *Magnificat and Nunc Dimittis in D major* were sung for the first time. The distinguished master of the College, Dr Whewell, and the scarcely less distinguished Professor, walked up and down the ante-chapel for some minutes before the service commenced, and I wish that it were in my power to place before the eyes of my readers the portraits of these two remarkable men as they are present to my own mind.

The composer was warmly congratulated, afterwards, on his vigorous and masterly work, and it was forthwith sung, from MS. copies at Ely and perhaps elsewhere, but was not printed until after his death in 1856. Many of us made our first acquaintance with the words of Sebastian Bach by hearing them performed by Walmisley in the chapel. I do not recall the great pedal-fugues; they could not have been played without awkward transpositions upon a pedal-board of twenty-five notes; but most of the "Forty-eight" became familiar to us as executed with great skill on the organ. At the service at Saint John's I believe I was only once present. It is not a little singular that after altering the Trinity organ to a C compass of manual and pedal, Walmisley should have promoted the erection of an F organ in the adjoining College. So it was, however. The instrument, one of very fine tone by Mr William Hill, built in 1839, had Great and Choir manuals to FFF, the 12-feet note; the Swell descended to FF. A coupler, uniting the Swell to the Great in the octave above, was a great novelty, and may have been almost unique at that time in England.

The Psalms were sung in all the Cambridge choirs from the Prayer-book only, without the aid of pointing. A pointed Psalter—possibly the first attempt of the kind—had been published by Mr Robert Janes, organist of Ely Cathedral, in 1837. He had had the great advantage and privilege of receiving hints from the learned Dr Mill, Regius Professor of Hebrew, and Canon of Ely, and his book—though much revised—is still in use. But it was never adopted at Cambridge.

The chants were of course Anglican, single and double, for the revival of the ancient Plain-Song, though not far distant, had not yet reached us, and if the vague word "Gregorian" was in use, it was only as applied to those barred chants in Anglican form, such as that so well-known as Tallis', founded on the ancient Tones, though having none of their freedom and spirit."

20

Presidential Addresses

Presidential Addresses given by G. H. G. at the Royal College of Organists on the occasion of the Presentation of Diplomas.

27 January 1979

No one can stand in the position I occupy at this moment and on this very important occasion, without recalling, with a judicious mixture of nostalgia and awe, the far greater names who, during the years, have, in their various capacities, been responsible for the administration of this College. Public acclaim is always a fickle and transient phenomenon: in some cases reputations have dwindled, in other cases (especially, happily, that of Sir John Stainer) their true worth as musicians has only become apparent comparatively recently. But the list in itself is quite daunting, ranging, as it does, from the giants of the nineteenth century to the great names of those who flourished in the first half of the twentieth century the purist Sir Edward Bairstow, the austere, erect, stiff-collared Sir Ivor Atkins, often complemented by the dapper, bow-tied Sir Percy Hull, Sir Walter Alcock, Sir William Harris, and many others who did so much to set a standard for us all to follow.

And when one thinks of standards in church and cathedral music one thinks of all that our sister organization, the Royal School of Church Music, has achieved in these countries of Great Britain, and indeed throughout the world, under its three Directors, Sydney Nicholson, Gerald Knight and Lionel Dakers. And we recall how fortunate we, in this College, have been to have had the benefit of Mr Dakers' wise guidance and cheerful encouragement over the last two years—we do indeed owe him a very considerable debt.

Next, I should like to congratulate very sincerely all those who have been successful in achieving their ambition of a diploma on this occasion. The standard we insist upon is an extremely high one, and it is right that it should be high. Nowadays there is an increasing tendency to promote races, both athletic and academic in which *all* participants win a prize; and logically there is no reason why all *our* candidates should not be successful. But this is not true to life and so, inevitably, there are those who are unsuccessful. If there are any in that category present this afternoon, I hope they will regard their presence in it as temporary, and that they will try again, or again *and* again, until they are successful. The thought is aptly expressed in an old Welsh proverb. "Dyfal donc a dyr y garreg"—"it is persistent blows which break the stone." Or, in other words, "Keep trying!"

The profession of Organist and Choirmaster is, in many ways, a strange one. For hundreds of years, before the days of radio, the gramophone, and the television, and when rapid communication between our cities and towns was unknown, the cathedral organist was the musical leader of the whole district. His salary was low, it is true, but he was usually able to eke it out with various small perquisites—

often by teaching, or perhaps by copying music for the use of his choir. Others had more colourful side-lines—an 18th-century Organist of Chester Cathedral, for example, held for many years the additional post of Dean's Barber—a subtlety of temptation of which even the Devil might have been proud! No doubt they all enjoyed comfortable lives: which they occupied in the cathedral itself. They were much more servants than colleagues; they were required to do what they were told, always.

In this century many things have changed, though not, I regret to say, the low salary. In some cathedrals the Organist is invited to Chapter meetings; his views are rightly considered to be expert views, and eagerly sought—and sometimes even acted upon. But elsewhere, in very recent years a certain type of churchmanship has sought to turn those cathedrals in which it bears responsibility into places where it is taught that the only music acceptable to the Almighty is that of congregational hymns, sung loudly. Here, the cathedral organist has one of three choices—firstly, either to give in to what is nothing more than a tyranny, a tyranny which is no less real because it happens to be imposed by well-meaning clergy under the cloak of Christianity, or secondly, to fight to keep some semblance of a cathedral tradition alive, with all the rancour that this course of action often involves (is it really true that last year, in one cathedral, the choir was only permitted to sing one choral service a fortnight, and that grudgingly?)—or, thirdly, to resign. And this is what a number of organists have been doing in recent years. It is indeed sad that members of our profession should ever be faced with this dilemma, but the really frightening aspect of it all is that, in some cathedrals, the whole edifice of choral worship could crumble almost overnight at the passing whim of an over-zealous Dean or Provost. It is easy to destroy a tradition—we saw that during the time of the Commonwealth: it is very much harder to resuscitate it—we saw that at the Restoration of the Monarchy in 1660. And it is, I believe, part of our duty as members of this College to give support, in as practical a way as possible, to any of our colleagues unfortunate enough to find themselves faced with this particular situation.

But the outlook is not wholly gloomy. There is, in general, a much happier spirit of co-operation between the clerical and musical sides of our cathedrals and churches these days—and this was exemplified last November when there was held, in Westminster Abbey, the first meeting of a group of Deans, Precentors, and Organists, under the skilled Chairmanship of the Dean of York. The complete success of this venture only made one the sorrier that it was being held for the first time. Discussion was frank, objective and friendly, and we all left convinced that a real step forward in the musical life of the Church of England had been taken.

And it is perhaps because of this growing spirit of co-operation that there is still no lack of young people whose burning ambition is to become an Organist and Choirmaster. They are not deterred by the low salary offered: in a real sense their work is a vocation, and is a specialist's work: it is also work which is unique to the English-speaking world. One hears abroad of Organists, and one hears of Choirmasters, but only in the Anglican Church is one person required to fill both positions with equal distinction.

And that brings one to the curious point that, although we are *described* as Organists and Choirmasters, most of us are only trained as solo organists. Especially is this to be seen in University Organ Scholarship Examinations, where it is quite common to find candidates who can dazzle with the brilliance of their technique in solo pieces, and yet whose knowledge of, and insight into, the subtle art of accompaniment is minimal. It may well be, now that the old apprenticeship system has disappeared, that we should offer more instruction in this, and perhaps our College should take a lead in helping people who have not had the benefit of sitting daily in a cathedral organ-loft watching, and therefore unconsciously assimilating, the techniques of accompanying a professional choir, as shown by someone skilled in the art.

It is much the same thing with choir-training. I suppose that few of us ever had any positive instruction in it: we learnt what we know through watching others (both good and bad), and by practical experience. It is indeed one of the most imprecise and personal of all the arts, and one must say that the actual *knowledge* required (apart from the necessity of becoming familiar with an extremely large repertoire) is not extensive. In the late 1940s some of us in Cambridge used to watch Boris Ord rehearsing his choir with little less than awe. We admired his technique but, above all, were electrified by his personality—and it was his *personality*, of course, which inspired his choir. It was partly to do with his choice of words, partly to do with the particularly characteristic sound of his voice (a sound which can never be forgotten by those who heard it!), partly to do with the precision and rhythmic vitality of his gestures, but, above all, to do with his eyes—it is in the *eyes* of a conductor that a member of a choir finds inspiration. And Boris Ord's eyes were magnets which drew members of his choir into a share of a quite unique musical experience. He always had his own conception of how the work under rehearsal should ideally sound, and the achieving of this conception was his only aim. Choir-trainers of his genius are rare indeed—and they provide an example and an inspiration without parallel.

So our work goes on. We know that, on this side of the grave at least, none of us can achieve perfection in any aspect of it, so we are always forced to compromise. And the contented Organist and Choirmaster realizes this and accepts it. Life is short; we can but do our best, hoping, when it comes to the point, that our own feeble efforts will, miraculously, somehow be helped by a much more skilful Conductor in another place.

21 July 1979

It is sometimes asserted by foreigners, no doubt completely without foundation, that one of our chief characteristics in this country is to denigrate ourselves in public at every possible opportunity—we accept our defeats philosophically, it is said, with just the faintest hint that the referee might conceivably have been, in some slight way, biased in favour of the other side. We accept our victories almost with an apology, being careful always to give the impression that we expected no less anyway. To many, this is a maddening and an incomprehensible attitude; as well as being, I imagine, somewhat dangerous from a medical point of view. For myself, I should this afternoon rather wish to echo the advice given by Saint Paul to the Romans, "Rejoice with them that do rejoice, and weep with them that weep." And so I ask you, first of all, to share in the pleasure and joy of our new diploma-holders on this fine summer's day. Do not feel it sufficient to clap politely—think carefully of that nervous opening of the fateful envelope with the dread words "The Royal College of Organists" printed on it, the quick glance, and then the enormous satisfaction, pleasure and pride that one of life's many obstacles has been overcome—and applaud them all with the utmost enthusiasm.

But think also of those who have *not* been successful on this occasion, those who have worked hard but who have failed this time to *satisfy the examiners,* as the phrase goes. It is, for them, a time of disappointment, but also, I hope, a time of resolution. And nothing would give the College Council greater pleasure than to see them all receiving their diplomas in January 1980. "We are none of us infallible—not even the youngest of us," wrote William

Hepworth Thompson—and this is worth remembering, too.

I ventured, in January, to speak a little about some of the problems facing the Organist and Choirmaster in this distracted age. I mentioned that attacks being made on traditional forms of cathedral worship—had I been bolder I might have gone on to express the exasperation which so many of us feel with the system that can bring into positions of responsibility and authority in the Church of England priests whose aim is, or seems to be, to destroy the *nature* of cathedral worship, as it has been handed down to us. And this, I believe, happens as much in the Catholic Church as it does in the Anglican Church. The terrible fallacy in the reasoning of these high-minded but misguided people is that they believe that *traditional* forms of worship are despised by the young. Not only is this not true, but rather does tradition often prove an attraction for young people, because any element of permanence in religion provides a bulwark, a comfort, something to hold on to, a vision of an eternal truth, in an impermanent and often frightening world. It is the middle-aged and elderly trendies who are out of touch with today's youth. Our experience at Cambridge in recent years is that young people are returning to the churches and college chapels and that they are particularly attracted to those places where the forms of worship are traditional and dignified and not experimental; they are attracted to those places where the Almighty is addressed with at least the same degree of deference as one would use to the monarch, rather than as if one was meeting a chance acquaintance in a pub, or in the street.

A tradition is easily lost, it need only be discontinued for a few years to disappear completely (one has only to recall George Orwell's *Animal Farm* to realize the truth of *that*). And this was a fate that very nearly happened to plainsong in quite recent times. There have been many attacks on it as a form of religious art during the centuries

and these have multiplied in the last twenty years. There
was even a period a few years ago when it almost seemed
that the Anglican Church would have to take sole
responsibility for its survival. But the scholarship, the
devoted skill and the hard work of a number of wise people
and, in particular, Dr Mary Berry, have borne fruit in a
remarkable way. Plainsong choirs are now being formed
up and down the country, plainsong conferences and
retreats are being held in increasing numbers, and the
old chant is being revived with love and enthusiasm. I
sometimes imagine a confrontation between Dr Berry and
Dr S. S. Wesley, who wrote "Some would reject all music
but the unison chants of a period of absolute barbarism—
which they term Gregorian. These men would look a
Michelangelo in the face and tell him Stonehenge was the
perfection of architecture!" Would the old man have been
so bitter if he could have heard the ravishing beauty of
the Office or the Mass as sung by the Monks of Solesmes,
or indeed by the monks of their sister house in Quarr,
in the Isle of Wight? We shall never know; but what is
certain is that, far from being the barbarism as described
by Wesley, it is a form of art so subtle as almost to defy
notation, a form of art with which one has to live and
grow—and, at the same time, a form of art which adds
an indefinable dimension to all worship. Its future now
seems more certain from day to day—and one even hears
suggestions from time to time that it might play a slightly
greater part in our examinations here at the Royal College
of Organists than it does at present. That, to say the least,
would not be difficult to achieve!

　　And just as is the case with plainsong, so there are
a number of other areas too, which are barely touched
by our work in the College; and one which springs
immediately to mind is that of music in the Nonconformist
churches. Quite often, and especially in rural areas, there
is no choir to lead the choral music; but this is not

necessarily a great loss when one considers the wealth of congregational singing that one meets within those services, though what has always seemed strange is that so few of those magnificent 19th- and early 20th-century hymn-tunes of Nonconformist origin are known in the Church of England. Nonconformist music is essentially congregational in character—and the often uninhibited nature of this congregational response is a characteristic from which many of the other Christian churches can learn. But there has been no real musical tradition, except for a small group of writers, one of the leaders of whom was Eric Thiman, who was, as Erik Routley put it, "the Bairstow and the William Harris of Nonconformity." He stood almost alone in rejecting the unworthy legacy of anthems in use in the Nonconformist churches, many of them discarded from the standard Church of England repertoire—and, in their place, trying to fill the gap with easy, dignified, uncomplicated music. To him the hymn-anthem was almost a god-given form—and what form could better be used for its purpose? It was simple, short and made a direct appeal, and the lack of variation in style was a small price to pay when one considers the often unworthy music it replaced. As Routley wrote, "there is an almost obstinate lack of surprise in [Thiman's] music. But fairness demands an historical recognition that to have forced the pace of the entrenched reactionism of English Nonconformity of 1925 would have been to invite complete rejection. . . . Thiman's technique was infiltration not aggression."

Quite apart from this choral music his contribution to the literature of organ music was extremely influential. His pieces, most of them conceived for church rather than for recital use, are always unpretentious and rather short. And perhaps this last characteristic is especially necessary in the Nonconformist churches because so often, as soon as the service ends, the congregation, with noisy alacrity, picks up its belongings, gets to its feet and walks out, immediately, and as a body. This means usually that, within a dozen or so bars of the start of the voluntary, the church or chapel is empty. Nothing could be more demoralizing for an organist, particularly if he has taken time to practise the piece he is playing. Small wonder then that some never play a piece afterwards—they make do with playing either a hymn-tune (no bad thing perhaps in itself) or the first and last pages only of a printed voluntary, so there is little organ-playing of any consequence. Congregations have declined in Nonconformist chapels—encouraging their musicians to play a fuller and more worthy part in their services would be an elementary step in attempting to reverse that decline. To the Nonconformist organist the watchword would seem to be "do the simple things well"— play correct notes, play in correct time, play music which is fitting, and hope and pray that one's efforts will eventually meet with approval and encouragement by those in authority, and by congregations.

Musicians *need* encouragement as plants need water— there is no doubt about that—and, in many ways, indifference is worse than open opposition. We need not apologize for this as we are dealing with people's emotions to a greater degree perhaps than is any other art. To do this successfully and sincerely we must bring our *own* emotions into play in which nationally is a most uncharacteristic manner, especially when we recollect that we are dealing with words which are often cataclysmic in conception. Emotion is all-important in choral music, especially in sacred choral music; an over-concentration on technique is always fatal. The really successful performance is one which succeeds in *moving* the listener and, at the same time, exciting his admiration. In order to do both these things one has to get the proportions right, and one has to be *helped* to get the proportions right by encouragement. And even when one gets so far, one realizes that what one has finally produced is ephemeral, fleeting, transient.

And in this respect, organists and choirmasters are perhaps in a very similar position to that of country clergymen—about whom one of their number, that wonderful poet R. S. Thomas, wrote so movingly—

They [leave] no books
Memorial to their lonely thought
In grey parishes; rather they [write]
On men's hearts and in the minds
Of young children sublime words
Too soon forgotten, God in His time.
Or out of time, will correct this.

From these words all organists, all choirmasters, can take heart.

26 January 1980

Once again it is my pleasant duty to congratulate our new Associates and our new Fellows. They have been successful in passing what are perhaps the most arduous and difficult examinations of their kind in the world.

At the same time that we share the joy and pleasure of those who have been successful, we should also remember the disappointment of those who have been unsuccessful on this occasion. I hope they will persevere and that they will achieve their aim.

A few months ago the Saint John's Choir undertook a tour of the United States and Canada. We did most of our travelling by coach, and went as far as Indianapolis. Then we turned north and aimed for Canada. And if you approach the Canadian border going north from the mid-west of the U.S.A. you will, almost certainly, come within sight of Detroit, a large sprawling metropolis, with all the usual problems that face most American cities these days, and which are just now beginning to affect many cities in England, too. Detroit is a city whose economy and whose prosperity largely depend on the motor car, and with the motor trade in recession in the U.S.A. now, there is a renewed anxiety amongst its inhabitants. And for Detroit's dependence on the motor car the late Henry Ford was almost entirely responsible. Henry Ford was a comparatively uncomplicated man whose ability to make money was boundless, but whose academic interests were limited. He was, it would appear, the epitome of the plain, blunt, northern Englishman, who so often confuses sincerity with rudeness. And this bluntness was nowhere more apparent than in the witness-box during his celebrated libel action against the *Chicago Tribune* in July 1919. He was asked his opinion of history by defending counsel—"history" said Ford "is bunk." I would never dream of suggesting, of course, that a similar view is taken by any who take the College examinations, but is has often seemed to me, as an examiner, that history is regarded by many candidates as something of a poor relation, when one looks dispassionately at the Associateship and Fellowship examinations as a whole. So often one has to read strings of facts without any attempt having been made to place them into an historical context. Details of a composer's life are almost always of less significance than his works, and to understand a composer's *works* means that one must be able to place them in an historical context. Surely Ralph Waldo Emerson was writing with his tongue in his cheek when he wrote "There is properly no history; only biography." And it is this preoccupation with bare facts, without an ability to make deductions from them, which is, in my opinion, the root cause of so many abjectly poor history papers in our examinations.

How should one prepare for the History papers? There are few, if any, lectures on historical topics available, so one is almost totally reliant on books and gramophone recordings. But books do not only exist to impart facts (about which there can be no argument); they also exist to offer the considered opinions of their authors on those facts (about which there should always be discussion). Perhaps the most important first step in approaching musical history is to acquire the ability to distinguish between fact and opinion; there is much more to a book than just the reading of it, a sober consideration of what one has read is at least as important. The purpose of our History papers is not to see who can quote the largest chunks of the standard text books, and candidates who favour answering the questions in this mechanical way should reflect that the literature on the subject is small anyway, and that therefore there is a very good chance of the examiners recognizing such quotations. Received opinions quoted without acknowledgement are always sterile and often insincere.

In short, one should, from time to time, ask oneself *why* one is reading a particular book. Michel Quoist wrote "some people read books primarily to find confirmation of what they already believe. They are not open to the thoughts and experiences of the author, and they do not find what a particular book has to offer. Instead they spend their time seeing what is not there, and bewailing what they do not see."

And nowhere, to broaden the argument a little, has this lack of reasoned judgment, this propensity for accepting received opinions uncritically, been more apparent than in a consideration of mid-Victorian church music in England. Sir Henry Hadow wrote "there are three diseases from which religious music can suffer: the disease of virtuosity, which over-elaborates the technique of composition and so tends to lose sight of its meaning; the disease of theatricalism, which over-emphasizes the *meaning* at the expense of true dignity and reverence; and the disease of sentimentalism, which enervates the meaning by relaxing it into a soft and facile prettiness." And he went on to say that it was this *third* disease which, in his opinion, attacked English church composers of the mid-Victorian period.

But let us examine Hadow's three "diseases" a little

closer. It is still generally recognized that J. S. Bach stands amongst the elite of church composers—yet in the German magazine *Der Critische Musikus* of 14 May 1737 appears the following piece written about him by the noted critic Scheibe—"this great man would be admired by the whole nation had he more agreeableness, and did he not keep naturalness away from his compositions by employing bombastic and intricate devices, and darkening beauty with over-elaborate art . . . all the ornaments, all the little grace-notes, are written out in full. Therefore his compositions are deprived of beauty, of harmony, and of clarity of melody, since the melody is unrecognizable. His inclination towards extravagance leads him both from naturalness to artificiality, and from the sublime to a want of clearness. With him one admires the laborious effort and the exceptional work, but both are expended in vain because *neither* is conformable to reason." To understand the relevance of this seemingly outrageous criticism one must understand Bach's relationship to the new rationalistic doctrines of the early 18th century, and in particular one must understand the relationship of these doctrines to the music of the time. Then, and only then, can the true nature of Scheibe's criticism be understood, and evaluated.

Similarly with Hadow's "disease" of theatricalism. The Masses of Haydn and Mozart have often fallen under this condemnation but, again, this criticism takes no account of either the setting for such performances, the particular church architecture, the particular place of music in the Mass at that time, and the particular outlook of the composers. Alec Robertson recalls that Haydn once said that he could set *qui tollis peccata mundi* joyfully, because he thought not of the sins so much as the taking away of them! The inordinate length of some settings of the Benedictus of this period has been put forward as an illustration of the composer's lack of proportion—but when one realizes that it was necessary to fill in the space between the Consecration and the Pater Noster the disproportionate size becomes logical. Given all these things, one can almost come to the conclusion that *no* music could be more fitting for those sumptuously coloured and decorated churches in Austria and Germany in which it was customarily performed. To some the Baroque is an extravagance; to others, like Nicholas Powell "it is the mirror of heaven—of the unattainable to which so many still aspire. Never in the history of modern art was there a more happily conceived intention. Never were the essence of belief and its outward signs more brilliantly portrayed."

And so to Hadow's third disease, that of sentimentalism—with particular reference to the works of Garrett, Barnby, Stainer and Dykes. Like most cathedral musicians of middle-age I was brought up to regard the music of these men as retrograde, with the exception of some hymn-tunes and Anglican chants. Their anthems and services had been completely discontinued in cathedrals, almost without a single exception, by the late 1930s because that was the accepted thing to do.

If ever there was a case of a received opinion being universally accepted this was it—and, at one and the same time, 16th-century music was being approached and evaluated in the same uncritical way. Tomkins' sometimes absurd word-setting was condoned—the superbly emotional music of Tallis was regarded as being rather less inspired than that of Byrd—while that great master, Christopher Tye, perhaps the greatest of all the English Tudor musicians, whose settings of the Mass for mixed choir tower above those of his contemporaries, was known only for some rather dull transcriptions from his setting of the *Acts of the Apostles*. But these comments would have been regarded as heresy in the 1930s.

However, to return to the 19th century; Garrett and the others used the conventional harmony of their time, and they wrote sincerely for the kind of services they found in their cathedrals, and for the musical forces which they found there. There is much in their work that would repay study, and in studying works that make considerable use of chromatic harmony it is important to get the speeds correct. If these pieces are taken too quickly they lose dignity; if they lose dignity they become trivial. To make them moving and inspiring is indeed a worthwhile task for any conductor—there is little in any of them which is inherently *bad*.

So this really is a plea for a more rational approach to the History section of the College examinations. Perhaps some lectures or seminars in this building would help. But in the long run it depends on the examination candidate himself; the history of music is so intertwined with the history of the other arts, with social and political history, with economic History, that for any to consider it in isolation is a nonsense. As Curt Sachs wrote in the Preface to his *History of Music* (1949) "Even the most elementary history book should impart to its students a notion of the limited scope of the time in which they live, and a sense of the vast horizons that a knowledge of the past unrolls." He later writes that he has taken care to "restrict the number of names and the biographical details as much as possible.

Instead, characteristic changes in musical language, life, performance, in form, notation, printing, and the construction of instruments" have been concentrated upon. This, I believe, is the correct and scholarly way in which to approach the History papers in the examinations of the Royal College of Organists. As James Westfall Thompson put it "Narrative history has the merit of telling *what* happened. But the reflective mind wishes also to know *how* things happened and *why* things happened." Let us, in the History papers of the College examinations, encourage "the reflective mind."

26 July 1980

Once again we meet to share the joy of the new Associates and new Fellows of the College. They have all been successful in the most demanding of examinations, and, as a result, their achievement will be recognized and their ability taken for granted in all parts of the world. They will have worked hard and long, and probably at considerable expense, to reach their goal. They will, deliberately, have set either ARCO or FRCO as their target because they know these diplomas to be the most sought-after in our branch of the profession. But, in congratulating them, let us also spare a thought for those who, temporarily one hopes, have been unsuccessful. I hope that the reverse that they have suffered on this occasion will only make them the more determined to succeed next time.

But let us also recall the extreme importance of *maintaining* the standard of our examinations. Many things have changed in our society and in our countries since the Royal College of Organists was founded as the College of Organists on 12 March 1864—indeed, life itself has changed—but, and this is one of the greatest strengths of our College, the standard of our examinations, in spite of attempts through the years to persuade us to make our diplomas easier of attainment, has remained high, perhaps the highest in the world, and I believe that we should do everything possible to *keep* that standard. There is no merit in uniform mediocrity; as Arthur Conan Doyle said "mediocrity knows nothing higher than itself."

In less essential matters of course we *have* changed. At the Annual General Meeting held at 8 pm. on 26 July 1904, Sir Frederick Bridge said "We should have a man in uniform [at the front door]. Has the uniform been ordered for the Porter?" Dr E. H. Turpin replied, "The order has been given. It is to be a light brown suit, with frock coat, and on each shoulder will be the initials RCO, and, on the cap, RCO in gold letters." I do not know what happened subsequently either to the Porter or to his uniform, but I do know that the *present* staff, all of them devoted to the College in the most extraordinary way (even though they are provided neither with a frock coat nor even a cap with the initials RCO on them), do work extremely long hours with skill, enthusiasm and cheerfulness on our behalf. We owe them all an enormous debt of gratitude.

Last January I dared to offer a few remarks on the History questions in our Paper Work examinations, in the hope that they might provide some food for thought and perhaps even a little help to those contemplating them. I should like to turn, this afternoon, to another aspect of the examinations which, in the view of many examiners, although fundamental, is something that seems not always to be given its true weight either by pupil or by teacher. I refer to speed, or *tempo.* How often does one hear a piece of music which is just that little bit too slow, so that the phrases sag and the forward impetus is completely destroyed? And how often, similarly, does one hear works played or sung just that little bit too quickly, thus conveying flippancy instead of dignity, impotent bustle instead of tidy clarity? There is very little margin in the middle, between these two extremes, although a very dry or an over-resonant acoustic does, of course, make a slight difference. C. P. E. Bach, as usual, defined the point with his usual clear thought; "The pace of a composition," he wrote in his *Essay on the True Art of playing Keyboard Instruments,* "is based on its general content as well as on the fastest notes and passages contained in it. Due consideration of these factors will prevent an *allegro* from becoming rushed, and an *adagio* from being dragged." And one might add to that the general proposition that "the simpler the melodic line, the slower should be the tempo, commensurate with the phrase-lengths." There is a pernicious habit in some places of worship of taking hymns too quickly—one hears notable tunes like *Nun danket, Aberystwyth, Adeste Fideles, Blaenwern* and others, taken so quickly that they become merely jingles—and this excessive speed is responsible, to a larger degree, for the weakness of congregational singing in so many of our churches at the present time. Congregations, especially of the older kind, easily become flustered if called upon to sing too quickly, and rather than run the risk of making an audible mistake usually prefer not to sing at all. Not only that, but many choirmasters are unable to *sustain* a given *tempo,* and one hears the most inappropriate *rallentandi,* at the ends of verses, regardless of the sense of the words. As C. P. E. Bach says, "In sad passages the performer must grow sad—however, the error of a sluggish, dragging performance, caused by an *excess* of sadness and melancholy, must be avoided." So, essentially, this is a plea for much more thought in determining logical and musical speeds, whether the music is slow or fast, whether it is simple or complex. And, from the point of view of the College examinations, it is applicable as much to the playing of pieces as it is to the various tests.

But although I have rather concentrated on examinations so far, I should not like it to be thought that the College regards them as the sum total of its work. There have been a number of significant events held here during the academic year, and I should like particularly to mention the splendid series of Bach recitals given by James Dalton. Attendances have been uniformly good, and the informal atmosphere, coupled with a uniquely satisfying union between composer and performer, have combined to produce an unforgettable series. Then I hope you will notice, with due pleasure and pride, what has been done to make the College Library an attractive place in which to work. Our plan, though well-advanced, is still not finished in all its details, but we look forward to its completion within a few months.

The Library itself is of great interest, particularly as it now incorporates the large amount of organ music left

to the College by the late Mr Albert Sowerbutts. This
collection includes almost everything of value published
during the last 70 or so years, and especially interesting
are the pieces, often of considerable musical worth, which
have never achieved, or which have lost, public acclaim
without valid reason. One can think of many superb works
for the organ which fall into this category, and perhaps
at the forefront of these are the splendid sonatas by Herbert
Howells and Percy Whitlock. English organ sonatas are
few and far between, and the neglect which these two fine
pieces have suffered is completely irrational. Then there
are the many works, both large-scale and small-scale, by
C. H. H. Parry and by C. V. Stanford; most of these are
well worth the effort of learning them, as long as one
considers them in their historical context, rather than as
out-of-date contemporary pieces. Of more modern British
composers one thinks immediately of Arnold Cooke, the
distinguished pupil of Paul Hindemith, of Hugh Wood, and
of other equally notable writers for the instrument. If only
some of our recitalists would admit that Dupré, Messiaen,
Langlais, Peeters and Vierne were not the *only* contemporary composers of worthwhile organ music!

Public taste is a strange phenomenon, formed partly by
the vast army of critics in all sections of what is nowadays
called the media, and partly (and this is certainly true in
respect of the pop music subculture) by big business. There
are occasions, of course, when the critics who have so much
influence over public taste are right—there are other
occasions when their prejudices override their judgment.
Berlioz, for instance, condemned Handel as "a barrel of
pork and beer"; he wrote that Palestrina had "no spark
of genius"; but he regarded Beethoven as "a Titan, an
Archangel, a Throne, a Domination." On the other hand,
the first public performance of the *Eroica Symphony* on 7
April, 1805 was reported in Vienna as follows: "The
symphony would gain greatly if Beethoven would make

up his mind to cut it, and to bring more light, clarity and unity into the whole." Another critic, on hearing the same work, goes on to fear that "music can become so complicated that no one but experts will be able to take any pleasure in it: that everyone will leave the concert hall with a feeling of fatigue, depressed by too many incoherent and overstuffed ideas as well as by the perpetual noise of all the instruments." What is one to make of these two diametrically opposed comments? Simply that the uninformed man-in-the-street should be bold enough to make his own judgment on a work of art, using his *own* knowledge, and allowing himself to be swayed by his *own* prejudices into a subjective evaluation which is, to the person making the judgment, much more valid than any second-hand opinion, however distinguished the quarter from which it emanates.

This is the last occasion on which I shall have the privilege of addressing you as President. I look forward to the continuing progress of our College; may it always be true to the high ideals of its founders; may it continue to serve music by maintaining its standards; and may those who have taken its examinations remember that as the old Welsh proverb has it "ymhob braint y mae dyletswydd" ("in every privilege there is a duty")—and our duty, and theirs, in this particular instance, is having passed its examinations, to continue membership of the College, and therefore financial support of it, in the years to come.

Index

Printed by Paraclete Press
Orleans, MA 02653
1-800-451-5006
FAX 508-255-5705